D1095648

Gender Identities and Education

Gender Identities and Education

The impact of starting school

Barbara Lloyd and Gerard Duveen

Harvester Wheatsheaf

St. Martin's Press

First published 1992 by
Harvester Wheatsheaf
Campus 400, Maylands Avenue
Hemel Hempstead
Hertfordshire, HP2 7EZ

A division of
Simon & Schuster International Group

and in the USA by St. Martin's Press, Inc.

For information, write:
Scholarly and Reference Division
St. Martin's Press, Inc.
175 Fifth Avenue
New York, NY 10010

Typeset in 10/12 Baskerville
by Keyboard Services, Luton, GB

Printed and bound in Great Britain by
BPCC Wheatons Ltd, Exeter

British Library Cataloguing in Publication Data

A catalogue record for this book is available from the
British Library

ISBN 0 7450 0781 3 (hbk)
ISBN 0 7450 0782 1 (pbk)

Library of Congress Cataloging in Publication Data

Lloyd, Barbara B. (Barbara Bloom), 1933–
  Gender identities and education : the impact of starting school
Barbara Lloyd and Gerard Duveen.
    p.   cm.
  Includes bibliographical references.
  ISBN 0-312-09120-6
  1. Sex differences in education.   2. Gender identity.
3. Socialization.   4. Sex differences (Psychology)   I. Duveen,
Gerard.   II. Title.
LC212.9.L58   1993
370.19′345--dc20   92-32400
                                                             CIP

ISBN 0-312-09120-6

1 2 3 4 5   92 93 94 95 96

Contents

Preface

Gender Identities and Education is the product of an intellectual collaboration which has continued for over a decade. Originally begun in the context of doctoral supervision, it matured into a reciprocal exploration of ideas and data. Our use, throughout the text, of the pronoun 'we' reflects our shared intellectual perspective.

Barbara began to study aspects of gender and gender socialization in the early 1970s (cf. Archer and Lloyd, 1974; Smith and Lloyd, 1978) and at the same time supervised the completion of Gerard's doctoral research (Duveen, 1984). Gerard had investigated children's friendship patterns and developed new theoretical tools with which to conceptualize children's understanding of the social world.

The two enterprises were brought together in our effort to explain the relation of the individual to society (Duveen and Lloyd, 1986). In this theoretical statement we proposed that a particular concept of social identity, one based upon individuals' re-construction of a sense of self in relation to the social representations of significant groups in their society, might best describe the individual–society interface. Rather than being separate entities, the identities of individuals were construed in terms of group membership, and this membership was held to entail the adoption of the values, ideas and practices of the important groups in their society. These ideas were explored using data from Barbara's empirical studies of gender-marked behaviour and awareness in mothers of infants, and in children from 1½ to 4 years of age (cf. Lloyd, 1987; Lloyd and Duveen, 1989).

Equipped with a conceptual framework which had already proved serviceable, we secured funds from the Economic and Social Research Council (C000232321 September 1986–September 1989) to explore the effects of entering formal education on the social gender identities of children. We were fortunate both in gaining funding for our study and in securing the cooperation of teachers, head teachers, parents and children. While undertaking ethnographic observations in two schools, we realized the need to study language more carefully and became aware of the limits of our research resources. We secured further funds from the Spencer Foundation of Chicago to support a sociolinguistic study of children's natural discourse and their understanding of the use of linguistic forms to express social gender identities.

The structure of this monograph reflects our concerns with theory and with data. In the first part we introduce our theoretical model and describe our research strategy. We present the results of our empirical studies in reception classes in the second part. In the third part we return to our theoretical concerns.

In Chapter 1 we use our concepts of social gender identity and social representation to consider the ideology and practices of primary schools. We also begin our exploration of the difficult and confounded concepts of sex, gender and sexuality. In the second chapter we explore the terms 'social identity' and 'social representations' in a precise manner and employ them to examine dimensions of gender socialization in primary schooling. The first part concludes with Chapter 3, in which we describe our research strategy and show how our methods have been influenced by our theoretical perspective.

The six chapters which comprise the second part of the book contain our findings. Chapter 4 describes our particular approach to ethnographic investigation, presents some of our observations and demonstrates the contribution of this work to the development of our quantitative measures. Chapters 5, 6 and 7 are based upon our systematic observations of children in four reception classes. In Chapter 5 we describe the development of a measure of gender identity derived from these classroom observations. In Chapter 6 this measure is used to explore changes in gender identities in Land and McCarthy schools across the year. Observations collected only in the autumn term in two additional reception classes are analysed along with the original observations in Chapter 7. Chapter 8 is based upon our interviews with children about their understanding of gender. In Chapter 9 we report the results of our study of natural discourse in Land School and show how girls and boys use language to mark gender and to explore sex-group relations.

In Part III we return to our theoretical model of the development of social identities and re-examine it in the light of the results of our investigations of changing gender identities in the first year of formal education. We argue for the importance of distinguishing sex-group membership and gender identity. We also consider the location of social representations of gender in specific social contexts.

Preface

Throughout our report we have maintained the anonymity of the individuals we have studied. The names of schools as well as those of the teachers and children are fictitious. This handicaps us in making public our gratitude for the generous support and cooperation we received. We hope, none the less, that this anonymous expression will serve to convey our appreciation. We are happy to acknowledge our debts to the Economic and Social Research Council, to the Spencer Foundation of Chicago and to the individuals who have worked with us. Mr Nicholas Barley, Dr Marion Smith and Mrs Karen Wraith assisted us in our empirical studies.

Professors Jenny Cook-Gumperz and Peter Lloyd provided intellectual support; Professor Paul Rosenblatt succeeded where others had failed in seeking out an obscure reference, and Professor John Archer helped us sharpen our conceptual framework. Finally, various aspects of our work have been presented at seminars and conferences, and comments from colleagues in social anthropology at the University of Sussex and from Professor Robert Hinde provided considerable stimulus to our reflections.

The transformation of technical papers and end-of-grant reports into a coherent book owes much to our editor at Harvester Wheatsheaf, Farrell Burnett. We are indebted to David Lloyd for preparing the indices.

Part I

The new pupil as a social actor

1

The emergence of gender and sexuality in the primary classroom

We confronted challenging and thought-provoking events in our very first observations in reception classes. Perhaps none was richer and more intriguing than the episode of Seth dressing up. As our understanding of the processes through which children entering school has become more coherent, so our interpretation of this episode has become more complex. Initially we had sought to describe the social representation of gender which the primary school offered and observe children's re-construction of it. Episodes such as Seth's dressing up brought an awareness of the multiplicity of gender structures operating in reception classrooms from the earliest days of children's entry into school.

We report the dressing-up episode here just as Gerard recorded it on 17 September 1986, for it gives us the opportunity to outline a number of the major themes in our account of children's re-construction of their gender identities in the context of starting school.

> 9.29 am Seth selects the orange/pink nightie from the dressing up rack, though he has a lot of trouble getting it on before he finally succeeds. Then he tries to put the white tutu number on top. More difficulty. Great concentration. No-one really takes much notice. One girl, Charity, does come up to him and says 'It's not for you Seth'. He looks a bit bemused, but goes back to struggling with the white tutu. After a great deal of trouble he takes it to the teacher and asks her to put it on him. 'Oh no Seth, that's the smallest dress we've got, you won't fit into it. Let's look for something else.' [The teacher suggests.] Seth chooses a skirt. Teacher says 'That's nice' and also encourages him to put on a waistcoat.

Seth was the principal actor, but his only speech was a request for help in putting clothes on and included nothing indicative of his construction of a gender identity. We reconstruct it from his action rather than from his

3

words. Charity verbalized her views fairly succinctly. The teacher's message can be read both through language and in deeds. Each viewpoint provides different resources for the construction of a gender identity and each of these perspectives reflects a theme which is pursued in the chapters that follow.

Charity's admonition, 'It's not for you Seth', offers a window on the young child's categorical construction of gender. Charity reminded Seth that objects are gender marked and that white tutus bear the invisible but readily recognized label, 'for girls'. The rules of the gender game are usually unambiguous and unequivocal for 4–5 year olds. In the chapters which follow, we review the processes through which such young children re-construct their own society's gender code.

Our analysis of the teacher's response to Seth is considerably more complex. We were given documentation about the organization of primary education in the county at the beginning of our research work. It alerted us to the efforts which the authority was making to eliminate sexism from its schools. Against the background of these directives, the teacher might have felt uncomfortable suggesting to Seth that a skirt was unsuitable for him. Indeed, the teacher helped Seth find one which would fit and then validated his choice by saying, 'That's nice.'

In the teacher's interaction with Seth there is evidence of another ideological thread which runs through primary education, the child-centred approach. According to its precepts, teachers' interventions are designed to fit the specific needs of the individual child just as the skirt suited Seth's ample frame. Alongside the directives from county hall on sexism and those of the educational establishment on child-centred instruction, the teacher's addition of a waistcoat from a man's three-piece suit alerts us to her inclination to mark gender in a conventional, commonsense manner. Teachers are highly trained professional workers, but in a domain as important to social life as gender they encounter a struggle between competing representations. Authorities may identify approved attitudes but they cannot prevent teachers from holding other beliefs. The teacher's speech and action illustrate the articulation of competing representations of gender. In this chapter our examination of teachers' viewpoints on gender examines official anti-sexist and child-centred ideologies. We explore the interplay of different voices when we consider teachers' talk about gender in Chapter 4.

Seth's construction of a gender identity is perhaps the most ambiguous and difficult to interpret. It introduces another significant theme; the relationship between sex, gender and sexuality and the recognition that membership in a sex group does not constrain all individuals within that category to construct their sexual and their gender identities in the same fashion. Scarcely more than 4 years old, Seth was large for his age. He was

4

chunky and somewhat clumsy. In the playground he was often involved in rough-and-tumble play with other boys, yet his dressing up in the home corner might be construed as 'feminine'. In studies of young children there has been a tacit assumption that membership in a sex group defines gender identity, but issues involving sexuality are rarely considered. Distinctions between sex-group membership and sexual and gender identities are often lost, and there is a tendency to assume that all boys are masculine and all girls feminine in their construction of a gender identity. Seth's dressing up calls into question both of these assumptions and highlights a need to scrutinize the terms 'sex', 'gender' and 'sexuality' carefully. Evidence for a link to sexuality comes from the referral of 4 and 5 year old boys for treatment from parents who fear that choice of girls' clothes and play is indicative of homosexual object choice in adult life (Stoller, 1968).

The overarching themes of this study are on the one hand, young children's understanding of sex-group membership and gender identity, and on the other, the approach of teachers to sex and gender. In the remaining parts of this chapter we explore these themes before examining the conceptual limits of a taken-for-granted understanding of the terms sex, gender and sexuality.

YOUNG CHILDREN'S UNDERSTANDING OF SEX-GROUP MEMBERSHIP AND GENDER IDENTITY

Evidence to support our assertion that it is often the children in reception classes who have the most rigid and stereotyped views of sex-group membership and gender-appropriate behaviour is available in many sources. Huston (1983) has provided a comprehensive review of know-ledge, attitudes and beliefs in this domain and has documented their developmental history. Trautner (1989, 1991) has offered a developmental model which encompasses a phase of rigid thinking about gender, and he has provided longitudinal data to support his model. Virginia Paley (1984) has furnished a vivid description of kindergarten life organized around the themes of superheroes and domesticity. Each of these contributions enriches our understanding of the social representations of gender which children bring to school, and which are expressed as they create their gender identities in the classroom.

Huston (1983, 1985) offers important guidelines in thinking about developmental changes in sex-typing; that is, behaviour which is differen-tiated according to membership in one sex group or the other. The term sex-typing, common in psychological research, collapses a distinction we have been drawing between membership in a sex group and gender identities. In order to investigate gender identities, psychologists identify membership in

5

a sex group and then investigate the dimensions which are associated with this membership by society. The system of associations can be described as social representations of gender. A similarity in our approach and that of Huston is indicated by her decision to give greater attention to reports of characteristics which are attributed in terms of membership in sex groups. She relied somewhat less upon an alternative empirical strategy, namely, considering *all* statistically significant differences between girls and boys as indicative of sex-typing regardless of whether they have ever been identified as masculine or feminine traits. This latter strategy is essentially asocial and atheoretical.

A second major motif in Huston's examination of sex-typing is the bipolar versus the multidimensional investigation of sex-typed characteristics. Until the 1970s psychologists tended to conceptualize masculinity and femininity as opposite poles on a single continuum, but Bem (1974, 1981) and Spence and Helmreich (1978) introduced scales which avoided this assumption. These scales, the Bem Sex Role Inventory and the Personal Attributes Questionnaire, are now widely used and the subsequent theorizing of the results they have yielded has lead to the acceptance of masculinity and femininity as independent dimensions.

This newer strategy allows questions to be raised about the relationship between sex-group membership and particular beliefs, preferences and activities. While it may be completely obvious that an individual could enjoy both football and cooking, we may find it more difficult to think about people being simultaneously assertive and cooperative. In terms of commonsense understanding, violations of role expectations based on behavioural bipolarity (for example, female coal miners or male primary school teachers) are easier to grasp than the independence of psychological traits which mark gender.

Huston offered a matrix framework within which to locate the variety of studies of sex-typing in infants and children. Central to her review, along with her empirical inventory, is a discussion of the major theories that have been offered to account for the development of sex-typing. We outline her matrix briefly, but refer the reader to Huston or other texts for a review of social learning, cognitive developmental and psychoanalytic theories of sex-typing.

Huston identified four groups of psychological constructs – beliefs, self-perception, preferences and behaviour – which have been studied in relation to sex-group membership. These form the columns in her summarizing matrix. The five rows in the matrix are defined in terms of five content areas or domains through which the four indicators of sex-typing are expressed. These five domains are: biological gender (a puzzling term employed by Huston), activities and interests, personal–social attributes, social relationships and symbolic content. Potentially all twenty cells in

Huston's matrix are relevant to our presentation of the social representations of gender which are available to 4–5 year olds when they begin school
and through which they express their gender identities. Here we con-
centrate on the dominant themes which Huston (1985) has identified, in so
far as they are relevant to 4–5 year olds starting schools. Our aims are
different from those of Huston, who sought to summarize developmental
findings derived from extant research. Her conclusions are shaped by the
conceptual concerns of contemporary studies. Our attention is constrained
by an examination of the child as reception class pupil, in terms of a theory
of social representations and social identities which we explore in Chapter
2.

Huston concluded that 4–5 year olds are skilled interpreters of gender
marking in the activities and interests content domain, in terms of both
their own and other people's behaviour. She surveyed evidence which
indicates that, almost as soon as children of 2–3 years are able to label
themselves as girls and boys, they can identify the gender marking of
domestic artifacts and familiar activities at better than chance levels. She
cited studies which show that 3–4 year olds can even identify the typical
occupations of men and women. By the time children are old enough to
begin formal schooling, they already voice occupational preferences which
are parallel with adult gender stereotypes. For very young children, gender
functions as a conceptual scheme through which other aspects of their
social world are assimilated (cf. Duveen and Shields, 1984). Huston's
conclusions are congruent with a major finding from our earlier studies
(Lloyd and Duveen, 1989). We reported that by 2 years of age, children
display a gender-marked behavioural preference and play more with
gender appropriate toys.

Our own and Huston's evidence in the domain of social relationships
provide a similar picture of sophisticated gender marking. Even before the
age of 3, children interact more with children of their own sex group.
Huston suggested a relationship between interaction and preference for
particular gender-marked objects and activities. Thus children who enjoy
enacting domestic scenes will find themselves playing with girls while those
who aspire to visit other planets will be engaged primarily with boys.
Huston's conclusions, based upon a thorough review of empirical studies, is
completely congruent with Paley's (1984) observations of American
kindergarten children of about 5 years of age.

While Huston found solid evidence that 3–5 year olds have considerable
knowledge of gender marking in two domains – activities and interests, and
social relationships – she noted a lack of evidence which would suggest that
children of this age are aware of, or display an understanding of, gender
marking within the domain of personal–social attributes. Very young
children are unable to assign traits such as assertiveness, cooperativeness

7

and independence to members of sex groups. Such findings are consistent with studies of children's perception of other people which reveal that it is only in middle childhood, from about 9 years of age, that personality traits are used by children to describe others (Livesley and Bromley, 1973). It is worth noting that the only personality trait for which Maccoby and Jacklin (1974) reported consistent empirical evidence of sex differences in their classic study was aggression. Although Bem (1974, 1981) and Spence and Helmreich (1978) found that adults systematically attribute personality traits to men and women, investigators have had little success in producing data for sex-group differences along such dimensions. In the adult world, psychologists have found that expectations about personality traits are systematically assigned on the basis of sex-group membership but that observable behaviour is less clearly differentiated (Deaux, 1984).

There is little doubt that children's understanding of their social world and the conventions relating to gender undergoes striking changes. A theme, with origins in Kohlberg's (1966) initial formulation of the cognitive developmental approach, is the qualitatively different, initially more rigid, and progressively more flexible gender awareness of children in early and middle childhood. Trautner and his colleagues (Trautner *et al.*, 1989) have proposed a three-phase model which describes the development of children's understanding of sex-typing. The first phase is characterized by unawareness of links between sex-group membership and traits. In the second phase, gender-marked traits are linked exclusively to sex-group membership. In the final phase, children display awareness that adherence to gender-marked traits varies within and between sex groups. In their longitudinal study of German children, Trautner and his colleagues showed that 5 year olds possess considerable knowledge of gender marking in the domains of activities and interests and of personal–social attributes, but that the peak of rigidity was reached at 6 years. Noticeable flexibility was recorded by 8 years and was linked to both general intellectual development and the social environment.

The evidence which we have considered thus far shows that children starting school have considerable awareness about the gender marking of objects, activities and occupations, even though they may be less sophisticated in their understanding of personal and social traits. In addition, they display a preference for interaction with children of their own gender, but the interpretation of this segregation in homogeneous sex groups raises important conceptual issues.

Although we have already noted that gender segregation may reflect gender-marked object preferences, Huston (1983) offers three interrelated propositions which cognitive developmental theory raises about the relationship between understanding and behaviour. First of all, knowledge, awareness or understanding would be expected to precede preferences or

8

behaviour, yet we have already noted that 3 year olds display a preference for gender-marked objects well before they can explain the bases of their choice. Huston suggests that only in later childhood does gender understanding guide behaviour. Second, she noted that there is only limited correlation between knowledge and preference. What is striking in the available evidence is that for boys there is a closer relationship between gender knowledge and preference than there is for girls. In fact Huston concludes that 'girls move away from feminine preferences and identity during the age period from about 5 or 6 until adolescence' (1985, p. 12), although their knowledge of gender stereotyping is increasing just as that of boys. Again, our own evidence confirms Huston's conclusion; girls and boys share a similar understanding of the gender marking of toys, but girls display less stereotypic preferences than boys in their play with toys (Lloyd and Duveen, 1989). Finally, Huston presents the discouraging conclusion that changes in understanding do not necessarily lead to changes in behaviour.

Although psychologists are concerned to account for relationships between understanding and behaviour, less attention has been given to the origins of gender knowledge. John Archer's recent review of the development of gender roles is typical. He suggests that 'Boys and girls gradually develop different subcultures within their segregated groups' (Archer, 1992, p. 35) and implies that boys' and girls' restricted interactions contribute to the construction of systematically distinct social worlds. We believe that this approach discounts the importance of the existing social order. We employ the theory of social representations, which is examined in the following chapter, to signal a need to specify the dimensions of the adult world which contribute to the development of these subcultures in childhood.

Returning to our initial assertion that it is often the children in reception classes who have the most rigid and stereotyped views about sex-group membership and gender appropriate behaviour, perhaps the final word belongs to Paley. She has noted:

> Kindergarten is a triumph of sexual self-stereotyping. No amount of adult subterfuge or propaganda deflects the five-year-old's passion for segregation by sex. They think they have invented the differences between boys and girls and, as with any new invention, must prove that it works. (1984, p. ix)

INFLUENCES UPON TEACHERS' APPROACHES TO GENDER

We have already noted that the two major professional influences on teachers' representations of sex and gender – explicit anti-sexism and a child-centred ideology – make it difficult for them to avoid holding conflicting views. The *naturalness* of girls playing in the home corner and of boys monopolizing the playground is so easily taken for granted that it escapes comment or is readily dismissed. We consider questions about the invisibility and naturalness of sex differences in the last section of this chapter, when we examine the conceptual limits of the terms sex, gender, sexuality and identities. Here we explore the power of explicit efforts to avoid sexism in primary schooling and the influence of a child-centred pedagogy in the reproduction of gendered identities.

Both the local authority and the head teachers in the schools we studied were aware of sexism and actively sought to combat it by encouraging teachers' sensitivity to issues concerning gender. The major thrust of their approach was to restrict divisions based upon sex and to avoid the association of specific objects, activities and beliefs with one sex group or the other. Teachers are aware of the issue of sexism and deliberately avoid sexist language. We routinely heard the term 'home corner' used to describe the domestic set-up of cooker, basin, table, chairs, plates and pans which was once known as the 'Wendy house'. This usage explicitly decouples the female and the domestic by substituting 'home' for 'Wendy', but other experiences reinstate the equation of domesticity and femaleness. Paley's book is a vivid account of the struggle of 5 year old boys to escape from home and domesticity in order to expand their horizons and to travel the universe – a voyage that girls seemed rarely to contemplate.

But even official policy is not free of contradiction. Although the register was segregated into lists of boys' names and girls' names, we were assured that this was designed to ensure that the collection of attendance statistics was efficient. In some classes the teacher took only a mental register and thus avoided making audible an administrative organization based upon sex groups. In others the list was further divided into whole- and half-day children, and this mixed boys' and girls' names.

Further efforts to provide an anti-sexist environment included the use of gender-neutral symbols such as flowers and pets to mark individual children's coat hooks and storage places in some classes. In one school the head and the reception class teacher debated the merits of this strategy, with the head advocating strongly the anti-sexist merits of such a procedure. We explore their dialogue in our examination of teachers' talk in Chapter 4. Occasionally a deliberately anti-sexist strategy produced such contrived classroom divisions at playtime or assembly as line-ups differentiating children wearing lace-up shoes versus others, or children wearing jumpers versus other kinds of tops. But as French (1986) reported, and we observed in the first section, perhaps the most sexist persons in a reception class are the children themselves. Anti-sexist ideology also encounters limits in the taken-for-granted, commonsense representations of adults.

10

When we carried out our empirical research in the latter half of the 1980s, English primary school education was still dominated by a child-centred ideology which had been officially advocated in the 1967 report of the Plowden Committee (CACE, 1967). A reaction against a nineteenth-century emphasis on adult authority and a narrow, immutable curriculum, the rise of child-centred ideology coincided with the introduction of compulsory elementary schooling in Britain (cf. Boyd, 1989). Its combination of emphases on individual development, the importance of play and the innocence of childhood produces a school environment which is readily recognizable. It is this specific type of English infant education which provided the setting for our research.

Although the ideology of the Plowden Report has survived, it has not been immune to criticism, and recently has been the object of political and professional attack (cf. *Teaching and Learning in English Urban Schools*, 1991). In addition, in many authorities primary education has been formally restructured twice since the Report was published. The primary schools described in the report included children from 5 years to 11 years of age. In the 1970s, secondary schools were reorganized and primary education was extended to include 12 year olds. In the earlier infant schools, which included only 5–7 year olds, classes were often composed of children of mixed ages. With reorganization and a wider age range, classes became more homogeneous according to age. Primary education was again reorganized in our local community, and nationally, in the 1980s, when a shrinking population of children threatened the viability of secondary schools. Once more the 5–7 year olds formed a separate school, but the earlier element of mixed-age classes was often abandoned.

The move away from mixed-age classes for the youngest children may have major implications for teachers trying to implement an anti-sexist programme. As we noted in the preceding section, children aged 5–7 years draw rigid boundaries between the sexes in their efforts to understand the gender system. Developmental psychologists have shown that children choose to play with peers of their own sex more frequently in groups which are homogeneous in terms of age (Maccoby and Jacklin, 1987). Thus age-banding may be contributing to a narrowing of children's experiences of mixed-sex peer interaction and reinforcing their already rigid beliefs about gender. Trautner and his colleagues (1989) noted that increasing flexibility was influenced strongly by social experience and in particular by 'perceived sex-role discrimination and its social endorsement' (p. 9).

Surface diversity in the organization and practice of English primary education might suggest that the three defining characteristics of the child-centred approach – emphasis upon individual development, the importance of play and the assumption of childhood innocence – have been lost. Yet Henry Pluckrose (1987), an experienced primary school head teacher,

11

has argued that this visible diversity cannot disguise a surprisingly uniform and conservative curriculum. Primary school teachers have traditionally viewed themselves as generalists who would reply to the question, 'What do you teach?', by saying, 'Children'. Although this approach is currently under attack, they have seen their goals as helping the whole child to develop and find an individual personal identity. We question the extent to which primary school children can achieve an individuated identity when teachers rely upon their representations of such common social categories as age, gender, race, ethnicity and social class in their interaction with children and their organization of classroom life.

In a classic study, the sociologist Ronald King (1978) set out to describe the nature of infant education just as the first secondary school reorganization was getting under way. He approached these schools in an anthropological fashion and compared three schools in the same community, which drew their children from families that provided different social class upbringings. King explored many variables in his efforts to describe infant teachers as a group and to characterize the differences as well as the similarities between the three schools. Before examining the dimensions along which there was gender differentiation, we should note his stricture that, 'Explanations of social class differences in education that ignore sex differences are as unacceptable as explanations of sex differences which ignore social class' (King, 1978, p. 134). That said, our interest here lies in his description of gender differentiation as it has implications for the development of gendered identities. Undoubtedly, children also develop identities related to their membership in other significant social groups reflecting class, ethnic and religious affiliations. It is for analytic purposes that we focus upon the development of social gender identities.

King's description highlights the impact of the infant teacher on children's knowledge of gender, both when teaching is quite deliberate and when incidental instruction is provided. He notes that the things which happen in the classroom are arranged or allowed to happen by the teacher. The teacher creates the realities of the classroom and these include the story world of reading, the reporting and writing of news, and work in numbers and science.

We have already described the local authority's official attempts to combat sexism, so it is interesting to consider the influence of incidental teaching in conveying a gender prescription. King provides an example in a class discussion of christening. Following an interaction about telling baby boys from baby girls at birth, the teacher turned to the colour of the baby's clothes:

Teacher: What colour do we say for a boy as a rule?
Pupil: White.

Pupil: Blue.
Teacher: Blue for a boy and what for a girl?
Pupils: White!
Pupil: Green! Green!
Teacher: White or?
Pupil: Pink.
Teacher: Pink! Pink! That's right! (King, 1978, p. 46)

This is only one of a series of vivid examples of the incidental teaching which suggests that children's identities are shaped by the sex group to which they belong, whether they are girls or boys. Whether teaching is explicit or incidental, children learn that sex-group membership has inexorable consequences.

The christening example can be cited to illustrate aspects of an individuated teaching style which seeks to be responsive to the needs of particular children. None the less, behind teachers' use of 'pictures' of individual children designed to enshrine the uniqueness of each, King identified their use of two groups – girls and boys – to facilitate classroom control. This sex-based strategy was also evidenced in separate places for clothes, separate lines at playtime, separate administrative records, the separation of information such as heights or numbers of siblings in teaching displays, and the use of the two groups competitively to accomplish classroom chores such as changing for physical education or tidying up the room. When questioned about these practices, teachers said that they had never thought about them or that they were convenient or natural.

The Plowden Report asserted that, 'At the heart of the education process is the child' (CACE, 1967, p. 7). Although the child of child-centred ideology was presented as an individual, unmarked by membership in any social groups, we note, thirty years on, that the child was dealt with linguistically as the generic male. The sentence quoted above is followed by, 'No advance in policy, no acquisitions of new equipment have their desired effect . . . unless they are fundamentally acceptable to him.' At the time of the Plowden Report, gender had not appeared as a major issue in education. The differentiating characteristic which did receive attention was 'cultural deprivation', for it was held to limit the benefit children might gain from schooling. Teachers aware of differences in the achievement and adjustment of primary school boys and girls reconciled their experience with their beliefs by adopting a developmental view of boys as less mature than girls of the same age. For teachers these are 'taken-for-granted "natural" sex differences' (King, 1978, p. 69).

Teachers' beliefs in their prototypes of girls and boys as different kinds of pupils are repeatedly confirmed by the behaviour of girls and boys in their classrooms. King examined the contents of stories written by a group of children of almost 7 years old, and found that girls and boys had very different interests. Domestic settings of home and children provided the majority of themes for the stories of all the girls, while a third of the boys never wrote such stories. The dominant themes of boys' stories – rockets, planes, fighting and accidents – were only occasionally employed by girls, and then only by two thirds of them. One third of the girls never used boys' themes. Although two thirds of girls and boys occasionally wrote stories containing themes of interest to the other sex group, there was little overall similarity in their creative writing. Paley's (1984) observations of American children are reproduced in the written work of these English children, despite the fact that King studied primary school pupils at least two years older than the kindergarteners. Domesticity is the dominant theme for girls and adventure that of boys.

Examination of several hundred assessments by teachers of the academic progress of children in their classes provided King with further evidence of sex-group differentiation. He reported not only that girls were rated more highly in general but that, in the two schools in which he identified different social class upbringing, the gender differences were greater than class differences.

Issues of naughtiness offer a similar picture of readily observable differences in the behaviour of girls and boys. In the educational priority area school in which King worked, there was a special 'adjustment class' established for children experiencing severe academic or behavioural problems. Of the fourteen children in this special class, ten were boys. The four girls were all described as slow rather than as presenting behavioural problems. The boys in this special class were viewed as typical of boys in the school by the head, who described boys as responsible for 90 per cent of the trouble in the school. In the more middle-class school, teachers more often described boys as being sillier than girls, but here they were not seen as being troublesome. Teachers' expectations that boys are livelier is typified by the comments of two teachers in the most middle-class school; they wished that their boys might be, 'more spirited', or more, 'boyish' (King, 1978, p. 118). The view of boys as more difficult was also seen in teachers' more frequent admonishment of boys than girls. Although a child-centred ideology represents each pupil as an individual, sex remained a major organizational principle in the primary school classrooms which King observed. Confronted by behaviour which is differentiated in terms of sex-group membership, teachers often rely upon their commonsense expectations about the development and behaviour of girls and boys, although it may be rationalized by appeals to ideology.

THE CONCEPTUAL LIMITS OF SEX, GENDER AND SEXUALITY

Until now we have assumed that our use of the terms sex, gender and sexuality is intelligible to the reader, but this strategy masks considerable divergence about the application of these concepts in psychological and social research. Money (1988) popularized the term 'gender' in the 1950s in the context of his work with babies whose genital sex was ambiguous. These individuals were assigned to a sex group, either male or female, and reared according to this designation even though their genital or chromosomal sex might be incongruent with the assignment. In the face of such incongruence Money believed that it was illogical to describe these individuals as having a male or a female sex role and instead suggested the terms 'gender role' and 'gender identity'.

A convention which became popular in the 1970s was to use the word 'sex' to refer to a binary division between male and female based upon biological criteria, and to employ the term 'gender' to describe an often parallel differentiation deriving from the social construction of appropriate activity for members of these two groups (Archer and Lloyd, 1986; Kessler and McKenna, 1978; Oakley, 1981). Money (1988) was critical of this approach, which he viewed as reductionist since it allows both biological and social scientists to focus on their own domain and to ignore each other's work. He argued that it is impossible to study pure biological maleness or femaleness, and proposed instead a typology of gender differences which reflects the exclusivity of their gender distribution and the mutability of the traits.

We heard echoes of a biological–social, sex–gender distinction in our conversations with teachers. Systems of sex differences and gender differentiation appear to function side by side, although teachers do not use the terms 'sex' and 'gender' explicitly or systematically. They do, as King (1978) documented, see sex differences as natural, biological and unchanging when they comment 'boys will be boys, they just take up more space'. Here their observations take on a certainty which derives from a belief in the biological origins and immutability of the differences they report. In their efforts to implement anti-sexist directives, teachers learn to say 'home corner' when before they talked about the Wendy house; in this usage their understanding is closer to that of social constructionists and reflects faith in processes of social learning. Gender-differentiated social practices are viewed as being similar to language – arbitrary and changeable; a new, more egalitarian symbol system is deliberately employed to replace one based upon sexist inequality.

In her influential textbook on social development, Maccoby (1980)

15

explicitly rejected the use of 'sex' to indicate divisions employing biological criteria and gender for social convention. She believes that such systematic usage carries with it a commitment to the specific causal explanations we observed in conversations with teachers. Thus sex differences would be viewed as biologically determined and unchangeable, while gender differentiation would reflect social influence. Rather than prejudging issues concerning the origins of behavioural differences through the choice of terminology, Maccoby determined to avoid this device. In addition, she proposed that methodological considerations support her conceptual objections. The sex–gender distinction arose in the context of the study of transsexuals, who deliberately reject their biological sex and struggle to become a member of the other gender group (Neitz, 1982). Most individuals' membership in a gender group is the same as their sex-group classification. Certainly, in studying children, psychologists rely upon the children's membership in a sex group in order to classify them, and then observe the similarities and differences between the two groups. Indeed, this is the process which parents, peers and other adults and children use in helping very young children in their re-construction of an appropriate gender identity.

The objections Maccoby raises about linking the term 'sex' to biology and 'gender' to social convention are formidable, and the methodological problem of identifying children through their membership in a sex group and then seeking to study the development of a gender identity haunts us throughout this study. None the less, there is a conceptual gain in examining sex-group membership and gender identities separately. It allows us to escape from the assumption that all members of a sex group adopt gender rules in a similar manner. In other words, in distinguishing sex and gender we are able to consider variation in gender-marked behaviour within sex groups. But there are issues other than those of origins which are raised by trying to separate sex and gender neatly. These include questions concerning the definition of difference, the nature of biological knowledge and the role of sexuality.

So natural is it to assign children to groups as girls and boys that we may overlook important questions, such as how biological criteria function in our decisions, or how many groups we should form. When we look more closely we can see that we employ a biological distinction at second hand. The attending professionals, midwives and doctors, make the assignment when children are born, most often on the basis of external genitalia. Their decision is usually reinforced by gender-marked names, clothing and behavioural expectations, and it is these signs which signify 'boy' and 'girl'. But in the world of competitive, international sport, sex designation may become a matter of controversy and names, clothing and behaviour suspect when competitors are believed to be transsexuals. In this situation it is chromosomes and not external genitalia which are considered crucial. What, then, are to be the biological criteria which determine membership in a sex group, and how many groups are to be formed?

Again, there are taken-for-granted assumptions here. External genitalia may be subject to reconstruction; chromosomes do not deceive. But even here, where we assume that the answer is unequivocal – that the twenty-third pair of chromosomes being XX or XY categorically defines female-ness and maleness – ambiguity arises. Are the OX individuals, whose secondary biological features appear feminine, truly female when they are incapable of producing ova? And what of the individuals who carry mosaic patterns which include both Xs and Ys? They look masculine but are sometimes sterile.

Is it the knowledge that reproduction reflects the union of ovum and spermatozoon which suggests a simple binary division into male and female according to biological criteria? But the simplicity and certainty of a categorical distinction is also called into question by hormonal abnor-malities, which result in XX fetuses developing male genitalia and XY fetuses failing to differentiate as males (Money, 1988). As soon as we consider secondary sexual characteristics – those which are influenced by hormones but not absolutely differentiated, such as body hair, breast development and height – the situation becomes even more confusing, as these traits are not distributed exclusively to one sex group or the other. It is common knowledge that some women are hairier than some men, that some men have breasts and that the distributions of heights of men and women overlap.

These examples, which call into question the givenness of a simple binary division into male and female, serve to highlight the nature of biological knowledge. It too is a construction, the product of the community of scholars who work on genetics, endocrinology, molecular biology and related disciplines. Knowledge of the process of reproduction serves as a metaphor to organize thinking and to naturalize distinctions in related domains. It perpetuates the belief that a binary distinction is natural. The convention in the sporting world that it is chromosomes which determine membership in the sex groups, male and female, alerts us to the arbitrary nature of the division of individuals into two, and only two, non-overlapping groups.

But if sexual reproduction serves as a metaphor sustaining a belief in a binary division into male and female, it also serves to naturalize our views of sexuality. Human sexual behaviour is schematized by academics to preserve a clear dichotomy in the sexual behaviour of men and women (cf. Connell, 1987). Although it is almost one hundred years since Freud (1905) set out to show how sexuality is constructed in terms of its object, aim and source, it was Harlow's monkeys, raised in isolation, which offered

17

dramatic evidence that sexual responses are shaped by early experience. Without it these animals were sexual failures and their rehabilitation problematic (cf. Goldfoot *et al.*, 1984).

Money (1988), who has pursued issues of gender role, gender identity and erotic orientation for more than thirty years, can be seen as continuing Freud's project to promote an appreciation of the importance of childhood experience in the creation of those psychological representations or 'lovemaps', as Money terms them, which guide the choice of erotic partner and performance. From research with animals other than humans, he underscores the importance of childhood and in particular a period of juvenile sexual play. Indeed, he suggests that childhood sexual rehearsal play is a research priority if we seek to understand adult lovemaps. Our discussion of children's sexuality in Chapter 9 suggests that it may still be many years before such a study appears on a research agenda. There is little published research on the topic, and Best's (1983) insightful study explains why this is so. She suggests that children appreciate the discomfort their sexuality generates in the adults around them and carefully ensure that it remains *sub rosa*. Developmental psychologists have not shown any greater enthusiasm for tackling the issue than have other adults.

The anthropologist Davenport (1976) reminds us that, while sexual behaviour employs biological structures, the organization of sexuality is a cultural product. It is social convention realized through individual experience which influences the choice of partners, objects, places, times, frequencies, etc., of sexual behaviour.

Eating is also subject to cultural patterning, although beliefs may invoke biological explanations. Holmberg's (1969) description of Siriono taboos on eating snake illustrate the patterning of eating behaviour by biological and cultural factors. The Siriono believe that anyone who eats the flesh of poisonous snakes risks being poisoned, but the taboo extends to non-poisonous snakes as well. Although a chief had watched Holmberg eat a poisonous snake with no ill effect and had eaten a muffin cooked with the fat of the same snake, the chief regurgitated the lot when informed of the snake fat ingredient.

Despite the recognition that sexuality is shaped by social convention, the reproductive metaphor naturalizes our understanding of sexuality. In spite of Freud's initial insights, this even occurs in classical psychoanalytic theory, which defines normal sexuality in terms of heterosexual object choice and labels homosexual choice as pathological (Schaffer, 1977). Consideration of homosexual pairing helps to bring into question the reproductive metaphor which sustains a binary opposition in the biological domain of sex. Reproduction is viewed as given and immutable; in discussions of gender it naturalizes conventional definitions of masculinity and femininity, and in descriptions of sexuality it yields the labels 'normal' and 'pathological'. By giving serious consideration to the role of sexual object choice, heterosexual, homosexual and bisexual, theorists have been able to avoid employing binary divisions. An understanding of the construction of sexuality casts light on discussion of sex roles and sex identities, gender roles and gender identities (cf. Connell, 1987).

A consequence of child-centred pedagogical ideology, with its view of very young children as sexual innocents, is a failure to theorize sexuality and intergroup relations between sex-group members in primary school. The teacher who, upon seeing a 4 year old girl and boy cuddling under the table, said to us 'I'd rather not know what's going on' would probably invoke adult models of heterosexuality to understand their behaviour, if she allowed herself to think about it at all. The teacher's comments suggest that the precept of childhood innocence is in conflict with her everyday experiences in the classroom.

In our discussion of anti-sexist ideology, we described the belief that a more egalitarian gender system could be instituted by adopting a new set of words or symbols, but we have failed thus far to consider the most salient aspect of male–female relations, its hierarchical structure. Male hegemony has for millennia been the order of human social life. Whether we examine the classical one-sex model of woman as an inverted man or the Renaissance view of two distinct sexes which is supported by modern biological knowledge, women are devalued (Gould, 1991; Laqueur, 1991). So pervasive and enduring has been this structure that change is slow and difficult to achieve. The deliberate blindness to sexuality in primary education, which functions to naturalize social representations of sex and gender and is part of child-centred ideology, may also inhibit rapid progress towards greater equality.

2

Social representations, social identities and schooling

In Chapter 1 we used the terms 'social representations of gender' and 'social gender identity', assuming that they could be understood without systematic definition. In this chapter, we want to be more precise about the sense in which we use these concepts in our analysis of gender socialization in reception classes.

Moscovici introduced the term 'social representation' into social psychology. Social representations are the products or features of social groups, and form organized systems of 'values, ideas and practices' (Moscovici, 1973, p. xiii) which pre-exist the birth of any individual and, although they form the context of their lives, persist after an individual's death. It is through access to shared social representations that individuals are able to understand the structure of social life and to communicate with others. In the first part of this chapter we examine Moscovici's theory of social representation.

We have employed the concept of social identity in a particular sense, to help us maintain an awareness of individuals as they are constructed in terms of the groups of which they are members (cf. Duveen and Lloyd, 1986). Individuals' social identities reflect the social representations of the significant groups in society to which they belong. The development of social identities draws upon resources made available through the intern-alization of these social representations. Our basic premise is that individuals are so inextricably interwoven in the fabric of social relations within which their lives are lived that a representation of the 'individual' divorced from the 'social' is theoretically inadequate. There is no pure 'individuality' which can be apprehended independently of social relations. In the second part of this chapter we relate our use of the term 'social identity' to the theorizing of other social scientists.

Gender identity is a particularly difficult concept to place in terms of individuality and group membership. Because sexual behaviour is relatively private in our society, it may be tempting to think of gender identities as private and individual too. But social representations of gender cannot be understood unless account is taken of membership in a sex group. Though the terms are often confounded, social gender identities and sex-group membership are not completely overlapping and coterminous. However, in Chapter 1 we suggested that, when organizing classroom activity, even teachers enjoined by the individualistic philosophy of a child-centred pedagogy relied upon images which reflected their objectification of social representations of gender in terms of a bipolar classification of sex-group membership. As a consequence, membership in a sex group and a social gender identity appear to be indistinguishable.

In the final section of this chapter, we consider the extent to which primary schools offer particular social representations of gender which can function for their pupils as resources for the construction of gendered social identities. In order to do this, we examine the variables which have been identified as significant in gender socialization in school, and then return explicitly to the role which starting school plays in providing children with additional resources to be utilized in the re-construction of their social gender identities.

SOCIAL REPRESENTATIONS

Social representations as structures provide collectivities with intersubjectively shared means for understanding and communicating, but Moscovici also uses the term to describe the process through which these structures are constructed and transformed. The process of social representation is not bound by the canons of logical discourse, nor is it regulated by procedures of empirical verification or falsification. Rather, social representation is composed of two complementary functions, anchoring (whereby the unfamiliar or remote is absorbed into the familiar categories of everyday cognition) and objectification (whereby representations are projected into the world, so that what was abstract is transformed into something concrete). For example, the description of electrons circling an atom was *anchored* in an earlier physical model of planets rotating around a sun. Once *anchored* in this way the model is *objectified* so that the reality of the atom is construed in terms of orbiting electrons/planets. These two functions are interdependent, in the sense that a representation can become securely anchored to the extent that it is also objectified (made concrete) and, vice versa, that objectification would be impossible unless a representation was anchored (became familiar). Nevertheless, objectification and anchoring

21

are distinguishable analytically as two moments in the process of social representation.

In discussing the process of objectification Moscovici refers to the *figurative nucleus* of a social representation, which he describes as '. . . an image structure that reproduces a conceptual structure in a visible manner' (Moscovici, 1981, p. 199). The most graphic examples of iconic aspects of social representations of gender in our work are visible in children's evocations of sexuality in their pretend play which we consider in Chapter 9. In pretend play sexuality is represented as the union of bipolar opposites, and is celebrated in routine rituals of marriage and domestic life. The structure of a bipolar opposition is the connecting thread between sexuality, marriage and domestic life and each implicates the other. When one element is evoked in pretend play it readily leads on to the next.

Moscovici also makes a distinction between the consensual universe of social representations and the reified universe of scientific discourse, which respects the laws of logic and whose products are open to empirical investigation (1981). Moscovici is not proposing a particular philosophy of science, but focusing upon a distinction made in our society between everyday or commonsense understanding and scientific understanding. He proposes that these two universes, the consensual and the reified, correspond to a particular social representation in which common sense is distinguished from the realm of the scientific. Moscovici notes that while scientific understanding 'attempts to construct a map of the forces, objects and events unaffected by our desires and consciousness', social representation 'stimulates and shapes our collective consciousness, explaining things and events so as to be accessible to each of us and relevant to our immediate concerns' (Moscovici, 1981, p. 187).

In the first chapter, we observed that a scientific understanding of the process of reproduction influences commonsense understanding of gender, and this supports Moscovici's proposition. We went further and suggested that common sense has in turn influenced the scientific study of sexuality. Although scientific understanding and common sense may be differentiated as distinct forms of thought, they are not, in practice, exclusive. When we bring scientific understanding to bear on gender relationships in society, we cannot step completely out of the world of social representations into a totally logical and objective realm of science.

This issue is clarified by examining the theory of social representations alongside other constructivist approaches in psychology and the social sciences. In all of them, the subject and object of knowledge are viewed as correlative and co-constitutive and not as terms which designate independent entities. The ontological corollary to this position is that social representations are constitutive of the realities represented, a construction affected through anchoring and objectification. Accordingly, the *content* of what is constructed has the same significance as the process of construction. Moscovici's dictum that social representations are always the representation *of something* reflects this theoretical position (Moscovici, 1984).

As well as being the representation of something, social representations are also representations *of someone or some collective* (cf. Moscovici, 1984). The interdependence between social representations and the collectives for which they function means that social life is always considered as a construction, rather than being taken as a given.

The duality of social representations in constructing both the order of social life and an understanding of it recalls a similar duality in Piaget's conceptualization of operational knowing. The availability of scientific knowledge which could serve as his point of reference facilitated Piaget's empirical research but in the consensual universe of social life there is no privileged vantage point. In his study of psychoanalysis, Moscovici (1976a) took the body of psychoanalytic theory originating in Freud's work as an objectified point of reference from which to compare and contrast the social representations of psychoanalysis constructed by different social groups. He observed the transformation of this body of knowledge as it was reconstituted in the network of representations held by different groups. A reference point in the domain of gender is more difficult to establish.

We have taken social representations of gender as our reference point for analyzing social gender identities. We have used the knowledge about gender which has been accumulated in the past thirty years as a reference point for our study (cf. Archer and Lloyd, 1986; Maccoby and Jacklin, 1974; Walum, 1977). In the final section of Chapter 1 we examined the contemporary use of the term gender and considered the relation of gender to sex and sexuality. Here we examine the salient features of social representations of gender as they are diffused in common-sense understanding. The most obvious aspect of social representations of gender in our own society, and many others, is the differential and primarily positive evaluation of masculine practices and objects. Related to this is the hierarchical pattern of social relations, with masculine roles generally being more positively perceived (Bem, 1991).

There is a repeated asymmetry in gender evaluation which means that membership in the male sex group entails privileged access to resources, be they intellectual, interpersonal or economic. This is a shorthand way of describing the differential prestige which attaches to pursuits and objects which are designated as masculine. In the intellectual sphere, the sciences are accorded greater honour than arts subjects and are described as masculine (Weinreich-Haste, 1979). In the interpersonal realm, the boss, usually a man, is accorded greater status than the secretary, usually a woman, and consequently has a larger work space and the right to initiate interactions and to expect deference (Henley, 1977). In the economic sphere, jobs which are usually filled by men attract larger remuneration as well as greater prestige; bosses are paid more than secretaries. This pattern of male hegemony is repeated in all areas of social life despite the challenges of the second wave of feminism.

For the past twenty years this asymmetric pattern has been described in terms of the patriarchal organization of society (Mitchell, 1974). In the writings of Lacan, this asymmetry is raised to a principle of mental life, as the name of the father and the phallus are proclaimed as the foundations of the symbolic order. Even as staunch a feminist as Juliet Mitchell sees little immediate possibility for change.

Perhaps the most revolutionary challenge to patriarchy comes from lesbian and gay movements. As long as heterosexuality was seen as the dominant and normative form of sexual expression, the social regulation of gender, expressed in terms of two reciprocal and hierarchically ordered social categories, was readily interpreted as natural, biologically determined and unchanging. The possibility of other family structures and other sexualities undermines the biological basis of patriarchy and allows the circulation of new social representations of gender (Connell, 1987).

The influence exercised by social representations on individuals takes different forms (Duveen and Lloyd, 1990a). Some social representations impose an imperative obligation on individuals to adopt a particular social identity. This is the case, for example, with representations of age, gender or ethnicity, where individuals are generally constrained to construct prescribed social identities. In these domains there is an external obligation which derives from the ways in which others assign individuals to age, sex, racial and national groups.

In other instances, the influence of social representations is exercised through a contractual obligation rather than an imperative one. In these cases, an individual joining a social group contracts to adopt a particular social identity. Social representations of psychoanalysis provide an example of a contractual obligation. As a body of knowledge, psychoanalysis exercises no external obligation on individuals to interiorize the categories of analytic thinking as psychologically active constructions. But entry to some social groups (principally that of psychoanalysts themselves, but also other groups of carers of whose world-view an analytic perspective forms part) is dependent upon individuals contracting to construe the world in terms of psychoanalytic categories. The lively controversy occasioned by Masson's (1984) claim that Freud had suppressed the truth about his female patients' childhood seductions can be seen as a contractual dispute. Membership in the group of classical analysts entails a contractual obligation to accept Freud's interpretation of patients' verbal accounts of childhood seductions as evidence of infantile sexual fantasy.

A developmental perspective is a further dimension of a theory of social representations, one implied by its constructivist approach. We have interpreted Moscovici's formulations within a *genetic* structuralist framework, viewing a structure as the relatively enduring organization of a function, and a function as implying its organization in a structure (Duveen and Lloyd, 1990a). From this developmental perspective we have distinguished the following three types of transformation associated with social representations:

1. *Sociogenesis*, which describes the construction and transformation of the social representations of social groups about specific objects.
2. *Ontogenesis*, which describes the development of individuals in relation to social representations.
3. *Microgenesis*, which describes the evocation and transformation of social representations in social interaction.

Moscovici's (1976a) study of psychoanalysis is an example of sociogenesis, the diffusion of scientific knowledge through the community as it is reconstructed by different social groups. But it is not only knowledge originating in scientific discourses which gives rise to social representations; other themes also circulate in society through the medium of social representations. Beliefs about health offer a contemporary example of sociogenesis. The impact of ideas about preventive medicine on social representations of health has lead to a dramatic reduction in cigarette smoking and to changes in rules concerning smoking in public places. As we can see from this example, sociogenesis takes place in time. When social representations are investigated at a particular moment, the resulting description needs to be viewed in an historical perspective. The changes in gender relations which occurred in the 1970s have been described as the second wave of feminism. The contemporary social identity of feminists is thus distinguished from that of the individuals who struggled for the enfranchisement of women at the beginning of the century.

If, as Moscovici asserts, the society into which children are born is a 'thinking society', it is social representations which constitute the 'thinking environment' for the child. We have described the development of the competence to participate as actors in this thinking society as the ontogenesis of social representations. Through ontogenesis, children reconstruct the social representations of their community and create various social identities, but the process is not restricted to childhood. Across the life-span, individuals – adults as well as children – engage with novel social representations in order to participate in the life of a group. Both when starting school and when moving into a retirement home, new social identities are constructed.

Interpersonal communication entails a third developmental aspect of social representation. The evocation of social representations in social interaction occurs as individuals construct an understanding of the situation and locate themselves and their interlocutors as social subjects. In many circumstances, a mutuality in the understanding constructed by different participants may reduce the need for any explicit specification or negotiation of social identities. But where a mutuality of understanding cannot be taken for granted, or where an assumed mutuality breaks down, the negotiation of social identities becomes an explicit and identifiable feature of social interaction (cf. Gumperz, 1982). In these circumstances, the negotiation of social identities may involve the coordination of different points of view and the resolution of conflicts.

Some examples may help to illustrate the possible relationships between these three types of genetic transformation. Consider first of all a scientist who proposes a new theory, and let us assume that we are dealing with an Einstein or a Freud proposing a radical new interpretation of human knowledge or human experience. Through various forms of social interaction (publications or lectures), the scientist tries to communicate his or her theory to colleagues. The communication is successful to the extent that other scientists understand the concepts being proposed, and also accept that these concepts are well-founded and themselves begin to use them. The outcome will be ontogenetic transformations in the representations held by these scientists as individuals, as well as a sociogenetic transformation in the representation held by the scientific community as a social group.

By contrast, consider children as they grasp some social representation of their community – gender or ethnicity, for example. Children need to receive some communication, whether through interaction with other children or adults or from the public representations provided in the media for this development to occur. These microgenetic processes may lead to ontogenetic transformations in the child's representation of the world, but the social representations of their community are unlikely to be influenced by these particular microgenetic processes. In this case there is ontogenesis without sociogenesis, a state of affairs which is a characteristic feature of childhood, given the negligible influence which children are able to exert on the representations held by their community.

In both of these examples ontogenesis and sociogenesis are the consequences of microgenetic processes. Indeed, microgenesis constitutes a motor for the genetic transformations of social representations. When children enter the school classroom, interaction is a central arena for the ontogenesis of social representations of gender.

One of the central theses of this study is that starting school is a significant moment in children's construction of their social identities. In order to understand this assertion, it is necessary to consider further both the concept of social identities and this new context of development.

SOCIAL IDENTITIES

In the preceding pages we have invoked the terms 'social identity', 'gender identity' and 'social gender identity' in a colloquial manner. The concept of identity has such wide currency that we have used it without questioning our readers' willingness and ability to follow our argument. None the less, as a conceptual tool in our study of children in reception classes, we employed a specific and limited definition of identity. The work of Moscovici in his theory of social representations, and of Tajfel (1981, 1982) in his formulation of intergroup relations, were the foundations upon which we established our concept of social identity (Duveen and Lloyd, 1986). We proposed that children are born into a particular society and become competent, functioning individuals with particular social identities to the extent that they re-construct for themselves the social representations of the significant groups in their society. Following Tajfel, we asserted that the expression of social identities was influenced by the dynamics of intergroup relations.

In drawing upon Tajfel's (1981) theory of social identities and inter-group relations, we shared his distinction between identity as a social formation and as an enduring and individual structure. Tajfel indicated the different aspects of identity in his statement that social identity is 'that *part* of an individual's self concept which derives from his membership of a social group (or groups) together with the value and emotional significance attached to that membership' (1981, p. 225). Social identities are not the whole of the self-concept.

Tajfel's definition alerts us to three features of social identities: their partial nature, their relation to social category membership and the emotional and value-laden aspects of such membership. In our discussion of social identities (Duveen and Lloyd, 1986), we explicitly acknowledged that there were aspects of the self which were not part of a social psychological discourse. We linked them to methodological issues and suggested that some aspects of the self might only be accessible to psychoanalytic inquiry. In the discussion which follows, other theoretical solutions to the partial nature of social identities are considered.

Tajfel's own, minimal group research has been important in illustrating the extent to which social identities are influenced by group membership and group behaviour. First of all, he showed that the identities of ingroup members were established in opposition to the identities ascribed to members of the outgroup. Second, his studies demonstrated that, although this process of differentiation occurs when little is at stake between groups, the sharper the conflict between groups the greater the need for comparison and the more clearly identities are distinguished.

27

Tajfel's stress on the emotional and evaluative significance of group membership is particularly important when considering gender. Social representations of gender offer a virtually universal advantage to membership in the male group. Eckert (1989), a sociolinguist, has proposed that the reciprocal nature of male–female sex-group relations, along with the asymmetry of gender which values things male above the female, may distort intergroup dynamics. She suggests that, unlike ethnic group identities, gender comparisons are made within the ingroup; that is, men compare themselves with other men because the comparison with women is demeaning. In consequence, women compare themselves with other women, although they are sensitive to men's definition of their status.

Eckert's hypothesis derives from an analysis of research on adult speech. It invites speculation about the developmental trajectory of the comparison effects she has proposed. Perhaps children first re-construct social representations of gender and establish firm ingroup–outgroup boundaries, and only then turn to the ingroup in the construction of social gender identities. Such a history would accord with Paley's description of her 5 year olds revelling in sex differences, and with other reports of rivalry and avoidance between primary school girls and boys (Thorne, 1986).

We have considered our particular definition of social identity, but the term 'identity' occupies an important place in the social sciences and is used in many senses. Our particular usage reflects our theoretical interest in the social psychological theories of Moscovici and Tajfel and our empirical research into the development of gender understanding. The concept of identity has been taken up and transformed through social representation into the commonsense usage which we invoked in Chapter 1. Erickson's (1946, 1950) use of the psychoanalytic concept 'ego identity' introduced the term into the social sciences. Two themes are distinguishable in Erickson's original formulation (Gurin and Markus, 1990). The first relates the concept of identity to the individual's persistent sense of an enduring self across the life-span, and has been developed and studied principally by psychologists. The second – the persistent sense of sharing significant characteristics with others – is more typical of sociological investigations. Erickson used the concept of identity in order to explain the influence of nature and culture in the development of personality and the construction of inner reality.

Three American sociological psychologists have traced the history of the term within their discipline (Weigert, Teitge and Teitge, 1986). They suggest that, in his use of the term 'ego identity', Erickson was able to unite the concepts of human nature and social reality and 'opened up a tremendous epistemological space for analyzing the human condition' (p. 8). Erickson focused simultaneously on the continuity and self-sameness which individuals create for themselves and present for others, uniting psychological and sociological concerns. In addition, he stressed the constraints which the context or the historical moment imposes upon individuals in achieving their developmental goals. From his psycho-analytic perspective, Erickson sought to describe the children's construction of a functional sense of self across the interpersonal and biological changes of youth.

Highlighted by its pivotal position between childhood and adulthood, it is in adolescence that issues of identity were seen as particularly salient. The problems which the scope and rapidity of social change in the years following the Second World War posed for adults were objectified in Erickson's concept of an 'identity crisis'. His technical concept was transformed through sociogenesis, and the notion of 'identity crisis' was diffused throughout society.

The concept of identity was developed within sociology by symbolic interactionists and European social phenomenologists, groups with their own projects. Stone's definition of identity in terms of the meaning that an individual attributes to the self 'situated – that is, cast in the shape of a social object by acknowledgement of his participation or membership in social relations' (Stone, 1962, p. 93) is typical of the symbolic interactionist position. Stone went on to add a developmental perspective by stating that identity 'is intrinsically associated with all the joinings and departures of social life' (p. 94). Alongside our attention to social representations, Stone's emphasis upon the situation can be construed as an alternative structure within which to consider the content of social life and the social relationships which are a part of it. The particular situation in which we are studying the development of social identities is reception classes, but we acknowledge that children's social identities are already constructed in the context of the family before they enter school.

Goffman's (1963) description of three types of identity – social identity, personal identity and ego or felt identity, conceptualized as a sense of existential continuity – was a further progression within the symbolic interactionist tradition, and reflected his efforts to explain performance in social life. Our designation of only two types of identity collapses, within the concept of social identity (Duveen and Lloyd, 1986), an interpretation of the individual in relation to cultural institutions and products, which Goffman described as a social identity, and the personal identity which was particularly important to Goffman, and which he held an individual negotiated through interaction with others. We did not follow Goffman in identifying the impact of social life on identities separately in terms of social organization and interpersonal relations.

Recently Habermas and his colleagues (Dobert, Habermas and Nunner-

Winkler, 1987) have produced a theory of identity with a cognitive-developmental dimension by drawing upon Piaget's theory. Their formulation of identity theory is centred upon Habermas' concept of interactive competence. They have explored the issue of identity in the context of empirical studies of adolescence, and have integrated Habermas' theory with the ego psychology of Erickson and sociological theories of the family, as well as the epistemological theory of Piaget.

Habermas and his colleagues (Dobert *et al.*, 1987) cast their identity theory in a constructivist model and view the self – or, as they note, its sociological equivalent, identity – as a symbolic structure which ensures 'continuity and consistency under changing biographical conditions and different positions in social space' (p. 276). They connect both personal identity and social identity to the structures of social life, and consider the interactive context as the matrix from which each develops.

The developmental process is described in terms of an initial phase in which the very small child differentiates the self from the environment and constructs a *body-bound identity*. This process is viewed as 'natural', in the sense that even plants and animals have a unit status. Following this initial differentiation, and as a consequence of the child's participation in the symbolic world of family and, later, school, the child constructs a *role-bound identity* which is based upon and reflects the repertoire of roles offered by the child's social world. With increasing symbolic competence, the young adult is eventually able to create an *ego identity*, which is not limited by the behavioural expectations inscribed in an early ego-ideal, and which facilitates complex social interaction. In order to appreciate this formulation fully, it is necessary to acknowledge debts to the psychoanalytic perspective which is employed to describe the consequences of an internalization of the symbolic order.

In relating role theory and the individual's quest for biographical meaning, Berger (1963) presented a European epistemological account of identity. Grounded in concern with the self, he bypassed the psychoanalytic theorizing of Erickson and attributed origins to Cooley and Mead. He also established links with symbolic interactionism by placing importance on social interaction in the establishment and maintenance of identities. In his influential work with Luckmann, Berger not only emphasized the socially constructed nature of the self, but gave a central position to the human dialectic which links the individual's body and the social meanings which exist beyond that body (Berger and Luckmann, 1966). We acknowledged the significance of the body, and in particular the genitals, as a sign in our semiotic analysis of the development of social gender identities, but we brought our own perspective, informed by the theories of Moscovici and Tajfel, to issues concerning the significance of the body for socially constructed identities (Lloyd and Duveen, 1990).

Weigert, Teitge and Teitge's (1986) analysis of the concept of identity grapples with the central question raised by social interactionists and social phenomenologists: 'Who am I?' Their formulation of identity as both a structural concept which locates individuals in a social world, and a processual concept to the extent that the product depends upon ongoing interactional processes of identification, unites the two approaches. Their sociological grounding is revealed in their belief that social organization structures identity organization. Our social psychological affiliation is reflected in our dependence on Moscovici's notion of social representations to fill the same epistemological space.

This brief survey of the history of the concept of identity in the social sciences is evidence of the constructedness of not only social scientific concepts, but the facts or evidence which they marshal in support of their claims. Goldmann suggested that, from the analytic perspective of the social theorist, the subject of knowledge 'has the function of rendering the facts we propose to study intelligible and comprehensible' (1976, p. 92). We argue that our concept of social identity can be construed in precisely the same terms. In other words, we have constructed a particular concept of social gender identity, one in keeping with our aim of explaining the impact of school on children's understanding of gender. We employ it to explain the use to which children put their knowledge of the gender-marked aspects of their material and interpersonal environment. Our formulation of a social gender identity offers only a partial view of the self, one which takes into account sex-group membership and in which gender is valorized in terms of social representations.

Our debt to Tajfel can be seen in our choice of sex-group membership and resulting social gender identities as our objects of study. Here we are in agreement with both symbolic interactionists and social phenomenologists in their emphasis on the organization of social life. Age, sex and ethnic origins are significant categories in social life. Individuals can be assigned to categories on the basis of eye colour or handedness, but social identities deriving from membership in these categories are rarely significant in social life. How often does one hear 'What do you expect, he has hazel eyes!' as an explanation for a social transgression?

In the developmental re-construction of the social representations of different groups in society, not all groups are equally significant for the child. Age, gender, social class, ethnicity and religious affiliation exert great influence on interpersonal relations and endow these groups and their social representations with salience. In addition, we expect that the more saliently marked social groups will be the first to be re-constructed by the young child. Our own evidence (Lloyd and Duveen, 1989) and that reviewed in Chapter 1 suggest that social representations of gender are among the first which children re-construct, and that this process begins

31

almost as soon as young children are capable of symbolic function. By the time children begin formal schooling, they have considerable understanding of the social representation of gender in the domains of activities and interests, and the social relations of adults as well as children.

To support our assertion that starting school is a significant moment in children's construction of their social gender identities, it is necessary to establish the nature of this new context of development. As a societal institution, formal education provides a setting and a set of expectations which differ considerably from the family. It is useful to examine the contrast between these two contexts in terms of Habermas' theory of communicative action (cf. Habermas, 1984; Furth, 1983). Habermas distinguishes the field of communicative action, which is personal and consensus-oriented, from that of strategic action, which is systematic and success-oriented. He also suggests that a central developmental task is the uncoupling of systematic, strategic action from personal, communicative action.

In the context of our study of the impact of schooling on social gender identity, it is sufficient to note the discontinuity between the personal world of the family, where authority is parental and based upon generation, and the public arena of school and peer relations, which are essentially egalitarian and require the construction of new interactive roles. It would be an oversimplification to associate the family exclusively with the field of communicative action, and the school with the field of strategic action. There are systematic aspects to family life, and also communicative aspects to school experience. Nevertheless, with respect to the processes through which gender is uncoupled as a system from the field of personal communicative action, the school has a particular role to play. As an institution, the school not only represents gender to children as a 'system of values, ideas and practices', but it also legitimatizes this social representation of gender in relation to the social world beyond the family. Categorizations which remained implicit within the personal relationships of the family nexus become explicitly elaborated in the context of the school. 'Like Mummy' or 'like Daddy' are extended to become 'ladies' and 'men' (cf. Lloyd, 1987). For the child, the re-construction and understanding of sex-group membership is one of the major tasks of the primary school years.

DIMENSIONS OF GENDER SOCIALIZATION IN
PRIMARY EDUCATION

In order to describe the progress which has been made in identifying the dimensions or variables of gender relevant in primary education, we examine a recent review of research on the educational experiences of girls and boys by two psychologists, Paul Croll and Diana Moses (1991). Their review supplements but in no way contradicts the work of King which we considered in Chapter 1. Their descriptions of the influence of gender are even more extreme than those of King. 'Primary classes are made up of little boys and little girls rather than little children and reference to this and use of it for organization, control and class management is a routine feature' (Croll and Moses, 1991, p. 224). They report that Hartley (1985) has extended gender-sensitive observations to a Scottish primary school. His descriptions of adults' use of gender in organizing the life of the school are complemented by descriptions of children's use of sex-group membership in forming friendships.

The most innovative aspects of the Croll and Moses chapter are their emphasis on classroom interaction and their attempt to explain the discrepancy between the primary school and later adult performance of girls. Since King's original research, gender-marked dimensions of class-room interaction have been the focus of a great number of studies, and differences in the attention given to girls and boys have been cited as a source of girls' later disadvantage. Dale Spender (1982) originally claimed that girls received little more than half as much attention as boys, even when teachers attempted to right their hitherto unrecognized preference for classroom interaction with boys. Alison Kelly's (1988) meta-analysis, based on eighty-one quantitative studies of primary and secondary schools, showed that boys received 56 per cent of all classroom interaction, while girls received 44 per cent. Alongside quantitative information, Kelly provides qualitative assessments and locates her results conceptually in terms of other classroom research on gender.

There are few surprises in Kelly's findings: overall, 35 per cent of teachers' criticism is directed at girls, and only 32 per cent of criticism about behaviour is focused on girls. The view that girls are deprived of equal attention from their teachers may be partially supported by results indicating that 56 per cent of teachers' questions and response oppor-tunities are offered to boys, although 52 per cent of hands raised in response are those of girls. But girls fail to assert their desire to respond: only 41 per cent of answers are shouted out by girls. Despite teachers viewing boys as less academically able and more troublesome, they receive 52 per cent of teachers' praise in classroom interaction.

Croll and Moses (1991) argue that, although the descriptions of the types of interaction in which girls and boys engage are important, few of the studies Kelly analysed were carried out in English primary schools (less than 20 per cent). They examined five observational studies of English primary classroom interaction. Even here, four out of five studies were carried out in junior school classrooms. The first large-scale study in

English primary classrooms was concerned with teaching styles rather than gender differences. Although individual pupil interaction produced proportions similar to those of Kelly's meta-analysis, with girls receiving 46 per cent and boys 54 per cent, the inclusion of whole-class interactions reduced this discrepancy to 49 per cent and 51 per cent (Galton *et al.*, 1980). Croll and Moses' (1985; Croll, 1986) own study of both primary school children with special needs and a second-year junior classroom yielded similar results. These supported the finding that the majority of classroom interaction in junior schools was on a whole-class basis and not differentiated by gender. The other study, which revealed more individual teacher interaction with boys, was conducted in inner London junior school classes. Here boys received 54 per cent of teachers' attention in the second year and 48 per cent in the third year.

Croll and Moses' conclusions leave us with a paradox. They are in no doubt that gender is highly marked in primary classrooms. We (Lloyd and Duveen, 1991) know that children already arrive at school with a great deal of gender knowledge, with names and clothing that are usually gender differentiated, with interests, play-styles and peer preferences that are gender marked. In the classroom, teachers use sex groups to organize activity, and have different images of what girls and boys are like. Yet Croll and Moses (1991) are aware that the disadvantage they seek to explain is difficult to identify in terms of the variables which have been studied in primary school classrooms. Girls are reported to like school more and be more motivated, to perform slightly better, particularly in language skills, and to be rated more favourably for progress by their teachers. They contend that studies of teacher–pupil interaction suggest that boys receive slightly more attention, that they appear more self-confident and sometimes perform better at mathematics. Their overall conclusion is that 'The research reviewed here cannot be regarded as supporting the thesis that gender differentiation in the primary school contributes in any substantial fashion to the disadvantages females suffer in the outside world and, in particular, in the world of employment' (p. 288). Indeed, they conclude 'Although girls are differentiated at primary school the evidence suggests that they are not disadvantaged' (p. 289).

Tests of achievement at the end of the primary years reveal no deficit, but perhaps it is girls' very capacity to learn, and in particular their reconstruction of social representations of gender which value things masculine more than things feminine, and which place men in a more privileged position, that is the ultimate undoing of girls. In the first section we showed that feminine activities and objects are widely held to be less prestigious and less advantageous than things masculine. A few women may manage to become high court judges, consultant neurosurgeons or even prime ministers, but most primary school girls learn the lesson that to be assigned membership to the female sex group implies feminine gender traits. If, as Eckert suggested, men compare themselves with other men, and women with other women, it is this lesson, which confounds gender-appropriate behaviour and sex-group membership, which turns girls away from mathematics, science and technology, and not any intellectual failing.

The confounding of social gender identity and sex-group membership is not a problem restricted to primary school girls. One way to analyse the provocative conclusions of Croll and Moses – that girls evidence no deficit in primary school achievement – is to suggest that they, too, have confounded sex-group membership and gender.

Any disadvantage girls may experience in primary school is to some extent a matter of judgment, but Kelly's (1988) conclusions certainly sustain the hypothesis that girls learn that they occupy an identifiable and different place in the educational system to that of boys. Again, sex-group membership and gender socialization are confounded. This is borne out by Kelly's conclusions that:

> This meta-analysis has confirmed, extended and made more precise our knowledge of gender differences in classroom interaction. It is now beyond dispute that girls receive less of the teacher's attention in class, that this is true across a wide range of different conditions. It applies in all age groups . . . , in several countries, in various socio-economic and ethnic groups, across all subjects in the curriculum, and with both male and female teachers . . . Boys get more of all kinds of classroom interaction . . . The discrepancies are just as large in teacher-initiated interactions as in pupil-initiated interactions. (1988, p. 20)

Girls learn their place; they make fewer demands and are accorded fewer resources.

In the terms of our analysis, the study of teacher–pupil interaction sustains our earlier description of the most salient characteristics of social representations of gender. In school as in other areas of social life, masculine activities and objects are more highly valued. In so far as girls in secondary school, with the advent of puberty, are turning to their own sex group in assessing their behaviour, they confront a shared representation of disadvantage. Girls who pursue academic excellence, careers in science and technology, or positions of leadership find themselves challenging the dominant view of femininity. The prospect of pursuing these goals without risk of ridicule has prompted some feminists to raise the issue of single-sex schools, as environments which are less restrictive and allow girls to pursue a variety of social gender identities.

The provocative analyses both of Croll and Moses and of Kelly demonstrate the difficulties in separating sex-group membership and social gender identity. In both reviews the unit of analysis – girls and boys –

derives from sex-group membership. Yet in their explanations the authors use the language of gender as though the two discourses – of sex-group membership and of gender socialization – were the same. In Chapter 1 we discussed Maccoby's decision to avoid any systematic use of the terms 'sex' and 'gender'. Although the conceptual and methodological problems are not easily solved, we continue to differentiate membership in a sex group and social gender identities because we believe this differentiation encourages a more precise understanding of the choices and decisions both children and teachers make in the early school years.

3

Investigating gender identities in the classroom

In this chapter we introduce our research strategy for studying social gender identities and describe the specific techniques which we employed. This discussion is presented within the framework of the theoretical issues which informed our thinking about gender in reception classes; these were examined in Chapters 1 and 2. We begin by offering a sketch of the state primary system as it functioned at the time of our study, and then describe the schools in which we worked for two years.

The examination of our research techniques is presented in two sections. The first deals with our ethnographic investigation, and the other with our assessment of social gender identities through the use of quantitative measures, observational methods and interview techniques. Finally, we note the collection of additional quantitative data from two schools chosen to be similar to those in which we carried out both ethnographic and quantitative research.

PRIMARY EDUCATION IN ENGLAND

When we began our study in 1986, state education was coming under closer public scrutiny. The government published a White Paper in 1985 and brought forward legislation in 1988; yet, in broadest outline, the path through the educational system for the children we studied will not be radically altered. After their first year in a reception class they will have a further six years of primary schooling, followed by five years of compulsory secondary education. An additional two years of secondary education are available for pupils seeking access to tertiary education or to work requiring higher qualifications. Children are legally bound to start school when they reach 5 years of age; then they remain in primary school until they are 11 years old. In East Sussex, part-time primary schooling is offered to children who have reached 4 years of age by 1 September, though they are only permitted to attend full time in the term in which they become 5 years old.

Our major concern is with the first year at school, but we have adopted a wider outlook, one reflecting the framework of educationalists. We have already examined two ideological threads which run through primary education in England and Wales, an explicit anti-sexism and the child-centred approach.

In England and Wales, primary schooling may take place in an infant school from which children move on to a physically separate junior school after three years. At the other extreme, children may be housed in a single building where only the names 'infant school' and 'junior school' separate the 5–7 and the 8–11 year olds. These two different modes of organization were realized in the two schools in which we spent two academic years studying children in reception classes, Land School and McCarthy School.

Land School

Land School is a modern infant school built on one level. It is part of an educational complex in a park setting which includes three secondary schools, playing fields, and a middle school housed in the building which once held primary school children of all ages. It is in a popular, middle-class residential area but includes a small council estate. With over ninety children in a three-class entry, and similar numbers in each of the other two infant school years, Land School is larger than McCarthy School, but the children in the school range in age only from just 4 to 7 years.

For children entering Land School, reception classes were divided according to age, so that one class consisted of children who would be 5 years old by Christmas and who attended school full time in the autumn term, another of those children whose fifth birthday occurred before Easter and who became full-time pupils in January, and the third of those who only became full-time pupils after Easter. For the first two terms, this class was divided into two groups, with one attending school in the morning and the other in the afternoon. Across the two terms, each group had the opportunity to attend school in the morning and in the afternoon. In the summer term, all the children attended school full time together in one class. These were the children we studied. In the autumn and spring terms, each group contained eighteen children, but some children were trans-ferred to other reception classes when the groups were combined in the summer term. Figure 3.1 shows the plan of the classroom at the beginning of the autumn and spring terms in the second year of our study.

There were thirty-two children – eighteen girls and fourteen boys – in the

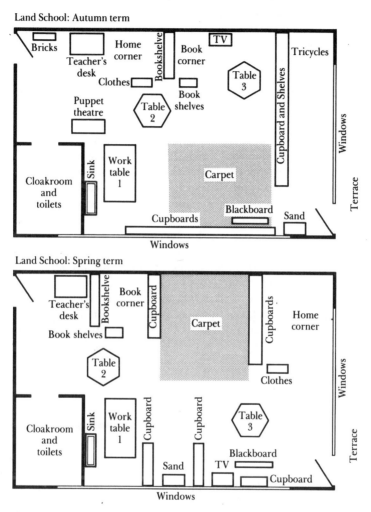

Figure 3.1 Reception class plan: Land School

combined class in the first year of our study. The reception class teacher was a woman, and she was assisted for much of the time by an auxiliary, who was also a woman. The head teacher was a woman and there were no men on the staff of ten. In the second year, the combined class in summer term included twelve girls and seventeen boys who attended school all year. Three boys joined this class in the summer term; they had attended nursery school in the earlier terms, and only began school after Easter.

The decision to add the children who attended nurseries earlier in the year to the youngest of the three reception classes highlights the educational dilemmas faced by the teacher who instructed these children throughout the first year. Although they were the age of children attending nursery, their parents had enrolled them in an infant school and expected that they would be taught accordingly. In similar fashion, the local education authority provided resources, specially teachers, in the ratio appropriate to primary school and not according to the child–adult proportions of nursery education.

In Land School, the first term in all the reception classes was seen as a period of adjustment, during which the teachers sought to establish 'good play habits'. The teacher we observed aimed to work individually with each child, so it was important that all her children could play productively until their turn came. There was little structured academic work in the first term, although the teacher introduced children individually to simple tasks which prepared the way for literacy and numeracy skills. There was no formal reading or counting. In the first few weeks, children played on a terrace adjoining the classroom, and only later joined the other reception classes and second-year children in the playground at morning and afternoon break. Only in the second half of the first term were reception classes taken to school assemblies, and only in the summer term, when children attended school all day, did they stay for lunch in school.

McCarthy School

McCarthy School is an example of a complete primary school. It is housed in a totally refurbished Victorian building, with vast ceilings and high windows built so that children can see little more than the sky. The school is near the town centre, in a predominantly working-class area which has seen an influx of more middle-class families, stimulated by rising house prices in the local community. The infant school occupies the ground floor, the junior school is on the floor above. There is only one class in each year group, and there are weekly assemblies which bring together children from 4 to 11 years of age.

In McCarthy School, the reception class we studied included a range of ages, from children who were just 4 years old to those who began to reach 5 years of age in September. The children who would reach 5 years by Christmas had lunch at school and remained there throughout the day. Those who would reach 5 years later in the year came to school only in the morning. Figure 3.2 presents a plan of the classroom and the adjoining play room which was shared with other classes.

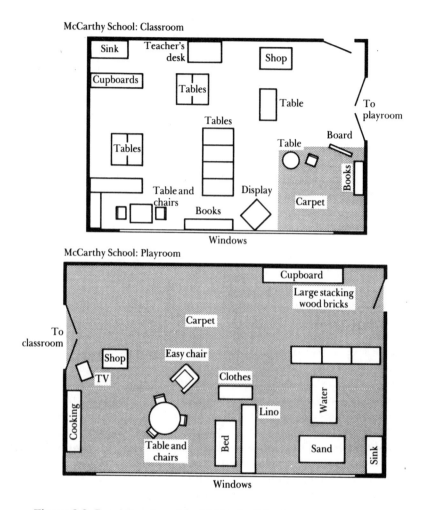

Figure 3.2 Reception class plan: McCarthy School

In the first year of our study, there were twenty-four children in the class
– eleven girls and thirteen boys – but only seven children attended full time
in the autumn term. The teacher, who was a woman, was sometimes
assisted by a student teacher, who was also a woman. The head teacher was
a woman but her deputy was a man. There was another man on the staff of
eight who taught in the junior school. In the second year, thirty-five
children – fifteen girls and twenty boys – were enrolled in the autumn term,
of whom five girls and ten boys were old enough to attend school all day. In

the summer term, there were only thirty-three childen, as two girls had moved house and consequently changed schools.

The adjustment period in McCarthy School extended for a couple of weeks. Early in the autumn term, the teacher organized structured lessons about nature or social studies, with the whole class participating, at the beginning of the morning. Instruction in reading and counting was soon included in the early morning lesson. Chidren joined other infant-class children for break on the playground from the very first day, and attended school assemblies in the first week.

RESEARCH STRATEGY

The structure of our research, which entailed an initial year of ethnographic investigation followed by a second year in which we studied individual children, ensured that we gained access to the social representations of gender offered by teachers in two very different reception classes before we assessed children's gender knowledge and measured their social gender identities. Our ethnographic investigations were based upon the assumption that social life revolves around collective systems of meaning, and that it is through the interrogation of the beliefs and practices of a community that these systems can be analysed. These presuppositions are shared by Moscovici's theory of social representations. It is this common conceptual ground which establishes ethnographic investigation as a necessary first phase in the study of developing social identities (cf. Jodelet, 1991).

The systematic observation and individual interviews employed in the second year of the study were developed in the light of the knowledge gained in the first phase of the research. These individual measures were used to assess children during their first term in school and towards the end of their first year. This longitudinal data enables us to describe the social gender identities and gender knowledge which children bring to school, and to measure the impact of schooling at the end of the first year.

Ethnographic investigation

The aim of our ethnographic work was to provide a description of the structure of the social representations of gender in the classroom. This autonomous investigation generated a descriptive framework, within which we examined and interpreted the actions of children as they sought to express their social gender identities. Before considering specific methodological issues related to the scope of our ethnographic observations and the character of the evidence it provides, we explain the precise nature of our ethnographic research.

42

In contemporary usage, particularly that of sociologists, investigations based upon participant observation and interviews with informants in field settings are usually referred to as ethnographies. Ethnographers commonly test the adequacy of the interpretations they construct of the events in which they participate and which they observe through a process of triangulation. To do this they re-present their own understanding to informants for comment and discussion. Although there is general agreement about these tactics, there is no single and definitive ethnographic procedure, as Agar (1986) has noted, and ethnographic investigations are conducted using many different interpretive strategies and terminologies.

Our ethnographic investigation differs from many traditional studies in that it was motivated by two specific concerns. First, we selected our theme, gender, *a priori*; we did not go into the field setting – Land and McCarthy schools – ready to work on whatever material came to our notice in the course of the research. We embarked on our study of children starting school with the belief that gender was a significant phenomenon in the organization of social life within the school. Second, in relation to the overall study, the ethnographic investigation facilitated the development of the quantitative, psychological instruments. We looked for phenomena marked for gender which would identify appropriate material for our observation schedules and interview questionnaires. Because of these focused concerns, we describe our method as *motivated ethnography*.

We have argued (Lloyd and Duveen, 1989) that all psychological research proceeds from ethnographic interpretation, but that it usually remains implicit. Researchers often rely upon their own intuitions, drawn from their participation in their own culture, to structure their understanding of psychological processes. Herzlich (1972) makes a similar point about the unacknowledged role of social representations in psychological research. A novel feature of this study is our explicit and systematic approach to ethnographic investigation. We acknowledge our reliance upon ethnographic procedures, but also realize the limitations of a motivated ethnography.

There were two explicit restrictions on our ethnographic observations of classroom interaction in the youngest of the three reception classes in Land School and the only reception class in McCarthy School. First of all, although we had ascertained the daily and weekly timetables at the beginning of the school year we made little effort to sample the school day or week systematically. In addition, our observations recorded what children and teachers actually did while we observed them in school, but we rarely treated teachers or children as traditional informants, interrogating them about their beliefs concerning the gender appropriateness of different materials or activities. Teachers, and sometimes children, offered spontaneous comments; these we recorded and they were given careful attention in our analyses of ethnographic data. While our data provides ample evidence of conspicuous marking of gender, we cannot conclude that children are ignorant when gender is not marked or when it is disregarded. Some boys sometimes allowed girls easy access to the trikes; yet on other occasions, they made clear through language and action their priority of access to these objects, which were generally seen as masculine. Our ethnographic observations allowed us to infer, through evidence of awareness of gender marking, the potential resources available to children for constructing social gender identities. Despite systematic patterns, the rules of gender marking were not binding in all situations.

In addition to more traditional ethnographic procedures, in both schools we occasionally made video-recordings of activities such as assemblies, playground breaks and plays. None the less, we sought to intervene as little as possible in ongoing classroom activity and wrote only skeleton accounts at the time. These notes were later elaborated when we entered them in our computer record. We began our research by meeting teachers in Land and McCarthy schools before children arrived in September 1986. Our visits and note-taking continued throughout two school years and focused on the following three areas:

1. Classroom interaction, in contexts of activity organized by children and by adults through which children expressed their gender identities.
2. Talk about gender in the classroom, in which children usually commented about the gender arrangements visible in their activity while adults employed gender to organize activity.
3. Institutional representations of gender offered in concerts, assemblies and exhibitions, organized by the schools for children and parents, and also representation of gender expressed in official school and local authority publications.

The major portion of our ethnographic evidence derives from our observations of practices in the classroom which involve gender differentiation, and from actors' talk about gender. This verbal discourse included actors' own reflections and inferences about gender marking. We elaborate upon this distinction in Chapter 4, when we describe the analytic framework we employed to organize our material in terms of six aspects of classroom life, and present the social representations of gender which it yielded. We drew upon this body of material when developing the individual measures described in the following section.

Quantitative investigations

From our ethnographic investigation we were able to identify aspects of the social representation of gender in the classroom. Our task, in devising measures of individual behaviour, was to produce data which would be indicative of children's individual expression of social gender identities through the use of these aspects. The measures we developed fall into two distinct categories; the first group is based upon observation, and the second is derived from interviews on various topics.

Observational measures

Spot observations Our initial aims in developing systematic classroom observation measures were threefold. First, we planned observations which would sample each child's activity, its nature and peer composition. Second, we wished to record children's proposals for activity and the response these received. Finally, we hoped to analyse teachers' discourse with pupils.

Our ethnographic investigations led us to modify our initial aims. We abandoned traditional time-sampling techniques in specific contexts, and adopted a method of spot observations constrained only by the need to sample particular children. Spot observations are a relatively unobtrusive, modified time-sampling procedure. The method involves making a 'mental snapshot' of a target child; the data sheet indicates the information which we sought to capture with each 'take' (Figure 3.3). Spot observations have been used by Whiting and Edwards (1988) to make cross-cultural comparisons, by Rogoff (1978) to compare the effects of family characteristics on activity, and by Wenger (1983) to investigate the amount of sex-segregated activity in children from 2 to 11 years of age.

Our ethnographic observations indicated that a time interval of fixed duration would contain a complex and changing set of interpersonal relations which spread across contexts. The method of spot observations permitted the identification of particular activities and the specification of contexts within which they occur. Target children were observed one at a time, and a pre-ordered list of names was used to identify them. Once the target child's location had been identified and all other peers and adults in the location listed, the other observational categories on the data sheet were completed.

The categories of our observational record coded three interrelated factors: the degree to which the activity was organized by the teacher, the gender composition of groups, and their location in the classroom. It can be seen from the sample data sheet in Figure 3.3 that we also recorded the materials with which the target child and others were engaged, and that we

45

School: McCarthy Date: 5 November 87
Observer: G.D. Time: 9.40

Target child	Location	Adults/peers	Speaking	Being spoken to	Conversation	Non-verbal communication	Listens to conversation	Listens to monologue/adults	Observing	Activity	Group	Distant	Pretend	Teacher/adult organized	Materials: Target child	Materials: Other	Notes
1. Hope	Sand														Sand		Entirely alone
2. Stewart	Table	Alan								U	✓				Playdough	Playdough	Table by wall
		David								U	✓				"	"	
		Keith			✓					U	✓				"	"	
		Neal	✓							U	✓				"	"	
3. Nina	Table	Alice												✓	Maths exercise	Maths exercise	
		Louise												✓	"	"	
		Lisa												✓	"	"	
		Adult												✓	"	"	

Figure 3.3 Spot observation data sheet

sought to categorize the nature of the social interaction – whether it involved, for example, conversation, observation or pretend play. Definitions of the categories used to complete the data sheet appear in the appendix to this chapter.

We identified four specific contextual influences from our own ethnographic observations and from published research, and incorporated them into the spot observation schedule. They served as dimensions in the analyses of our data. The first is a contrast between different *organizational contexts* – between those occasions when children are free to organize their activity in conjunction with their peers, and those when their activity is directly organized by the teacher. When children are free to play with each other, the reception classroom can resemble life in the playgroup or nursery (most of the children in our study had some structured pre-school experience). But schooling impinges most directly on children when the teacher actively organizes children's activity. In teacher-organized contexts, children develop a way of responding to new norms and expectations.

A second contextual influence on the expression of social gender identities is that of children's own *peer organization*. The groups which children form differ in their composition according to the sex of the children involved. When Maccoby and Jacklin (1987; also Maccoby, 1988) speak of the phenomenon of 'gender segregation', they provide a clear image of sex-group membership as a consistent feature of young children's social lives. As we shall see later, this extreme characterization of children's social lives is misleading in some important respects. Although many of our spot observations revealed the target child playing in single-sex groups, there was a variety of mixed-sex groups as well. Decisions children make about the sex-group membership of peers with whom they play are indicative of their own social gender identities. Single-sex and mixed-sex groups tend to engage in different activities, to use different materials and to be located in different areas of the classroom. These different aspects coalesce into a nexus of gender-related identifications. A child may join a particular group in order to play with some gender-marked material, or it may be that playing with a specific toy can lead to an association in a group with a particular constellation of sex-group members. In our analyses we have emphasized *group composition* as an influence, not because it need necessarily be assigned a primary importance in the expression of social gender identities, but because it is the most visible of this nexus of influences.

Third, there is the contrast between classrooms in different *schools*. There is considerable variation between schools and between teachers, both in their general educational approach and in their approach to gender issues in particular. Given this diversity, are patterns of gender identity consistent across different schools, or does a local gender culture emerge in each classroom? The research design for our observational study did not allow us to distinguish clearly between the effects due to individual teachers and those which result from some more general influence in the school, since we observed classrooms in different schools, and this should be borne in mind when we speak of school effects in our analyses. Although Chapters 5 and 6 record some such effects in the contrasts between the two schools in our longitudinal sample, this issue is considered in more detail in Chapter 7, where analyses of the cross-sectional data include observations drawn from reception classes in four different schools.

The three contextual influences described so far all have a synchronic character, in that they operate within any given situation. The fourth influence, *term*, is different in that it is diachronic, and refers to the impact of schooling on the development of gender identities over time. Longitudinal comparisons of children's activity in the autumn and summer terms of their reception year will establish the extent to which patterns of social gender identity become more consistent over time.

Spot observations are an attractive observational technique because high inter-observer agreement can be established in a relatively short time and a variety of information collected quickly. We monitored inter-rater reliability for the two observers who carried out the spot observations, Gerard Duveen and Nick Barley. We did this by making simultaneous observations on the same children in three sessions spread across the period of data collection. These joint observations yielded 1120 data points and provided an inter-observer agreement of 94.7 per cent.

We planned to collect twenty observations on each child in the reception classes in both schools at the start, and towards the end, of the school year. This schedule could not be maintained in the autumn term in McCarthy School because the younger children in the class only attended school in the morning. All of the analyses reported in Chapters 5 and 6 are based on a sample of children for whom at least eight observations were made. This criterion excluded three girls and three boys from McCarthy School. In the summer term all the children in McCarthy School attended full time and the difficulty did not arise. However, two girls from the school moved out of the locality and changed schools between terms, thereby reducing the number of complete data sets available for longitudinal analysis.

Natural discourse

Our ethnographic investigations sensitized us to difficulties in recording speech in the classroom. We recognized that we could not rely on hearing with accuracy or completeness the speech produced during spot observations. At the end of the first year of the study we obtained additional funding which supported the collection of linguistic data from one school to supplement our other material. These funds enabled us to study natural discourse which we analysed from video-recordings made during the second year of our research in the reception class in Land School.

To minimize the intrusiveness of the procedure, the apparatus was set up in a particular area of the classroom and allowed to run with as little attention as possible. Our ethnographic observations guided our choice of the home corner and the carpet area as the main locations. These recordings were only made after pilot testing with a tripod-mounted camcorder with automatic focusing in another reception class indicated that children usually ignored the apparatus after it had been set up for a little while. Occasionally the directional microphone became the object of children's play, but interventions were rarely necessary.

Autumn term recordings were made during normal class time, when as many as fifteen children might be present. Our procedure was revised in the summer term, when there were thirty-two children together in the classroom all day and recordings proved to be untranscribable despite the use of directional microphones. As a result we recorded during the lunch-time break, and invited eight to ten children to come into the classroom and play while we recorded them, using the same recording procedures as we had in the autumn term (focusing the unattended camera on the home corner and carpet).

Written transcriptions of the video record were made by two assistants, Marion Smith and Karen Wraith, who collaborated to produce agreed versions of the recordings. Despite many hours of effort, the transcriptions have not exhausted the information on the video record. Anyone who has recorded in classrooms appreciates the magnitude of the aural task. Besides problems with sound quality, children turn their backs to the camera or disappear from the camera altogether. 'Turns' were identified after a script was divided into topic episodes which comprised talk and action focused on a single game or conversational theme. This partitioning required careful reading in order to gain an idea of the overall shape of the games and conversation. Only those children whose speech or action contributed at least once to an episode were defined as actors and each of these active contributions were classified as a 'turn'. The transcriptions collected in the autumn term included over 2,200 turns, and in the summer term the recordings yielded over 2,800 turns.

Interviews

Our aims in constructing individual interview measures were to sample children's knowledge of the gender marking of various aspects of classroom life and to record their expressions of social gender identities. In particular we wished to assess children's understanding of gender rules relating to aspects of sex-group membership, material culture, activity and space. In practice, only components of the Object assignment, the Preference test

49

and the Figures test allowed the expression of a social gender identity. The Odd-one-out test and the majority of information generated with the other two tests supplied quantified information about children's gender knowledge. A modified version of Edelsky's (1976) measure of knowledge of linguistic stereotypes was used to assess children's understanding of gender differentiated use of language in order to determine their awareness of systematic gender differences which might be revealed in the recordings of natural discourse. All of these measures were administered twice, at the beginning and at the end of the school year.

Michael and Susan: Object assignment and Preference test The first interview measure we developed was based upon sex-role research with very young children – two and three year olds – undertaken by Danna Kuhn and her colleagues (Kuhn *et al.*, 1978). In order to assess children's understanding of the gender marking of activities, roles and traits, children were required to identify whether it was a girl, Susan, or a boy, Michael, who preferred to play with certain objects, to do particular things or behave in specific ways. During the first year of our study we piloted modified versions of this test, using photographs of thirty-three toys and other objects available in the two classrooms. Analyses of this data enabled us to identify those items of the material culture of the classroom which carried gender markings for the children.

Photographs of twenty items were selected for the final versions of the test. Sixteen of these twenty items had been categorized in similar ways in both schools and were used in both classes. They sampled a variety of classroom activities. These sixteen items were as follows:

- Blackboard.
- Bricks.
- Clothes.
- Cooker.
- Crayons.
- Doll.
- Farm.
- Jigsaw.

- Lego.
- Paints.
- Sand.
- Scissors.
- Story-book.
- Wordstand.
- Worksheet.
- Trike.

The four additional items comprised two sets of two each which were specific to each of the schools. In Land School these were photographs of a computer, which was available in the classroom, and Play-dough. In McCarthy School the additional items were photographs of Number Bricks and Hat People (the dolls that portrayed the characters from the reading scheme used for classroom instruction).

In individual interviews, children were shown photographs of a girl, who

50

wore a dress, had long hair and was named Susan, and a boy, who wore short trousers, had short hair and was introduced as Michael. The two photographs were placed on the table and the child's task was to decide whether Susan or Michael would like to play with each of the eighteen objects shown in the photographs. The set of photographs was shuffled before each interview to ensure that they were presented in a new random order to each child. In addition, the interviewers switched the positions of Susan and Michael from one interview to the next, so that neither consistently occupied the left- or right-hand position.

After they completed the assignment of the eighteen items to Susan and Michael, children were asked to choose the four objects with which they would most like to play. In this way we assessed children's knowledge of the gender marking of the objects in their classroom and their own preferences. We sought to measure both their understanding of the social representations of gender in relation to material culture, and their expression of a social gender identity. A majority of children were interviewed using this technique during the summer before they started school. At the same time we interviewed their parents, primarily mothers, and gathered the information on family backgrounds which we presented in the first section. The test was administered a second time at the end of the summer term.

Odd-one-out test   In the Odd-one-out test, sets of drawings were used to investigate children's conceptual understanding of an interrelationship between sex-group membership and the gender marking of material culture. Children were asked to identify the odd one out in six sets of three drawings, or triads. Each drawing showed a child playing with a toy. The actor could be either a girl or a boy, and the toy could be either a masculine or feminine marked toy. Each triad contained a girl playing with a feminine marked toy, a boy playing with a masculine marked toy, and one child playing with a toy marked for the opposite gender. In three triads the third drawing showed a girl playing with a masculine marked toy, and in the other three the third drawing showed a boy playing with a feminine marked toy (see Figure 3.4).

Children were interviewed individually and first asked to identify each of the three members of a triad and to say what they were doing, for example: a girl playing with a doll. After the three identifications were completed the child was asked, 'Which one is doing something odd?' On a given triad a child could nominate as odd either 1. the actor whose sex was discordant, e.g. there was only one girl and two boys, or 2. the toy with a discordant gender marking, e.g., one masculine toy midst two feminine toys, or 3. the drawing of a mismatch, showing a child playing with a toy marked for the opposite gender, e.g. a girl playing with a masculine toy. Only the third type of nomination provided evidence that a child perceived

51

Figure 3.4 A triad from the Odd-one-out test

an interrelationship between sex-group membership and the gender marking of material culture. The first two types of response are uni-dimensional and indicative, in the first instance, of sensitivity to sex-group membership, and in the second, to the gender marking of material culture.

The Figures test   This interview was developed to assess children's under-standing of the gender marking of classroom activity and their knowledge of

Table 3.1 Tasks, settings and styles for Figures test

Tasks:

Teacher-initiated	*Child-initiated*
Sand	Sand
Bricks	Bricks
Painting	Painting
Puzzles	Puzzles
Home corner	Home corner
Train set	Train set
Play-dough	Play-dough

Settings:

Teacher-organized	*Peer-organized*
Children to sit on carpet	Children arguing
Children to line up	

Styles:

Teacher-articulated	*Child-articulated*
Noisy	Girl being hit
Silly	Boy losing pencil
Quiet	Boy being hit
Naughty	Girl losing pencil
Bossy	
Helpful	

gender-differentiated behavioural styles. It allowed us to identify any differences in their understanding of gender differentiation in the contexts of teacher organization and ascription, and of peer organization and ascription.

The Figures test derives its title from the set of sixteen small, wooden figures, eight of boys and eight of girls, which children were asked to place on a stylized plan drawing of the classroom. The interview was conducted with each child individually, as a story about a morning in school, and each child was requested to allocate the figures in a variety of circumstances which assessed their gender-marked knowledge of the information presented in Table 3.1. For example, children were asked to place two figures on the drawing to show them carrying out each of the seven classroom tasks, both on their own and when organized by the classroom teacher. In a similar fashion, children were requested to choose the figures engaged in the two teacher- and one peer-organized setting. To assess knowledge of gender-marked behavioural styles, children were asked to choose the figure the teacher meant when she said 'Someone was being noisy, silly', etc. Similar choices of figures were required to identify the child who was hit or who had lost a pencil.

Modified Edelsky test Edelsky (1976) had tested American children of 6, 9 and 12 years, as well as adults, to determine their awareness of gender-marked, adult linguistic stereotypes. We modified her procedures by developing a story format within which to present eight linguistic forms to children, twice each in different contexts, making a total of sixteen items. Two of Edelsky's original items were adapted for English children – 'sweet' was substituted for 'adorable', which is not commonly used by English 4 year olds (or adults), and 'blast' was substituted for 'damn', which was believed to be too offensive for use in school. The test sentences were as follows:

Blast it, it's broken.
Blast it, I've spilt my tea.

I'm going to draw a *sweet* picture.
What a *sweet* bear.

Oh dear, I dropped the crayons.
Oh dear, I forgot my scarf.

Won't you please let me have the 'phone.
Won't you please let me have the teapot.

The water is *very* hot.
I am *very* tired.

We're friends, *aren't we?*
I can go on the slide, *can't I?*

Look how I go down.
Look at me swinging.

My goodness, it's time to go home.
My goodness, what a mess we've made.

The protagonists of the story, a girl (Jenny) and a boy (Simon), were described as playing together in school with a variety of toys. Children were asked to help make up a story about Jenny and Simon's afternoon at school. To make the task more interesting, a series of photographs of the toys was shown.

Children were interviewed individually and the test sentences were delivered as the speech of Jenny or Simon in reference to the activities. After each test sentence, children were asked who it was who had spoken – Jenny or Simon. All the children were asked on several occasions to explain their choices, but the number of times this probe, designed to elicit explanations for specific choices, could be employed varied according to children's attentiveness or restlessness.

This interview measure was only employed in Land School. Children in the top class – that is to say, children of 6–7 years – were also tested to determine the extent to which English children in the top infant class were aware of systematic, gender-marked differences in speech.

EXTENDING THE QUANTITATIVE INVESTIGATIONS

The quantitative findings derived from our studies in Land and McCarthy schools were supplemented by a further term of additional data collection in schools which the heads of Land and McCarthy schools identified as similar to their own. Newby School, chosen as similar to Land School, was situated in a modern building but located in a middle-class suburban area rather than on a campus. It had a two-class entry, and play and adjustment were emphasized in the first term. George School, like McCarthy School, was near the town centre and in a predominantly working-class area, although it was housed in a modern building. There was only one reception class, and older children attended all day while younger children came for one session only. Spot observations were collected and three interview measures – the Michael and Susan: Object assignment and Preference test, the Odd-one-out test and the Figures test – were administered. This material allowed us to compare the expression of social gender identities and gender

54

understanding of children in their first term in a reception class in four different schools.

APPENDIX: DEFINITIONS OF SPOT OBSERVATION CATEGORIES

1. *Location:* the physical setting of the target child's activity.
2. *Adults/peers:* each adult and peer in the same location as the target child listed in separate rows on data sheet. See definition 12, *Distant,* requiring the entry of others with whom the target child is engaged at a distance.
3. *Speaking:* the target child is talking to another at the moment of observation.
4. *Being spoken to:* another is talking to the target child; definitions 3 and 4 may occur simultaneously.
5. *Conversation:* entry made only when a second turn is heard following an initiation by either the target child (definition 3) or another (definition 4).
6. *Non-verbal communication:* gestures, sounds or actions which form part of the target child's interaction with the other in the absence of spoken communication.
7. *Listens to conversation:* target child listens to a conversation between others but is not an active participant.
8. *Listens to monologue/adults:* target child listens to utterances which are not specifically addressed to that child. These include the monologues of other children and adults' speech addressed to other children. When the adult is addressing a group including the target child it is coded 4, *Being spoken to.*
9. *Observing:* target child is looking at other/s but not engaged in monologue or conversation.
10. *Activity:* this category codes the modality of the target child's interaction with other/s as one of three types:
    (a) *Nothing* is entered when there is no interaction despite physical proximity to another;
    (b) *Coordinated activity (C)* is recorded when there is joint or mutual attention organized in terms of a common aim or goal, indicated by common action or a coordinated sequence of action. Conversation *per se,* in the absence of common action, does not merit the entry of *C*;
    (c) *Uncoordinated activity (U)* is entered when an interaction fails to meet the criteria listed above.

11. *Group:* this category is used to specify the relationship between the target child and individuals listed in definition 3. A *tick* is entered for each individual with whom the target child is engaged in a group, which is indicated by commitment to common activities involving mutual interpersonal attention through gaze, speech or physical orientation. Where others form a group in which the target child is not a member, a *cross* is entered in the appropriate row.
12. *Distant:* the target child is interacting with other/s in a location different from that of target child. (These locations are entered for other/s in definition 16.)
13. *Pretend:* the target child and other/s are engaged in a pretend game, usually indicated by speech which orders actions not part of the physical setting; for example, stirring imaginary food in a saucepan. Pretend in the absence of speech is also recorded; for example, in the puppet theatre or dolls' corner.
14. *Teacher/adult organized:* the target child is engaged in activity organized by the teacher or other adult, including work, tidying up or specific errands, such as bringing the teacher a specified object.
15. *Materials:* only the toys and other objects with which the target child and peers are engaged are recorded.
16. *Notes:* other comments/observations, and *Distant* locations, as appropriate.

PART II

Re-constructing gender in reception classes

4

Ethnographic observations and insights

Schools, as societal institutions, present children with sets of social representations of gender in ways which distinguish the school from the family as an ecological context. They not only represent gender to children as 'systems of values, ideas and practices' (Moscovici, 1973, p. xiii) but also legitimatize these social representations of gender in relation to the social world beyond the family. Categorizations which remain implicit within the personal relationships of the family nexus are explicitly elaborated and made public in the context of formal education.

Ethnography offers a useful means of identifying and describing the ways in which gender is articulated in the beliefs and practices of educational institutions. The body of ethnographic research on schools is, however, limited in two respects (cf. for collections of studies, Burgess, 1984; Hammersely, 1986). For the most part, research has concentrated on junior and secondary schools and, consequently, on a more formal classroom organization than is typical of infant schools. While the primary focus of this research has been processes of instruction and learning (for example, Edwards and Mercer, 1987; Streeck, 1983), gender has been examined to a limited extent (cf. Delamont, 1980; Delamont and Hamilton, 1984; Wilcox, 1982). Second, in the few available ethnographic studies of infant schools, gender has not been a prominent dimension in the analysis. We noted King's (1978) classic study in Chapter 1. Although he acknowledged the significance of gender, his aim was to describe the overall nature of English infant education.

Our ethnographic study provides a description of the structure of social representations of gender in classrooms within two schools, Land and McCarthy, with particular focus on the children in them. Schools as institutions are the focus for the activity of diverse groups of people, each of which introduces its own social representations. Schools also differ one from another in terms of the representations which circulate. But in all schools, there are professional groups which include teachers, head teachers and local authority officials; then too, there are parents as well as adult helpers such as the dinner servers and caretakers. Undoubtedly, all of these groups influence children's understanding of gender in the adult world. In Chapter 1 we examined the images of children contained within official ideologies. Images of children also circulate more widely in society (cf. Chombart de Lauwe, 1984; D'Alessio, 1990; Molinari and Emiliani, 1990). In this chapter, we examine the social representations of gender which circulate in each school, before comparing them.

As ethnographic observers, our own social representations of children affect our descriptions. We have been shaped by particular theories in developmental psychology. For example, we have been specifically influenced by certain Piagetian themes. As a result, we are sensitive to the social influence which adults exercise over young children. Piaget (1934) described this in one of his earliest books as the hegemonic influence of adults. In another early work (Piaget, 1926), he considered the problem of egocentrism which limited children's capacity for logical understanding, as, for example, when children failed to count themselves when asked about a sibling's brothers or sisters. More recently, Piaget (1977) described the limitations of young children's 'grasp of consciousness', when they are not yet able to provide an adequate explanation for problems to which they have found practical solutions. Each of these themes influences our ethnographic descriptions. Young children may be inhibited in talking to adult interviewers; they may have difficulty in communicating their understanding of events; their explanations may also lag behind their practice in logical sophistication. This representation of children's intellectual skills has influenced our ethnographic strategy. We do not expect children to act as ethnographic informants in the same manner as adults. Consequently, we have relied on observations more than on interviews.

The aims of our ethnographic investigation were limited by our developmental concerns and by our specific focus on social representations of gender. In Chapter 3, we described our concept of a motivated ethnography. In the first section of this chapter, we present the specific framework which we have used to analyse our ethnographic material. This is followed by descriptions of social representations of gender based upon talk about membership in the social categories of sex groups in Land School and in McCarthy School. We conclude the chapter by considering the insights which we gained from our ethnographic observations and used in planning the quantitative phase of the study.

60

ASPECTS OF THE GENDER MARKING OF SCHOOL LIFE

To enable us to order our ethnographic notes, we developed an analytic framework early in the first year of our study. Through it we sought to identify those *aspects* of the social representation of gender which function as resources for the expression of social gender identities. We list below the six aspects which we distinguished, and illustrate their use with examples.

1. *Social categories:* the verbal invoking of categories such as sex or age to organize or comment upon social interaction. For example, one of the teachers invoked sex groups as a significant social category when getting her children ready for playtime, by saying 'Let's see if the girls are ready and the boys are ready.' Children also invoke sex-group membership as a category. When jostling with four other girls at the end of a line, a girl protested 'I don't want to be by a boy.'

2. *Group composition:* our employment of categories such as sex and age to describe active participation in functioning groups. Our use of group composition to make sense of classroom interaction is evident in this account from Land School.

Two boys, Charlie and David, were playing on the carpet, fitting pieces together to make a slide for marbles. Although these boys were busy for a while, none of the other children showed any interest in their activity. David ran to the teacher and said 'Look what we have done!' She went over to their construction and two girls, Rosie and Gill, joined them. The teacher drew the girls into the game by encouraging one of them to take a turn on the marble slide. When the teacher left the girls stayed on, but after a minute, one drifted away, followed shortly by one of the boys. We noted that the teacher was instrumental in changing the sex-group membership of the activity and that her participation influenced group composition.

3. *Material culture:* the cultural marking of objects, so that, for example, dolls are identified as feminine and vehicles as masculine. We began Chapter 1 by describing an episode in which Seth attempted to dress up in a white tutu, and pointed out that while Seth ignored the gender marking of the dress, Charity appeared to be fully aware of its feminine marking. Children in both schools enjoyed dressing up, and the gender marking of clothes was well-understood and shared knowledge. The markings of particular objects could, in specific circumstances, change as they were incorporated in different activities. Boys who wished to be superheroes put on scarves which may once have adorned women, but in this context symbolized the cloak of a superman.

4. *Activities:* the cultural marking of activities, scripted play and ritual, which leads to the identification of specific roles and routines as masculine

and feminine. The most elaborate scripts children produced related to family life and were clearly marked for gender. In an example from Land School, Gerard asked two girls crawling about the book corner what they were playing. The girls replied 'Babies!' and took turns saying 'gooo-goo'. When Frank came over and said 'Don't be silly', Henrietta suggested that he, too, might be a baby. Frank rejected that offer but suggested that he was a daddy. Immediately, Susan acknowledged his role and greeted him, saying 'Good morning, daddy. I am going out.' In this evocation of domestic life, both Frank and the two girls recognized that Frank had chosen a domestic role congruent with his sex-group membership.

5. *Space:* though more transitory than the material culture aspect, areas of the classroom and playground may be differentially allocated to one sex group or another. An instance from McCarthy School illustrates the use of space to mark gender.

The teacher asked five boys to go into the adjoining playroom. The boys obliged, but no girls offered to join them, nor did the teacher ask any of the girls. After a few minutes, when a girl asked permission to join the boys, the teacher replied 'No, not yet. Let the boys finish first.' Soon there was complete sex-group segregation. All seven boys were in the playroom, engaged in either rough-and-tumble play or a running game involving trucks. The six girls sat on the carpet in the main classroom, having a tea-party with their dolls and the teacher. For a time, the playroom had become a masculine space and the carpet a feminine area.

6. *Behavioural style:* particular patterns of behaviour, such as forceful or assertive activities, are often labelled masculine, while passivity or compliance are construed as feminine. One morning in Land School several children, girls and boys, were building a rocket near the entrance to the classroom. The teacher and her auxiliary teacher were in another part of the classroom and could not see the rocket group clearly. Both of them asked the children to be a little quieter. Finally the auxiliary walked over to see for herself what was going on. She reported to the teacher that it was Kelly as well as Zara. The teacher replied 'Kelly as well? I knew it was Zara. Why do we always think it's the boys?' The auxiliary grinned in recognition, for she understood that noisy behaviour was assumed to be the product of boys' activity.

This last episode, in which the teacher mused on her assumption that the noisy children were all boys, provides empirical evidence to support our conceptual claim for the potential independence of sex-group membership and gender identity. By and large, teachers confound sex-group membership and gender-marked behavioural styles, and assume that they are isomorphic. The surprise and sly grin of the auxiliary are evidence of the prevalence of this assumption and of its violation in this episode. Just such a confounding occurred in McCarthy School when all the boys were in the playroom while all the girls gave a tea-party for their dolls on the carpet. At that moment, all six of our aspects were aligned: social organization was based on groups composed exclusively of members of a single social category, and material culture, activities, space and behavioural style were likewise divided between the two groups. But the auxiliary's discovery that girls were among the noisy children illustrates the potential independence of sex-group membership and gender-appropriate behaviour. By paying attention to the two classificatory aspects, 'social categories' and 'group composition', in conjunction with the four content aspects, 'material culture', 'activities', 'space' and 'behavioural style', we were alerted to mismatches and enabled to think about gender identities as potentially independent of sex-group membership.

These examples illustrate some of the consequences of undertaking a motivated ethnography. As we remarked in Chapter 3, our ethnographic observations and analyses were limited by our focus on gender and by the need to identify variables which could be measured quantitatively in the second phase of our study. In regard to these aims, it is important to remember that the aspects 'social categories' and 'group composition' function to identify gender issues. The four content aspects specify the direction of gender marking within these domains. Although we coded our ethnographic observations for each of the six aspects, the same incident might attract a number of aspect entries; that is to say, aspects are not independent categories.

The information which is coded in the aspect 'social categories' differs from that collected under the other five aspects in other ways. It is primarily based on the talk of children and teachers about sex-group membership, and usually includes specific comments about events. When social categories such as sex or age are invoked, they are used to comment upon or to organize social life. 'Social categories' is an empty or formal grouping, in the sense that gender is highlighted but not given a specific direction. The talk encoded in 'social categories' usually refers to other aspects, such as 'group composition', 'material culture', 'activities', 'space' or 'behavioural style'. Although we create interpretations based on the content of children's talk about sex-group membership, their statements provide us with our most direct access to children's own reflections on the gender system.

The other classificatory aspect, 'group composition', has a different analytic function. When we describe a scene, and identify a particular group composition in terms of sex-group membership, we can only assume that the setting we have described has the same gender salience for the actors in the scene. The observational evidence presented in Chapters 5, 6 and 7 is organized in terms of our understanding of the group composition of the classroom. Here our analyses focus on social categories. The emphasis on social categories not only gives us access to children's and teachers' observations about sex-group membership, but, in examining their evocation of social categories, we gain access to their gender representations relating to the other five aspects.

TALK OF SOCIAL CATEGORIES IN LAND SCHOOL

The focus of our attention was one social category – that based upon sex-group membership. We used this material to gain access to the gender marking of group composition, material culture, activities, space and behavioural style. We begin by examining teachers' talk and then consider children's evocations of sex-group membership as they were recorded in our ethnographic observations. Our transcriptions of natural dialogue, considered in Chapter 9, provide another way of accessing children's own reflections on gender.

Our notes contained over seventy-five instances in which adults in Land School specifically referred to sex-group membership in their speech. These entries ranged from the casual comment of the teacher to her auxiliary, musing on why it was they always assumed it was the boys who were noisy, to the invocation of the terms 'girls and boys' in directing the class to tidy up or prepare for break. In the first instance, the teacher was commenting upon her assumption that sex-group membership and gender-marked differences in behavioural style were isomorphic, while in the second, she employed sex-group membership to organize classroom activity directly, and in so doing made this social distinction salient to the children in her class.

Perhaps the first thing to note about teachers' use of sex-group membership to organize activity is that it calls into question the explicit ideology which condemns sexism. This is not to deny the importance of an anti-sexist ideology in Land School. The head of Land School set a clear example for teachers in her conscious awareness of gender issues. So pervasive was the rhetoric of equality that when a student working with us observing playground behaviour sought the head's permission to interview girls and boys in separate groups, the head asked the student whether she thought that her procedure was sexist. None the less, the head also commented to the student that she had observed girls and boys doing different things in the playground. She and her teachers were concerned that boys used most of the area and that girls were less active and largely on the periphery. In other words, the head proposed a relationship between sex-group membership and the gender marking of activities, space and behavioural styles. The head's acknowledgment highlighted a distinct feature of Land School. The talk of teachers, including the head teacher, was a mixture of egalitarian rhetoric and an uneasy recognition of differences between girls and boys. Since their training in child-centred methods and official authority pronouncements about equality provided no structure within which to interpret their observations, the adults in Land School often fell back upon notions of biological origins in trying to understand their experiences of differences between girls and boys.

The class teacher's most common way of employing sex-group membership and of highlighting social categories was by invoking the terms 'girls' or 'boys', either singly or together, to organize classroom activity. When both terms were used, the teacher was usually making an announcement to the entire class, such as that it was or soon would be time to tidy up. Since we did not sample systematically, we are unable to estimate how frequently 'boys and girls' replaced 'children' in these announcements.

The teacher often employed the terms 'boys' and 'girls' separately in her management of the class. She called out 'boys' to tell children, usually the same particular boys, to stop running around, to calm down and to be careful, a comment on their behavioural style. This usage is further evidence of her use of sex-group membership to give a gender marking to a particular behavioural style. In the language of the first chapter, she had 'naturalized' a particular gender identity; a noisy, active style was assumed to belong to all boys. Though 'Good boy' was used to give praise, it was more often employed in an attempt to restrain the behaviour of boys.

In contrast to the teacher, a mother, working as a temporary assistant and unfamiliar with the children, used social categories freely to organize activity when helping children change their clothes for physical education. She called a girl who was heading for a table where only boys were changing to come to the girls' table. She labelled the area the girls' table, despite the presence of two boys among the girls. She sought to direct the girl to an area which she viewed as a gender-appropriate space.

Teachers, who knew the names of all the children in their class, and who consciously subscribed to an anti-sexist ideology, actively discouraged children's use of sex-group membership or social categories to organize activities or space. For example, we noted on separate days that one boy's efforts to designate a work table as that of boys met staunch opposition from the teacher on both occasions. The first time he was told 'We don't have boys' tables', and on the second attempt the teacher said firmly 'We're not having boys' tables!', clearly implying that she would not tolerate it. From the children's perspective, adults appear to be sending conflicting messages: some give gender markings to areas of the room while others deny such meaning.

Children's reactions to these comments from teachers and other adults provide us with insight in their representations of gender. The boys who were told to stop running around or being noisy accepted the reprimands.

Indeed, in so far as these activities form part of the image of a 'boy', being told not to do it is a backhanded compliment on the extent to which a boy is acting in conformity with this representation of gender. By way of contrast, the boy who is told by his teacher that 'boys' tables' will not be tolerated showed only confusion and disbelief. Certainly, the first time he was told he complied with the teacher's command, but this was more a consequence of her authority than his acceptance of her point of view. Within a day or two he was again claiming the table for 'the boys'. These different reactions to the teacher's reprimands illustrate the expectations about gender which children bring into the classroom. When the teacher produces traditional expectations they are met, but when she offers egalitarian perspectives they are violated.

Despite conscious awareness and efforts to avoid sexism, teachers' talk also demonstrated that their social representations of gender contained established links between group composition and behavioural style. A girl who was known to have preferred the company of boys at nursery school was much talked about by the teacher and her auxiliary. They knew that they often blamed boys for misbehaviour in which this girl was implicated. But in acknowledging her membership in the social category 'girl', they commiserated about her plight when she and another girl were seated at a table of 'rough' boys. Here we have evidence that the adults themselves were aware of a conflict between the formal rhetoric of equality and their own everyday behaviour.

A further example of the issues surrounding the gender marking of behavioural styles is the teacher's talk about the naughtiness of boys; she suspected her own bias. While recognizing her tendency to blame boys, she also moderated it. On one occasion, the teacher accused a boy of causing another child to cry, and she later apologized to him for blaming him when she heard the whole story. Perhaps it was the teachers' belief in the 'unnaturalness' of naughty girls which led them to comment, during a staff-room discussion, that while naughtiness was rare among girls, when a girl was naughty she was worse, being spiteful and vicious.

Alongside the spontaneous speech of teachers, we also examined their evocation of sex-group membership in structured linguistic settings such as games and story reading. 'The farmer in his den' was the game which most consistently invoked rules about appropriate gender-marked behaviour based upon sex-group membership and social roles. Traditionally in this singing game a farmer is chosen, then the farmer chooses a wife, the wife a child, the child a nurse, the nurse a dog, and the dog a bone. Girls volunteering to be the farmer disturbed the conventional marking of the farmer's role as masculine. The teacher responded in different ways. Sometimes she suggested that children chose a boy, while on other occasions the choice of a girl was confirmed by the teacher, but then the girl

66

was labelled a lady farmer and asked to choose a husband. When a girl ignored the designation 'lady farmer' and chose a boy to be a wife, he staunchly refused to fill the role; the teacher supported his decision by suggesting that a girl be chosen. In the course of many enactments, we noted inconsistencies in the gender marking of the farmer and spouse roles, but teachers explicitly pointed out that the child could be a girl or a boy. The husband/wife roles were clearly fixed by adult conventions, which the teacher as well as the majority of children resolutely defended. Here we have an example of the incidental teaching of social representations of gender which King (1978) described.

Story reading was another setting which often involved the evocation of social category membership to mark activities and behavioural styles for gender. In the 'hen and the sly fox' story, the hen was described as very domestic, which the teacher glossed as meaning that the hen shops and sweeps. In another story, about a little girl and a burst water pipe, the little girl says that she does not know where to turn the water off and needs her daddy, who knows how to turn it off at the mains. Many of the stories which are read to children preserve existing social conventions, marking gender-appropriate material culture, activity and behavioural style.

In considering the impact of story telling on children's incidental learning, it is interesting to reflect upon their responses to the tale of Mrs Plug the plumber. This is a story which challenges social category membership and conventional adult occupational role assignment. When the teacher asked the children if they knew what a plumber was, only one child responded, and said 'a man'. The children seemed generally confused about the work of plumbers, and the author's attempt to challenge gender stereotypes was lost on these children. With little understanding of the work of plumbers, the gender marking of the role was its most salient aspect. While adults intent upon offering a non-sexist view of the world may produce stories such as Mrs Plug, with her gender atypical occupation and heroic behaviour, the capacity of young children to process such information may be limited. Children aged 4–5 are able to deal with teachers' questions about domestic roles – whether their mummy does the ironing, or statements about mummy going home to do the housework – but role reversal, especially that involving less familiar occupations, poses problems. When confronted with an unfamiliar concept, children dealt with the problem by employing a distinction which was familiar to them – gender. We noted this strategy in their talk about men nurses and lady doctors.

There was little difference in our ethnographic record in the numbers of times we noted teachers' and children's talk about social categories. Children's use of social categories in a reflective gender marking of social life is part of an ongoing process of development. Children are trying to make sense of their social world through the enactment of social roles in pretend play. At this age, children are actively exploring links between social categories and gender marking in the four domains included in the content aspects, material culture, activities, space and behavioural style.

Alongside observations about the gender marking of peer activity, children frequently talked about adult gender-marked roles. Almost two thirds of children's talk about activities related to adult roles, and it usually occurred as part of pretend play. It is a significant feature of the natural discourse described in Chapter 9. A good deal of this talk is about mummies and daddies. In our notes about pretend play, three quarters of children's comments about adult roles relate to pretending to be mummies and daddies. The picture which children draw in their pretend play and in their talk is a very traditional one. Daddies fix things, are aggressive and brave, and occasionally behave out of role, as in an episode when one of the fathers surprised his wife and delighted his daughter by fixing her hair. Mummies do the ironing, look after babies and wear fancy clothes. Children are keen to learn as much about the adult world as possible. The struggle this search for understanding sometimes entails is evident in the remark that 'Katie got married but is not having a baby; some people sometimes don't', which we explore more thoroughly in Chapter 9.

In stories read to children, from 'Goldilocks' onwards, the biggest character is identified as the daddy, the next as the mummy and the smallest as baby. That children puzzle about adult roles was apparent in our conversations with them and in those of our assistant, Nick. In a discussion about 'My little pony', Gerard was emphatically told that he was not supposed to own one because he was a boy. Nick found himself in a complicated conversation when a girl asked him if his mummy and daddy lay in bed together. Much of children's gender talk about adult roles reflects their efforts to understand the world in which they live.

Playing superheroes is a common pretend game among children of 4–5 years old and has been carefully observed (cf. Paley, 1984). While we recorded four instances in which boys described their behaviour as that of Superman or Spaceman, we noted only one episode in which a girl stated that she was Superman/Superwoman, and her assertion was prompted by a question from Gerard as she was putting a scarf on to serve as a cloak. We commented on this asymmetry in Chapter 1, noting Paley's observation that boys usually seek adventure while girls pursue domesticity. In the classroom, superheroes functioned to assert the masculinity of the boys.

A further assertion of masculinity by boys is seen in their evocation of group composition and space together, in relation to social categories, in their comments on the sex-group membership of work tables. For example, one boy, changing for physical education, noted that there were four boys and one girl at his table. The girl at his table was Zara, the child the teachers had identified as a tomboy, and it was Zara who had been shepherded to a table of girls by a mother helping in the class. Although Zara may have sought to assert a masculine gender identity, from this boy's perspective she was still a girl. Zara's presence at a table otherwise inhabited solely by boys did trouble the mother, who had explicitly tried to ensure congruence between the girl's sex-group membership and her use of space; the teacher, in the face of her formal commitment to an egalitarian rhetoric, found the girl's incongruous behaviour (assertion of a masculine gender identity) a spur to thought about gender.

In another observation about group composition and space, a boy commented that there were three boys at the Play-dough table. He included himself in this count, a cognitively sophisticated operation and one which may have been prompted by the discomfort boys feel in being in predominantly female company. Similarly, a boy was moved to count the number of boys when a girl at a lunch table in the hall announced 'There aren't many boys.' Again, counting himself, he remarked accurately and emphatically on the sex-group membership (social category) and group composition, 'There are three boys.' The tension between the sex groups may have spurred boys to the limits of their cognitive resources, but emotions are sometimes summoned to deal with intergroup tension as well. One of the five girls at the table retorted 'Boys are horrible!' Her attack shifted the ground and linked social category membership and behavioural style.

The behavioural style of boys was frequently evaluated negatively. For example, a girl and boy in conversation with Nick accused Nick of being naughty because he had spiky hair; yet a boy had run his hands through the spiky hair of the auxiliary and commented that it was nice. Children appear to echo their teachers in expecting naughtiness from boys. In the lunch-table incident, the whole category of boys was proclaimed to be horrible and a boy covered with sand was called 'Dirty boy!' Girls used naughtiness as an excuse to complain to the teacher either about boys monopolizing certain toys or about them invading their space; that is, to challenge boys' gender marking of material culture and space. Perhaps the 'invisibility' of girls, and their failure to prompt the negative remarks which are so frequently made about boys and their behavioural style, reflects girls' less frequent challenge to boys for resources in the classroom.

On one occasion, social category membership was invoked successfully by girls in order to gain play resources for their own sex group. The teacher reluctantly agreed to organize turns for boys and girls after complaints about boys monopolizing the big blocks. One of the boys tried to re-establish the rights of boys by pointing out that the girls were not using them at the moment, but the girls remarked sharply that boys were not allowed to play with the blocks at that time; it was the girls' turn. In another episode, girls asserted that the home corner was their house as some boys approached it. This occurred on the same day that one of these girls reported to the teacher that she had found a boy in the girls' toilet. The link between social category membership and the gender marking of content aspects is clear in these episodes. So, too, is the inter-sex group conflict which access to resources provokes, and the difficulty which the teacher experiences in resolving it in an egalitarian manner.

There were other comments about group composition, such as 'This is a boys' table', which, as we already noted, prompted the teacher to deny social category membership as a principle of classroom organization. When a boy at one table identified his own table as a boys' table but the next table as a girls' and boys' table, a boy at the second table protested and said 'This is a boys' table!' In a similar context, another boy commented 'Boys don't go on girls' tables', while yet another boy said 'That is a ladies' table, this is a boys' table.' In this context, the difference between the teachers' response and that of male peers is clear; boys seek to establish an exclusivity. Boys invoke space as a resource to assert a masculine identity. The teacher denies their marking of space and the importance of sex-group membership as a social category in the organization of classroom interaction. In this instance, the teacher asserted the formal ideology of equality, though in other circumstances, such as in organizing an event, she also invoked sex-group membership and social categories as a structural principal.

Children occasionally invoked sex-group membership in attempts to influence ongoing activity. Their evocation of social categories to organize activity is instrumental and parallels teachers' usage, though it is rarer and may be less successful. One of our observations of a boy invoking social categories in this fashion appeared to be a direct imitation of the teacher's style. He was trying to get other children to take part in his pretend game involving a 'dangerous plank'. He called out 'Come, girls and boys', but no one joined him.

Our records of children's use of gender categorization to organize their activity include a number of episodes relating to the 'farmer in his den' game. On two occasions, boys were chosen by other boys for the roles of nurse and wife, which they refused to fulfil. In both instances, the teacher stepped in and named some girls. However, when a 'lady farmer' chose a girl for her husband, amidst hoots of laughter and one child's comment 'What a funny husband', the girls persisted. When the 'bone' was finally chosen, a boy remarked 'All girls in the middle!' Comparison of these episodes indicates that it is easier for girls to accept gender-inappropriate role allocation than for boys.

Analysis of our notes on reflective gender talk revealed a further asymmetry. The observations of girls were made in a descriptive or sometimes defensive mode, while boys were exclusive and competitive. For example, a girl drawing on the chalkboard put in eyelashes and then said, 'This is a lady.' Labelling a drawing with the teacher, another girl said 'I am a girl.' In contrast, when a shy girl said 'Girls win', a boy standing nearby replied 'It's no race!', apparently needing to have the last word.

The use of gender to organize play and the developmental issues it raises are evident in problems posed by attempts to mark gender by evoking shared signs. This is illustrated in an episode which began when a girl seeking entry to a game was told that only people wearing skirts could play the game. The girl who gained entry by virtue of her dress then noted that one of the other girls already in the game was wearing trousers. The new girl asserted that the girl wearing trousers could not play, but the other girls continued to include her. It is through episodes of this nature that children re-construct and redefine social categories and their social gender identities.

TALK ABOUT SOCIAL CATEGORIES IN McCARTHY SCHOOL

We begin our examination of the evocation of social categories by looking at teachers' talk. We follow this by an analysis of children's talk about sex-group membership. A comparison of social category evocation in Land and McCarthy schools follows.

Teachers' talk

Our visits to McCarthy School were not as frequent as those to Land School, nor are our notes as extensive, but we recorded almost fifty instances in which teachers drew children's attention to sex-group membership. The reception class teacher in McCarthy School appeared more willing to ignore the explicit ideology of anti-sexism and frequently employed the terms 'boys' and 'girls' to organize classroom activity.

Calling the class attendance register in a manner which made membership in a sex group salient accounted for about a third of the evocations of social categories (sex-group membership). It was the custom for the teacher to name the boys first and then the girls, though the listing of full- and part-time children meant that boys, then girls, were followed by boys and girls again. We have an entry in our notes indicating that the usual classroom teacher varied her practice, following an innovation by the student teacher in her class. The student had mixed up the names instead of calling the boys as a group and then the girls.

The teacher in McCarthy School used sex-group membership to organize activities between girls and boys both in a competitive and in a friendly fashion, making gender salient in many contexts. She might separate boys and girls to see who could tidy up faster or line up faster to go to the toilet. But even such non-competitive activities as handing in name-reading cards were organized by invoking the categories 'girls' and 'boys'. We have already noted that boys might be sent to the play-room while girls held a tea-party for dolls on the carpet in the classroom, thus confounding social categories and social organization, and all the content aspects.

Material culture and activities were also marked by the teacher for gender appropriateness. During a class reading lesson which introduced a family of dolls, the gender-appropriate nature of their clothing was brought to the attention of the class. In one discussion, blouses and shirts were distinguished as being the objects of girls and boys respectively. The unconscious salience of gender for the teacher was evident in a conscious effort to avoid the worn categories of girls and boys; unwittingly, her statement 'Children who have grey skirts can go and play' only served to reinforce the notion that it is appropriate for girls to wear skirts. As we observed in Land School, the teacher, in an effort to avoid an isomorphism between social categories and social organization, used articles of clothing to form the lines for playtime.

Often the teacher encouraged gender-appropriate activities. She suggested that a boy might build a tower, while on another occasion she suggested to a group of boys that they might arrange the chairs so that they could play trains. We speculated that a boy may have been criticized by the teacher for pretend cooking because she viewed his behaviour as an inappropriate activity. Clear marking of feminine activities was seen in the teacher's request for a girl, but not for the three boys she was playing with, to tidy up. Again, girls were reprimanded when they failed to help in tidying up, but boys were not censured in this way. Boys were criticized for aggressive, violent and noisy behaviour, but the teacher's suggestion that they should not shout in school might be viewed as recognition that such action was typical of boys' behavioural style, but inappropriate in the confines of the classroom.

Children's talk

Children in McCarthy School shared their teacher's representations in marking behavioural styles according to sex-group membership. Rough-and-tumble play became salient and was censored if the actor was a boy, but tended to be overlooked if it involved girls. This was shown in a bus-riding episode. Annie tussled vigorously with Henrietta, trying to get her to sit in the pretend seat on the bus next to her (in the book corner, actually). They appeared to enjoy the physicality of their rough-and-tumble play.

Together the girls captured Chuck when he approached the book corner. Chuck seemed stunned by their move and interpreted it as aggression. He raised his hands with clenched fists as if to warn the girls to leave him alone. At this point the teacher intervened, reprimanding Chuck without a word to the girls. A little while later the scene was re-enacted, and again Chuck earned a reprimand from the teacher. Annie was free to pursue Henrietta, who by this time had escaped from the book corner. Henrietta attempted to deal with Annie's rough physical behaviour by saying 'I'm not your friend, Annie', but failed to discourage Annie's attempts at recapture. Eventually, when the teacher did intervene, it was to say to Annie 'I think that Henrietta is getting a little tired of you.' We can contrast this episode with the apology of the teacher in Land School when she realized that she had misjudged the 'naughtiness' of one of the boys in her class.

Games and story reading offered further evidence of the teacher's social representations of gender. 'Farmer in his den' was a popular game in McCarthy School, as well as in Land School. It offers a bridge between the world of the family and school, in that it builds upon the roles of mother, father and child, already familiar to the pupils. In an assembly, the head teacher recited the story of Adam and Eve. The traditional story and parts played by Adam and Eve may well suggest that male and female roles are natural and god-given. Perhaps the most blatant message communicated to children was the large mural prepared along a nautical theme for the summer fête. It boldly proclaimed 'All the nice girls love a sailor.'

Land and McCarthy schools compared

Our comments thus far suggest that egalitarian issues were ignored in McCarthy School. This was not the case. The head was sensitive to these issues and often challenged her staff. She questioned the reception class teacher about any procedures which the head believed revealed a sexist bias. We became clearly aware of these conflicting orientations when the head challenged the reception class teacher about the pictures she provided to the new children, for them to mark their places in the hanging area and work space. The teacher maintained that boys preferred pictures of masculine toys. While the head sought to induce change by challenging old methods, her younger class teacher may well have believed that she was keeping faith with principles of child-centred pedagogy. But these differences in orientation alone do not explain the contrasts between Land and McCarthy schools which we observed.

We need to avoid any suggestion that one school was egalitarian and the other sexist, as there were conflicting representations of gender in both schools. Teachers in both schools displayed sensitivity to issues of gender equality and taken-for-granted assumptions about differences between boys and girls. In our notes from McCarthy School, we recorded that the teacher read a story about a boy who was interested in making cakes, encouraged a boy to pretend to wash up and urged three boys to tidy the home corner. At the beginning of the first chapter, we reported the teacher's struggle in Land School to manage a boy's cross-dressing up. Although she could say 'there is no reason why a girl cannot be a wise man' when casting the Christmas play, we were aware that such a view was inconsistent with some of the social representations of gender that she had internalized.

We concluded from our ethnographic observations that there were inconsistencies and contradictions in the social representations of gender that both teachers presented. As we remarked in the first chapter, teachers are not immune from the conflicts involved in presenting gender, and as a consequence, the social representations of gender which a teacher gives to children are not straightforward.

One source of difference between the classes may have been the resolution the teacher in Land School achieved between conflicting social representations of gender. She was able to focus on traditional family roles and offer an image of equality of opportunity regardless of gender. In this she was supported by a consensus among the teachers in the school. She succeeded in assimilating them into one overall, encompassing set of social representations. This is a useful example of the complexity of the – often contradictory – interrelationships between the many conflicting voices that go to make up the set of social representations in a significant social domain such as gender.

In contrast, in McCarthy School the teacher displayed sensitivity to the preferences of the children, but showed little interest in explicitly anti-sexist material. As we observed in Chapter 1, 4–5 year olds have very clearly differentiated views of gender, so that in drawing upon children's attitudes, change is inhibited. On at least one occasion (the pictures), the teacher was dissatisfied with the anti-sexist representations that she was asked by the head to make. Other teachers shared her scepticism of overt attempts at change, and their willingness to espouse an older model could be seen in the nautical poster.

FROM ETHNOGRAPHY TO MEASUREMENT

The insights derived from our ethnographic observations shaped the measurement techniques which we employed in the second year of our study. In Chapter 3, we described our decision to employ spot observations rather than time-sampling techniques dependent upon intervals of greater duration and complexity. The insights which we gained in our ethnographic study helped us devise the categories which were completed for each spot observation.

Earlier in this chapter we demonstrated the salience, for children and teachers, of social categories (sex-group membership) in the organization of classroom life. Given this concern among the protagonists, we took care to identify, in every observation, each participant engaged with the target child. From this information, we developed a description of the different sex-group composition of the groups in which children participated. The contrasts between participation in these different types of group is described in Chapter 5, and it became the basis for our working measure of gender identity. We also differentiated activities influenced by the participation of the teachers from peer-organized events. While the two classificatory aspects, social categories and group composition, were important in our quantitative study based upon spot observations, we also recorded and analysed material objects, ongoing activity and locations (material culture, activities and space). From this information we were able to derive systematic assessments of the marking of gender through children's practical activity.

Our interviews sought to measure children's reflective understanding, as opposed to their practical understanding. Here we were guided directly in the choice of the objects, activities, spaces and behavioural styles by our ethnographic observations. In fact, the Figures test offered an image of the classroom and then required children to position boys and girls appropriately. While our ethnographic study yielded much material beyond the immediate concerns of this book, it both alerted us to the variables which we needed to quantify and assisted us in anchoring our structured observations and interviews in the life of the classroom.

5

Observing sex and gender in the classroom

In earlier chapters, we argued for the theoretical need to distinguish sex-group membership and social gender identity, and were critical of empirical studies which, by neglecting this distinction, confounded the two concepts. In general, such confusion has been characteristic of studies in developmental psychology, so that when Maccoby and Jacklin (1987; also Maccoby, 1988) argued that there was little theoretical utility in distinguishing sex and gender, their remarks had some foundation. Although many researchers have employed a theoretical distinction between sex and gender, there have been few attempts to distinguish between these concepts empirically. And if the distinction cannot be made in practice, then, as Maccoby and Jacklin argue, it holds little value for research. Yet the fact that a distinction between sex and gender has not been made in research does not mean that it cannot be made.

Our aim in this chapter is to establish the basis for making such a distinction. In the following chapter, we shall go on to demonstrate that, once made, the distinction between sex and gender can make a difference to the analysis of empirical data. In this way, we hope to support our contention that the two terms not only need to be distinguished theoretically, but that this distinction can be realized empirically and employed meaningfully.

In establishing the basis for an empirical distinction between sex and gender, this chapter provides a first analysis of the longitudinal data from our observational study. The chapter opens with a discussion of the difficulties of establishing an index of social gender identity from observational data. Given all of the information recorded in the spot observations, which elements should be used to create such an index? We shall argue that one aspect of children's peer associations – the extent to which they participate in homogenous, single-sex groups – can provide a first approximation of an index of social gender identity. The remainder of the chapter presents an analysis of patterns of children's peer associations and describes the construction of an index.

ANALYSING GENDER

The confounding of sex and gender in research in developmental psychology stands in stark contrast to the efforts made in social-psychological studies of adults to establish an empirical basis for distinguishing between these terms. As we noted in Chapter 1, on page 6, this work has the advantage of distinguishing masculinity and femininity as psychological dimensions from membership in a sex group (cf. Deaux, 1984). Since Bem's pioneering studies, we have thought of both men and women as combining differing degrees of masculinity and femininity. It then becomes possible for researchers to compare the attitudes and behaviour of men and women with similar masculinity or femininity scores. With children in reception classes, it is not feasible to assess gender identity with a questionnaire measure. As we indicated in Chapter 3, we did not measure gender identity directly. One of the first tasks in our analysis was to devise a measure using our data which could provide an index of children's gender identity. Rather than establishing gender identities through individual endorsements of items in a questionnaire, we looked for an index of gender identity in children's activities.

In our earlier studies with pre-school children (Lloyd and Duveen, 1989; 1990), we found that boys and girls made differential use of gender-marked toys. There was a marked asymmetry between the sexes, with boys focused on male-marked toys almost to the exclusion of using toys with a feminine marking, while girls spent virtually the same amount of time playing with masculine- and feminine-marked toys. This asymmetry was influenced by the type of group a child played in; boys playing with boys were more extreme in their toy choices than when they played with girls. In these studies the children were observed in pairs which we had organized, but in the classroom there is no systematic control over children's choice of companions. Teachers organize children into groups for both work and play activities, but for much of the time children are free to form their own groups. We suggested in Chapter 4 that children use their associations with their peers as a primary means for expressing a gender identity. There are substantial *a priori* reasons for isolating this variable as the key indicator around which a strategy for analysing the observational data can be elaborated.

Our own ethnographic investigation showed the importance and

77

significance of gender for children's peer associations. Indeed, a distinction between 'girls'' groups and 'boys'' groups was a persistent feature of the visible surface of each of the classrooms we observed. Both children and teachers regularly identified and commented upon this feature of classroom life in a way which indicated that, for all the actors in the classroom, peer association functioned as a primary indicator of social gender identities.

As well as ethnographic reasons, there are also theoretical grounds for selecting peer association as an indicator of social gender identities. In the world of the young child, social relationships are not differentiated from their external forms. To be friends with someone means to play with him or her, and it is this sense of 'being with' which young children use to characterize friendship (Duveen, 1984). Only as children develop an understanding of internal, psychological processes do they come to appreciate their role in social relationships, and to see that relationships can exist beyond the immediacy of contact with others. Association with others is the principal means through which young children express and manage their social relationships. In so far as gender is an important organizer of young children's social relationships, we assume that it is visible in patterns of their peer associations. The concept of a social identity carries with it a sense of *identification with* others in the same group, and, in relation to gender, it is this identification which can be given expression through associating with members of the same sex group.

Investigating social gender identities through observations of the practical activities of children marks a departure from the more familiar use of the concept of gender identity in developmental psychology, which derived from Kohlberg's (1966) theory and research. From his perspective, gender identity is a cognitive phenomenon, and its development is seen to result from the emergence of more complex cognitive capacities through early childhood. Indeed, so much research on the development of gender identity has been cognitively focused that the issue has rarely been addressed in practical terms. As we noted in Chapter 2, social representations are constellations of 'values, ideas and practices' (Moscovici, 1973, p. xiii), and from our perspective, which derives social identities from social representations, a purely cognitive approach is insufficient (cf. Duveen and Lloyd, 1986). In addition to the developmental issues already considered, the emphasis on analysing social identity through children's practical activities also reflects a social-psychological perspective, in which social identity is always considered to be situated within a context of institutional and interpersonal relations, which shape and structure its expression. It is this dimension of the contextual influences on a situated identity which is absent from most cognitive-developmental accounts of gender.

Despite sound ethnographic and theoretical reasons for employing peer associations as a significant indicator of young children's social gender identities, our approach entails certain difficulties. Gender identity and sex-group membership may be distinguishable, but they are also related. In many contexts, sex-group membership functions as a signifier of gender. In this sense, the situation of the child in the classroom is unlike that of the adult sitting down to complete a questionnaire on gender identity. Adults filling in forms are less influenced by the practical activities of other people around them. In the classroom, the child is continually responding to the influences of others, and a part of that influence stems from the general acceptance of sex-group membership as a signifier of gender.

As theorists we have argued for the conceptual necessity of distinguishing sex-group membership and gender identity. But this perspective is not necessarily shared by the people we observed in the classroom. The children and their teachers regularly confound this distinction; they too tend to see the world of sex and gender as overlapping, binary categories. This overlap, however, is not complete; exceptions are made. For example, a girl who takes on the role of a tomboy is able to participate in masculine activities with boys without other people finding this behaviour odd. There is, though, an asymmetry; boys engaging in feminine activities are more likely to be considered to be doing something unusual. Dressing up in female clothes, for example, is something which boys can do if they make a joke out of it; otherwise it is something which will draw adverse comment from other children, as we noted at the beginning of Chapter 1.

By and large, children perceive sex-group membership as indicative of a gender identity, and this principle may influence their choice of peers, leading them to associate with or to exclude other children. An index based on peer associations is unlikely to offer as simple and clear an indicator of gender identity as responses to a questionnaire, since it will reflect the active influence of sex-group membership. Nevertheless, we have used this measure as an index of social gender identity, which is distinct from sex-group membership. It may not be ideal in some respects, but, as a first approximation, it helps us to demonstrate that distinguishing between these two terms can reveal differences which remain hidden when empirical data is analysed in terms of sex-group membership alone.

PEER ASSOCIATIONS IN THE RECEPTION CLASS

The first step in our examination of peer associations was an analysis of the frequency with which each child was observed with every other child. To do this we used a graphical technique – correspondence analysis. The data were cast in the form of a matrix, with a row for each child in a class, and columns which indicated the number of times each child was observed with each other child in the class. The more frequently two children were observed together, the closer together two points appear in the resulting graphs. Separate analyses were undertaken for each school, and for Land School separate analyses were undertaken for the morning and afternoon groups in the autumn terms. As our interest here is focused on peer associations, these analyses included only observations which were recorded in peer-organized contexts. The plots of the first two dimensions in each analysis for the autumn term are shown in Figures 5.1–5.3.

A consistent feature in these plots is the separation between the positions of the girls and of the boys. To indicate this separation we have drawn a line on the graph, and for the most part the girls are plotted to one side of this line, while the boys are plotted to the other (the fact that these lines do not coincide with one of the principal axes in the plots suggests that neither of the first two dimensions in the correspondence analyses is equivalent to sex-group membership). In general, boys are observed associating more frequently with other boys, and girls with other girls. There are some exceptions to this pattern in McCarthy School. Two of the girls appear in the 'boys'' part of the graph, while a number of boys and girls are found along the line of separation, or very close to it. There are no exceptions in either the morning or afternoon groups in Land School.

A second feature of the social organization of reception classes indicated by these plots is the capacity of children to form stable peer groups. Clusters

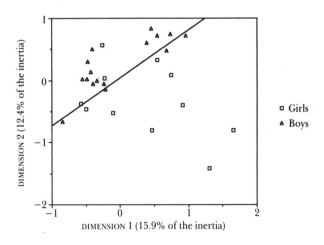

Figure 5.1 Plot of correspondence analysis for McCarthy School: autumn term

80

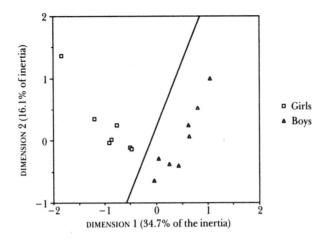

Figure 5.2 Plot of correspondence analysis for Land School:
morning, autumn term

of children who were repeatedly observed in each other's company are plotted close together. These clusters can be seen in all of these plots, among both boys and girls. For the most part, members of such stable peer groups are all from the same sex group. An exception can be seen in McCarthy School, where there is a large grouping of boys which includes one of the girls.

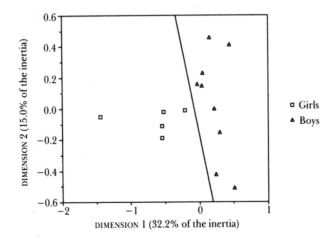

Figure 5.3 Plot of correspondence analysis for Land School:
afternoon, autumn term

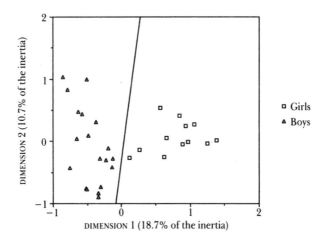

Figure 5.4 Plot of correspondence analysis for McCarthy
School: term 3

Both of these features also appear in the plots for the summer term data, where a single plot is provided for Land School, since all the children attended school full time. In McCarthy School (see Figure 5.4), the separation between girls and boys is more extreme in the summer term, with no exceptions. In Land School (see Figure 5.5), it is again possible to

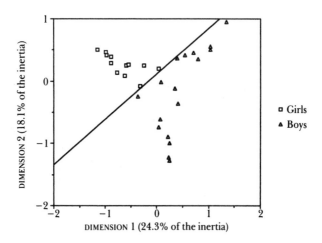

Figure 5.5 Plot of correspondence analysis for Land School:
term 3

82

draw a line which separates boys and girls exclusively, though one or two boys and girls are plotted very close to this line. In both schools, stable peer groups can be seen within each sex group.

These first analyses illustrate the significance of sex-group membership for peer associations in the classroom. None the less, it is worth noting that the proportions of inertia explained by the two dimensions plotted in the graphs are not large, ranging from about a third to a half in the different classes. In other words, sex-group membership may be a salient aspect of peer association in the classroom, but in itself it does not provide a sufficient explanation for the patterns of peer association which can be observed. Indeed, as well as the exceptions to the separation between boys and girls which we noted earlier, one can also see in these plots wide variations between children within both sex groups. Some children form more or less stable peer groups, while others were not regularly observed with any particular peers. There is considerable variability between children within the same sex group in their peer associations.

PEER ASSOCIATIONS IN DIFFERENT TYPES OF GROUP

Information about the other children present in each spot observation was used to classify the type of group in which the target child was observed. We have again used a correspondence analysis to provide a graphical overview as a first step towards a more detailed analysis of peer associations in different types of group. In the matrix for this analysis, each child is represented by two rows, one for each term, with five columns, one for each type of group. Figure 5.6 shows the plot of the first two dimensions for this analysis.

In this graph, when the points for two children are plotted close together it indicates that their profile of participation in all five types of group is very similar. Once again, it is possible to draw a line on the graph which separates children into sex groups, though it is noticeable that the division is by no means exclusive, with a number of children being plotted in the area of the opposite sex.

As well as indicating the position of individual children, correspondence analysis also allows us to plot the positions of the different types of group on the same graph. It is important to note that the line which separates girls and boys also divides the groups. On the whole it is boys who are more frequently observed in single-sex groups and groups of more boys, while girls are more frequently observed in groups of more girls, mixed even

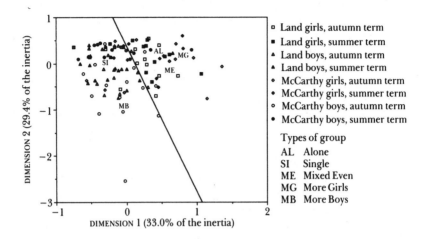

Figure 5.6 Plot of correspondence analysis for participation in different types of group

groups and alone. Again, this generalization on the basis of sex-group membership obscures a great deal of variability within each sex group.

A more precise estimate of the influence of sex-group membership on peer associations was obtained from quantitative analyses of the observational data. For these analyses, the frequency with which each child was observed in each kind of group in both peer- and teacher-organized contexts was expressed as a proportion of the total number of observations made on the child in each term.

The averages of these proportions are shown in Table 5.1, and they exhibit considerable consistency across terms. In both terms, about two thirds of children's activity is in peer-organized contexts, and about one third in teacher-organized contexts. Also, children were observed in single-sex groups about half of the time in each term, and such groups were far more frequent in peer-organized contexts than in teacher-organized contexts. Contextual influences on the formation of single-sex groups have been observed by a number of other investigators (e.g., Carpenter *et al.*, 1986; Huston and Carpenter, 1985; Serbin *et al.*, 1981; Thorne, 1986). In spite of the preponderance of single-sex groups, over a third of children's time is spent in mixed-sex groups of one type or another, and this is more evenly divided between the two organizational contexts. Thus the stereotypical image of children being segregated into sex groups in the classroom ignores the extent to which they are also involved in mixed-sex groups, even in peer-organized contexts. The total proportions of observations in each

Table 5.1 Mean proportions of observations in each type of
group, by term and organizational context (N=51)

Autumn term

Group	Peer-organized	Teacher-organized	Combined
Alone	6.6	4.5	11.1
Single	36.0	11.0	47.0
Mixed even	6.9	5.1	12.0
More girls	4.6	5.6	10.2
More boys	10.5	9.2	19.7
Total	64.6	35.4	100.0

Summer term

Group	Peer-organized	Teacher-organized	Combined
Alone	8.7	4.2	12.9
Single	40.8	9.2	50.0
Mixed even	5.4	4.4	9.8
More girls	7.1	6.2	13.3
More boys	6.3	7.7	14.0
Total	68.3	31.7	100.0

organizational context remain consistent across the terms, and are broadly
comparable for girls and boys (see Table 5.2). None the less, there are
differences between girls and boys in the proportions in which they are
observed in different types of group. Statistical analyses revealed significant
differences according to sex-group membership in all types of group except
'alone'.[1] Boys were observed more frequently than girls in single-sex
groups and in groups of more boys, while girls were observed more
frequently than boys in groups of more girls and mixed even groups.[2] In
addition, girls were observed in groups of more boys more frequently than
boys were observed in groups of more girls (cf. Table 5.2). This asymmetry
was observed even in teacher-organized contexts; indeed, the rate at which
boys participated in groups of more girls is extremely low in both contexts.

The only major change from the autumn to the summer term occured in

[1] Details of these analyses are reported in Duveen and Lloyd (in press). Separate analyses of
variance were undertaken for each type of group, with sex and school as between-subjects
variables, and organizational context and term as within-subjects variables. As the data
consisted of proportions, an arcsine transformation was applied prior to analysis in order to
stabilize variances (cf. Kirk, 1968).
[2] Main effects for sex (all df = 1,47) in analyses of 'single' ($F = 20.42$; $P < 0.001$), 'more boys'
($F = 8.59$; $P < 0.01$), 'more girls' ($F = 81.78$; $P < 0.001$) and 'mixed even' ($F = 7.43$;
$P < 0.01$) groups.

Table 5.2 Mean proportions of observations in each type of group, by term, sex and organizational context (N=51)

| | Autumn term | | | |
| | Peer-organized | | Teacher-organized | |
Group	Girls	Boys	Girls	Boys
Alone	9.8	4.5	5.3	4.1
Single	26.7	42.0	12.3	10.2
Mixed even	9.9	4.9	6.5	4.2
More girls	8.0	2.4	9.8	2.9
More boys	6.2	13.2	5.5	11.6
Total	60.6	67.0	39.4	33.0

| | Summer Term | | | |
| | Peer-organized | | Teacher-organized | |
Group	Girls	Boys	Girls	Boys
Alone	8.3	9.0	5.0	3.7
Single	33.3	45.7	4.7	12.1
Mixed even	6.3	5.0	6.0	3.4
More girls	13.5	2.9	11.0	3.1
More boys	5.3	6.9	6.6	8.2
Total	66.7	69.5	33.3	30.5

the formation of single-sex groups, and this change was most noticeable among the girls.[3] Girls' participation in single-sex groups in peer-organized contexts was greater in the summer term than the autumn term, but they were observed less frequently in teacher-organized contexts in the summer term. By the end of the year, there was less difference between girls and boys in their participation in single-sex groups when interacting with peers, but a greater differential in teacher-organized contexts.

Children in Land and McCarthy schools differed in their participation in single-sex groups in the two organizational contexts.[4] The difference in participation between the contexts was greater in Land School (mean when peer-organized = 42.3 per cent; mean when teacher-organized = 8.6 per cent) than in McCarthy School (mean when peer-organized = 33.3 per cent; mean when teacher-organized = 12.1 per cent).

[3] Sex by term by organizational context interaction in the analysis of single-sex groups; $F (1,47) = 6.04$; $P < 0.05$.
[4] School by organizational context interaction in the analysis of single-sex groups; $F (1,47) = 10.75$; $P < 0.01$.

CREATING AN INDEX OF GENDER IDENTITY

The analyses in the preceding section showed the extent to which children's participation in different types of group varied as a function of sex-group membership. It also showed that the overall rate at which different types of group were observed varied considerably, with single-sex groups the most frequently observed. In trying to use this information about peer association to construct an index of gender identity, we initially attempted to generate a measure which expressed the amount of time children associated with peers of the same sex. The more frequently children were observed with same-sex peers, the more they resembled the stereotypic images of 'girls' or 'boys'. Initially, we explored a number of ways of using the data about participation in different types of group. Our first attempt involved a combination of information about participation in different types of group (for example, calculating the difference between participation in 'more boys' and 'more girls' groups and adding this to the proportion of observations in single-sex groups; see Duveen and Lloyd, 1990b). Such a complex index created both statistical and theoretical problems. The statistical problem related to the contingencies between the proportions in which children were observed in each type of group. Given that a limited number of observations were made on each child, the more frequently a child was observed in one type, the less she or he was observed in others. Consequently, the data about participation in different types of group does not provide a set of independent items from which an index could be constructed. Statistical issues aside, we believed it was theoretically important to distinguish children who spent more of their time in single-sex groups from those who regularly participated in other types of group. However, when we compared the outcomes of analyses using different measures of gender identity, we found only minor differences. In view of the statistical problems which the earlier index raised, we finally decided to use the simplest measure – that is, the proportion of time spent in single-sex groups – as the basis for an index of gender identity.

In addition, in constructing an index of gender identity we have used only information about children's participation in single-sex groups in peer-organized contexts. As well as demonstrating the influence of sex-group membership on the formation of single-sex groups, the analysis in the previous section also showed the significance of organizational context. It is in peer contexts that children have the greatest freedom to organize their own activity. The index thus reflects the extent to which children associate exclusively with other members of the same-sex group when their activity is not directly constrained by their teacher.

As a proportion of observations in single-sex groups in peer-organized contexts, the index actually provides a continuous variable which could

Table 5.3 Numbers of children in low and high gender identity groups, and the median of proportions of observations in single-sex groups

Autumn term					
Gender	McCarthy School		Land School		
identity	Girls	Boys	Girls	Boys	Total
Low	4	7	6	7	24
High	4	7	6	10	27
Median	0.236	0.323	0.325	0.450	

Summer term					
Gender	McCarthy School		Land School		
identity	Girls	Boys	Girls	Boys	Total
Low	4	7	6	8	25
High	4	7	6	9	26
Median	0.275	0.425	0.325	0.450	

range from 0 per cent to 100 per cent, although 80 per cent was the highest proportion we recorded. In order to use the index in analysing other observational data, a median split has been made to separate children into two groups, those with a low gender identity index and those with a high gender identity index. As participation in single-sex groups varies between boys and girls and between schools, this division was made separately for girls and boys within each school. Thus the meaning of low or high gender identity varies across sex groups and schools. Table 5.3 shows the number of children in each of these categories for each term.

Although the numbers of children in each category are similar across the year for both sex groups in each of the schools, there is considerable variation between terms. Of the twenty-four children in the low group in the autumn term, eleven were classified in the high group in the summer term, and of the twenty-seven children in the high group in the autumn term, twelve were in the low group in the summer term. As Table 5.4 shows, this variability is spread across sex groups and schools.

Table 5.4 indicates the considerable variability which existed from the autumn to the summer term, although statistical analysis failed to show any significant differences. This variability does not arise as a consequence of creating a categorical variable from a continuous variable. The correlation between the proportion of observations in single-sex groups in the autumn and the summer terms is 0.4, and although this is significant at a conventional level ($P < 0.01$), it is low enough to indicate that it is

Observing sex and gender in the classroom

Table 5.4 Cross-tabulation of gender identity index across terms

McCarthy School

Summer term

	Girls		Boys	
	Low	High	Low	High
Low	2	2	5	2

Autumn term

| High | 2 | 2 | 2 | 5 |

Land School

Summer term

	Girls		Boys	
	Low	High	Low	High
Low	2	4	4	3

Autumn term

| High | 4 | 2 | 4 | 6 |

impossible to predict with any certainty what a child's summer-term rating would be from her or his autumn-term rating. Social gender identity, as measured on this index, is not consistent, but dependent on context. In analysing the longitudinal data, we are interested in the process of the formation of social gender identity through the reception year, and, accordingly, it is the categorizations in the summer term which have been used to define levels of gender identity for the analyses which follow in Chapter 6.

In devising a categorical index of social gender identity, we have used the labels '*high*' and '*low*' to distinguish between different types of children. Given that the index is based solely on the proportion of time children spend in single-sex groups, these terms reduce the complex phenomenon of social gender identity to a single empirical dimension. Undoubtedly the proportion of time which children spend in single-sex groups is a very narrow basis for an index of social gender identity. In using this measure in this way, we are not claiming that it provides an ideal index, but we do assert that it provides the best available point of departure for an empirical analysis which seeks to distinguish between sex-group membership and social gender identity. Trying to make this distinction on the basis of observations of children's activities is a step into the unknown. In time, it may become possible to establish a more adequate index. For the present, taking the first step is important if the conceptual distinction between sex and gender is to have any empirical validity.

6

Gender identity as an influence on classroom life

Familiar images of social life in the classroom distinguish stereotypical masculine and feminine styles. For example, a boy who participates in all things which are given a masculine label would be described as exhibiting a highly consistent masculine style. He would tend to associate with other boys in particular areas of the classroom, playing with specific items of material culture. This image of how we expect boys to behave in the classroom is matched by its converse, which describes girls exhibiting a highly consistent feminine style. But how true are these stereotypical images to the practical realities of classroom life? The images or social representations which circulate in society tend to be ones in which sex-group membership and gender identity are confounded, and because they are confounded the issue of within-sex-group variability in gender identity has been neglected.

In Chapter 5, we established an index of gender identity based on the proportion of observations in single-sex groups. In this chapter, we trace the influence of gender identity on other aspects of children's social life in the reception classroom, in particular its influence on group size, the use of material culture and the use of space. All of these aspects of classroom life potentially carry specific gender markings, and can serve as resources for the expression of gender identities.

Our index divides both girls and boys into two further groups: those who spend a great deal of their time in single-sex groups (a *high* level of gender identity) and those who spend less time in such groups (a *low* level of gender identity). We have employed this index as an independent variable to investigate within-sex-group differences in the ways in which children use other resources in the classroom.

Some caution is required when considering these analyses. In Chapter 5, we noted a considerable asymmetry between the sexes in the development of gender identities. Our studies of pre-school children showed that boys more readily marked a distinctive gender identity through their use of masculine-marked toys. Associating with other peers of the same sex provides children with another resource for expressing their gender identity. The analyses in Chapter 5 showed that the asymmetry in the development of gender identity persists into the reception year: boys, on the whole, spend more time engaged in single-sex groups than girls. This difference in patterns of association led us to question the meaning of same-sex peer association for girls and boys. If the norm for boys is different from the norm for girls, we cannot assume that high or low gender identity carries the same meaning for both sexes. A girl who associates predominantly with other girls is not necessarily asserting a gender identity which is the same as that of a boy who associates predominantly with other boys. Both children would be rated as having a *high* gender identity on our index, but if the social rules regulating the construction of femininity and masculinity are asymmetric, then the girl may be asserting an identity which goes against the prevailing norm while the boy is behaving in accord with the prevailing norm. This makes it difficult to consider as a single group children of both sexes who achieve similar levels on our measure of gender identity, which is primarily intended to enable us to investigate differences *within* each sex group.

GROUP SIZE

There was considerable variation in the size of groups recorded in the spot observations (ranging from two to twelve children), although in approximately three quarters of all observations, target children were recorded in groups with between two and four participants. Separate analyses of variance of this data were undertaken for each type of group,[1] with the size recorded for each observation as the dependent variable, and sex group, gender identity, organizational context, class and term as independent variables.

Across the year the size of single-sex groups varied according to sex,[2] though not gender identity. Girls were observed in larger groups in the summer term (mean = 3.2) than in the autumn term (mean = 2.6), while the size of group in which boys were observed remained more or less the same across the year (mean for the autumn term = 3.3; mean for the summer term = 3.3). By the end of the year, girls were observed in single-sex groups as large as those formed by boys.

---

[1] Mixed even groups were excluded from these analyses, since the size of such groups could only be even numbers.
[2] Sex group by term interaction: $F = 6.12$; $df = 1,864$; $P < 0.05$.

Differences across the year between the schools indicated that the size of single-sex groups did not depend on the number of children present in the classroom.[3] In Land School, where children were divided into morning and afternoon groups in the autumn term, and only combined when they all attended full time in the summer term, the size of single-sex groups increased from the autumn term (mean = 2.99) to the summer term (mean = 3.48). In McCarthy School, on the other hand, single-sex groups were larger in the autumn term (mean = 3.41) than in the summer term (mean = 2.94), even though children who had attended school only in the morning during the autumn term were present full time in the summer term.

Larger 'more girls' groups were observed in teacher-organized contexts (mean = 4.65) than in peer-organized contexts (mean = 4.09),[4] a difference which may reflect the capacity of teachers to act as mediators between the sexes. It is worth noting that neither sex group nor gender identity influenced the size of these groups.

The mean scores in Table 6.1 show a more complex picture for participation in 'more boys' groups.[5] In McCarthy School, the size of these groups is only influenced by sex-group membership; boys are observed in larger groups of more boys than are girls, irrespective of gender identity. In Land School, however, gender identity is an important influence for girls, though not for boys. Low gender identity girls are observed in larger groups of more boys than high gender identity girls. Indeed, girls with low gender identity are observed in larger size groups than are the boys.

As a whole, these analyses for different groups indicate that associating in large groups is not a specifically masculine style. By the end of the year, the size of single-sex groups is the same for boys and girls. And where gender identity does exercise an influence, in 'more boys' groups, it is an influence which operates only for girls in Land School. As this result indicates, the expression of gender identity can indeed take a different form for girls and boys. The difference between the schools also indicates that the expression

Table 6.1 Mean scores for the gender identity by sex by school interaction in the analysis of the size of 'more boys' groups

Gender identity	McCarthy School		Land School	
	Girls	Boys	Girls	Boys
Low	4.41	4.92	4.87	4.60
High	4.38	4.94	4.50	4.61

[3] Class by term interaction: $F = 22.99$; $df = 1,864$; $P < 0.001$.
[4] Main effect for organizational context: $F = 8.88$; $df = 1,184$, $P < 0.01$.
[5] Gender identity by sex group by class interaction: $F = 4.68$; $df = 1,271$; $P < 0.05$.

of gender identity may be responsive to the local conditions within a classroom.

MATERIAL CULTURE

In Chapter 4, we identified material culture as one aspect of the classroom which carried gender markings. Although there was broad similarity between the schools in the kinds of material available for children to use, specific items varied between the classrooms (cf. the selection of items for the Susan and Michael test in Chapter 3). Access to materials also varied with the teacher's organization of the school day. Many of the materials were available to children in free play, while some were used only in the context of teacher-organized activities. In order to analyse the spot observations of material culture, the data was grouped into six categories, determined in part by these constraints and the type of play with which they were associated.

In labelling these categories we have used the term 'play' in the sense employed by the teachers. They were keen to stress that in the reception class work and play should both be seen as contributing to the child's learning and development, rather than as clearly differentiated activities. The children, though, did not always appreciate the subtlety of the teachers' perspective and continued to distinguish between work and play, or at least between situations in which their activity was constrained by the teacher and those in which they were free to engage with their peers.

Our interest in analysing children's use of the material culture in the classroom is focused on the ways in which it contributes to the expression of their gender identities. But gender identity is only one influence among many in children's selection of materials. Some materials were more commonly used in one organizational context than another, and some materials were more frequently associated with members of one sex group rather than another. These overlapping influences are reflected in the way we have categorized material culture, a categorization which is based on distinguishing between types of play:

1. *No materials*. The target child was not engaged with any materials. This does not mean that he or she was doing nothing; he or she might be involved in other kinds of interaction, such as conversation.
2. *Creative play*. This category included Play-dough, water and sand, as well as art materials such as pencils and crayons, which children were able to use without direct supervision.
3. *Role play*. Role play included any items which were used to sustain pretend play, including dolls, prams, crockery and houseware from the home corner, dressing-up clothes and hats.

4. *Activity play.* This category included items such as tricycles, slide, ball games, climbing frame and see-saws, which involved considerable physical activity, and, often occupied a great deal of space.
5. *Constructive play.* This category included a variety of construction toys, such as large wooden bricks, lego, train and road layouts, and jigsaws.
6. *Directed play.* This category included all the materials which were used in teacher-organized contexts, such as books, reading schemes, writing materials, craft materials and a computer. Some items included in this category were also accessible to children in peer play.

The frequency with which children were observed using the different categories of materials varied considerably, both between categories and across organizational contexts. Table 6.2 shows the mean proportions of observations in each term in which children were recorded as using each category of material.

There is consistency in the pattern of toy use across the school year, and in both terms there is a similar difference between the two organizational contexts. The most frequently observed categories are constructive play,

Table 6.2 Mean proportions of observations in which different categories of materials were used

	Autumn term		Summer term	
	Peer-organized	Teacher-organized	Peer-organized	Teacher-organized
Nothing	11.4	2.5	14.9	4.7
Creative	9.7	5.4	8.1	5.7
Role	8.3	1.5	8.3	0.4
Activity	10.8	0.3	8.3	0.4
Constructive	22.1	2.9	23.8	3.2
Directed	3.4	22.4	5.4	17.1
Total	65.7	35.0	68.8	31.5

Table 6.3 Mean proportions (as %) for each category of material culture for each sex

	Girls	Boys
No materials	8.2	8.5
Creative	10.1	5.4
Role	10.9	6.7
Activity	6.8	11.4
Constructive	7.7	16.5
Directed	14.4	10.5

which accounts for about a fifth of observations in peer-organized contexts in both terms, and directed play, which accounts for a similar proportion of observations in teacher-organized contexts. Activity play, role play and creative play each account for about a tenth of the observations in peer-organized contexts, but much smaller proportions in teacher-organized contexts. Indeed, activity play and role play were so rare in teacher-organized contexts that it was not possible to undertake a statistical analysis of the influence of organizational context for these categories.[6]

As we anticipated, sex-group membership exerted a significant influence on the use of different categories of materials. We can see in Table 6.3 that girls were observed more frequently in creative play, role play and directed play, while boys made greater use of constructive play and activity play materials.[7] The only category for which there was no difference between girls and boys was 'no materials'. These results offer verification for our ethnographic work, which suggested that the use of materials was influenced by sex-group membership. Our concern in the present chapter is to examine the extent to which the use of these different materials also varied according to the gender identity of girls and boys.

The analyses of creative play and role play failed to show any influence of gender identity. For the remaining three categories – activity play, constructive play and directed play – our analyses showed that gender identity as well as sex group influenced children's use of these materials.

Girls with a high gender identity engaged in activity play much less than girls with a low gender identity, or than boys in either category of gender identity (see Table 6.4).[8] Girls who interact primarily with other girls do not engage in the physical activity characteristic of this type of play.

A stereotypic image of large activity games being dominated only by groups of boys is not borne out of this data. Low gender identity girls made as much use of these materials as boys of either category. Nevertheless, high gender identity girls may avoid using these games because they view them

---

[6] The analyses which follow are based on five-way analyses of variance, with gender identity, sex group and school as between-subjects variables, and term and organizational context as within-subjects variables. For activity play and role play, organizational context was omitted, and a four-way design was used to analyse the data for peer-organized contexts alone. As the dependent measure was the *proportion* of observations for each target child in the appropriate category, an arcsine transformation was applied to the raw data prior to analysis (cf. Kirk, 1968). For ease of legibility, scores have been converted back to proportions in the text. Where specific differences between mean scores are noted, these are based on *post hoc* pairwise comparisons using Tukey tests.

[7] For all of these categories of materials, there were main effects for sex group (with df = 1,43 in each case): creative play F = 13.88; P < 0.001; role play F = 7.27; P < 0.05; activity play F = 12.16; P < 0.001; constructive play F = 54.63; P < 0.001; and directed play F = 11.75; ' P < 0.001.

[8] Gender identity by sex group interaction F = 11.06; df = 1,43; P < 0.01.

Figure 6.4 Mean proportions of activity play, by gender, identity and sex

Gender identity	Girls	Boys	Combined
Low	10.6	11.1	10.9
High	3.0	11.7	8.4
Combined	6.8	11.4	

as carrying a masculine marking, or because when they are in single-sex groups they engage in play which carries a feminine marking. When groups of girls do engage with activity play materials, boys (believing them to carry a masculine marking) may intervene to repossess what they consider to be their property. In Land School we observed three different boys tell a girl riding round on a trike, to get off. None the less the proposition remains a hypothesis, as it goes beyond the limits of our observational data. We shall return to issues concerned with children's knowledge of gender markings in Chapter 8. For the present, we note that children's representations of the gender marking of materials might explain the variations in the frequencies of activity play related to the gender identity of girls.

The use of constructive play materials was influenced by a complex combination of gender identity, sex-group membership, organizational context, school and term.[9] In particular, there was a great increase in the use of construction play by high gender identity girls in Land School in peer-organized contexts. These girls used constructive play materials more in the summer than in the autumn term, and more than the low gender identity girls in Land School in the summer term (though not in the autumn term). In addition, comparisons between the use of these materials by girls and boys were significant in all cases except among high gender identity children in Land School in the summer term. By the end of the year, these girls were using constructive toys just as much as the boys (see Table 6.5).

The increased use of constructive play materials by high gender identity girls in Land School contrasts starkly with the use of these materials by the same category of girls in McCarthy School. By the summer term, these girls were making very little use of these materials. Comparisons between the two schools show that while no difference was observed for these girls in the autumn term, a large and significant difference emerged in the summer term.

Among the boys, in peer-organized contexts the use of constructive play varies across the year for those with low gender identity, though the variation takes different forms in the two schools. In McCarthy School, the

[9] Five-way interaction F = 6.40; df = 1,43; P < 0.05.

97

Table 6.5 Mean proportions of constructive play in peer-organized contexts, by sex, gender identity, school and term

Girls

Gender identity	McCarthy		Land	
	Autumn term	Summer term	Autumn term	Summer term
Low	13.7	11.2	9.3	15.0
High	9.7	2.5	12.9	27.5

Boys

Gender identity	McCarthy		Land	
	Autumn term	Summer term	Autumn term	Summer term
Low	34.9	21.4	21.1	35.0
High	33.2	30.7	28.4	28.7

use of these materials by low gender identity boys decreased from the autumn term to the summer term. In Land School, there was an increase in the use of constructive materials by low gender identity boys across the year. Among high gender identity boys, no differences were observed across the year.

Constructive materials are often interpreted as an indicator of a masculine identity, but these results illustrate the way in which the practical expression of gender identities through the use of these materials can take different forms in different classrooms. Although the differences among the boys are slight, the results for the girls make this very clear. While the high gender identity girls in Land School were able to use constructive play materials as much as the boys by the end of the year, in McCarthy School the high gender identity girls were characterized by the lowest frequency of any group of children in the use of these materials in peer-organized contexts (as low as their use in teacher-organized contexts by most children). In McCarthy School, girls with a high gender identity express a femininity through avoiding the use of a masculine-marked resource. In Land School, the teacher went to some lengths to ensure that girls had access to constructive play materials. Her intervention reflected her observation of the way the boys monopolized these materials. Challenging the boys' implicit assumption that these toys carried a clear masculine marking was one example of the way this teacher sometimes employed a strategy for equality of opportunity in the classroom. Yet it was a strategy which had mixed results, for the high gender identity girls made much greater use of these toys than the low gender identity girls.

The strong association between high gender identity girls and the use of constructive materials in Land School needs to be considered carefully in relation to the measure of gender identity we have used. High gender identity girls were those who were frequently observed in single-sex groups with other girls. By creating a time when these toys were only accessible to girls, the teacher's intervention may have had an impact on this measure of gender identity. How great an impact it is difficult to assess precisely, since the measure of gender identity was not derived only from observations when children played with these particular toys. But the teacher's intervention also highlights a deeper issue in the interpretation of our analyses. Did the increased use of constructive toys reflect the wish of high gender identity girls to play with other girls or with these materials? The results for McCarthy School, where the teacher made no direct intervention in the way these toys were used, also raise a similar problem of interpretation. Did the low level at which girls with high gender identity used constructive materials arise because the presence of boys playing with these toys meant that it was not a viable activity for them if they wanted to play with other girls, even if they wished to play with these things?

Our data do not allow us to distinguish clearly between these possibilities. It is difficult to distinguish causes and consequences within our observational data. What these results do indicate is the subtle and intricate ways in which the establishment of gender markings and the expression of gender identities are interwoven. Both need to be negotiated within the local context of a reception class, and teachers as well as children can influence this process.

As well as being influenced by the organizational context, the use of directed play materials was also influenced by gender identity, sex group and term (see Table 6.6).[10]

In the summer term, high gender identity girls made greater use of directed play materials in peer-organized contexts. In this term they used these materials more than low gender identity girls, and more than either · category of boys. Use of these materials in peer-organized contexts provided these girls with the opportunity to express a distinctive gender identity. Yet in teacher-organized contexts, the high gender identity girls were observed using these materials less frequently in the summer term than in the autumn term. One image which is used to characterize femininity in school children is that girls become more obedient and compliant to the teacher. Using these materials in peer-organized contexts may reflect an attempt by some girls to please their teachers, who, seeing them engaged in 'work' activities, feel they have less reason to intervene and organize them to do so. The capacity for high gender identity girls to organize themselves in

[10] Four-way interaction $F = 6.64$; $df = 1,43$; $P < 0.05$.

99

Table 6.6 Mean proportions of directed play, by gender identity, sex, activity context and term

Peer-organized Contexts

	Girls		Boys	
Gender identity	Autumn term	Summer term	Autumn term	Summer term
Low	4.0	3.5	3.6	5.0
High	4.9	10.5	1.9	3.8

Teacher-organized Contexts

	Girls		Boys	
Gender identity	Autumn term	Summer term	Autumn term	Summer term
Low	19.7	23.5	22.0	14.7
High	32.8	16.5	18.0	15.6

directed play may explain why teachers in primary schools spend less time with girls than with boys (cf. Croll and Moses, 1990).

Beyond the overall differences between girls and boys in their use of materials, these analyses have shown that gender identity also contributes towards an understanding of the way in which material culture is used in the classroom. The analyses of activity play, construction play and directed play all produced results which showed differences between high and low gender identity children of the same sex. In particular, high gender identity girls emerged as a group with a distinctive pattern of use of these materials. This pattern is clearest in activity play, where high gender identity girls made less use of such materials than any other group of children in peer-organized contexts in both schools and in both terms. Across the reception year, differences also emerged for directed play materials in peer-organized contexts, with the high gender identity girls making greater use of these materials in the summer term. For both activity play and directed play, the differences between girls took a similar form in both schools. For constructive play, however, differences emerged in the summer term which reflected the local conditions and circumstances in each school. In McCarthy School, high gender identity girls were rarely observed to use constructive materials in the summer term, while in Land School the high gender identity girls not only used them more than the low gender identity girls, but used them as frequently as did the boys.

Overall, our index of gender identity based on the proportion of observations in single-sex groups has been more successful in distinguishing between categories of girls than categories of boys in their use of the material culture of the classroom. Material culture does not appear to be an arena in which boys differentiate among themselves: single-sex groups of boys play with the same materials as boys in mixed groups. Boys playing with other boys or in mixed groups employ a style which is learnt before they come to school, a style in which feminine toys are rarely used.

Finally, the results for constructive play are particularly interesting, since they show that similar groups of children can use the same materials in quite different ways in different classrooms. The high gender identity girls in Land School make as much use of these toys as boys, while in McCarthy School such girls eschew these toys. The gender meaning associated with construction play can be defined differently in different contexts; it appears to be open to negotiation between teacher and children as well as among children. Even if the teacher's influence in Land School encouraged girls to use these materials, the high gender identity girls were able to use this to greater advantage than the low gender identity girls. Whatever the extent of the teacher's influence, particular materials can acquire different meanings, as a local gender culture is elaborated in the classroom.

SPACE

Along with group composition and material culture, space was also an aspect of gender in the classroom identified in our ethnography. Different areas of the classroom become gender marked, so that playing in a particular space provided children with a further means for expressing their social gender identity. On the basis of our ethnography, we divided the space of the classrooms into six zones, the majority of which were defined by the presence of particular pieces of furniture. In general, teachers used the available furniture to divide the classroom into defined areas (see the class plans, Figures 3.1 and 3.2), and our classification follows these divisions. The zones which were recorded for each observation were as follows:

1. *Home corner.* An area usually marked by such play furniture as cookers, sinks and fridges and including dolls, prams, dressing-up clothes and other domestic objects.
2. *Carpet.* A carpeted area used as a space to assemble children at the beginning of the day or when the teacher instructed the whole class, or for story time.
3. *Book corner.* An area marked out by shelving which contained a variety of reading materials.

4. *Open spaces*. Large empty play spaces available in each classroom, as well as the terrace in Land School, which was available to children in fine weather.
5. *Table*. This zone included all the work tables available to children.
6. *Other spaces*. This residual category included areas which children rarely visited (such as the sink or the cloakroom), as well as observations made when target children were in movement between one space and another.

Table 6.7 shows the proportions of observations in each of these zones for girls and boys in each activity context in each term. As we observed for material culture, there is a good deal of consistency across terms in children's use of space. Three zones predominate in peer-organized contexts, the carpet, open spaces and the table; while only the table is extensively used in teacher-organized contexts (indeed, the home corner, book corner and other spaces are so little used in teacher-organized contexts, particularly in the autumn term, that the analysis of these zones was undertaken for peer-organized contexts only).[11]

Clear differences between sex groups in their use of space are also shown in Table 6.7. Boys were observed more frequently on the carpet and in open spaces, while girls made greater use of the home corner and table.[12] Again,

Table 6.7 Proportions of observations in different zones, by sex, activity context and term

Autumn term

	Peer-organized			Teacher-organized		
	Girls	Boys	Both	Girls	Boys	Both
Home corner	8.6	5.1	6.5	0.3	0.5	0.4
Carpet	11.6	24.3	19.3	1.5	2.1	1.9
Book corner	2.7	1.2	1.8	1.0	0.2	0.5
Open spaces	16.1	25.3	21.7	1.2	2.1	1.8
Table	16.2	8.6	11.6	35.1	27.3	30.4
Other spaces	5.2	2.6	3.6	0.5	0.6	0.6

Summer term

	Peer-organized			Teacher-organized		
	Girls	Boys	Both	Girls	Boys	Both
Home corner	9.0	6.0	7.1	0.5	0.7	0.6
Carpet	6.3	22.2	16.0	2.0	5.7	4.2
Book corner	3.0	4.4	3.8	0.3	0.8	0.6
Open spaces	16.8	22.0	20.0	1.3	3.1	2.4
Table	25.5	11.0	16.7	28.3	19.2	22.8
Other spaces	6.0	3.9	4.7	1.3	1.1	1.2

Table 6.8 Mean proportions of observations in the book corner, by gender identity, sex and term

	Low gender identity		High gender identity	
	Girls	Boys	Girls	Boys
Autumn term	4.2	1.4	1.3	1.1
Summer term	1.0	4.7	5.0	4.1

these data provide a useful triangulation on our ethnographic observations of the differences between girls and boys in their use of space. In addition to sex-group membership, gender identity was also found to influence the use of three zones, the book corner, open spaces and the table.

As the mean scores in Table 6.8 show, the book corner was generally used more in the summer term than in the autumn term, an increase which may reflect children's growing interest in books and reading as an activity. However, low gender identity girls are an exception to this pattern, making less use of the book corner in the summer term than do the high gender identity girls.[13] While the reasons why this group of girls made less use of the book corner in the summer term are difficult to identify, the educational implication of this result is a cause for some concern if it means that some girls may be foregoing access to an important resource for literacy.

The analysis of open spaces once again focuses attention on differences among the girls in the two schools,[14] as the mean scores in Table 6.9 indicate. In McCarthy School, the use of this zone by the girls varied across the year. While the low gender identity girls increased their use of it, the high gender identity girls made less use of it in the summer term. In the summer term, the high gender identity girls made less use of this zone than did the low gender identity girls. By contrast, in Land School there was no differentiation within sex groups in the use of this zone in either term.

These results echo the findings in the analysis of constructive play materials described earlier. Although the high gender identity girls in McCarthy School made scarce use of this resource in summer term, the high gender identity girls in Land School used this resource as much as the

[11] Analysis of each zone was based on a five-way design, with gender identity, sex group and school as between-subjects variables, and term and organizational context as within-subjects variables. For the home corner, book corner and other spaces, where the frequency of use in teacher-organized contexts was extremely low, only the data collected in peer-organized contexts was analysed, using a four-way design. The treatment of the data followed that used in analysing material culture.

[12] Main effects for sex group (all df = 1,43): carpet $F = 57.97$; $P < 0.001$; open spaces $F = 16.69$; $P < 0.001$; home corner $F = 7.17$; $P < 0.01$; table $F = 47.46$; $P < 0.001$.

[13] Gender identity by sex group by term interaction $F = 7.99$, df = 1,43, $P < 0.01$.

[14] Gender identity by sex group by school by term interaction: $F = 5.15$; df = 1,43; $P < 0.05$.

Table 6.9 Mean proportions of observations in open spaces, by gender identity, sex, school and term

McCarthy School

	Girls		Boys	
Gender identity	Low	High	Low	High
Autumn term	8.3	5.6	9.7	12.4
Summer term	13.1	1.3	9.6	13.2

Land School

	Girls		Boys	
Gender identity	Low	High	Low	High
Autumn term	10.9	8.9	14.5	17.2
Summer term	9.6	10.8	10.8	15.4

boys in the summer term (when the teacher had intervened to ensure that girls had access to the constructive toys). The parallel is not quite perfect, since in this case the low gender identity girls in Land School also used the open spaces as much as the boys. The imperfect match arises because the open spaces were zones in which only some of the toys included in constructive play were used, as well as being a zone in which materials from other categories were also used. Yet, as with the analysis for constructive play, the results for open spaces indicate the way in which a local gender culture was negotiated in each classroom through the course of the year.

Children's use of the table zone was influenced by a complex combination of all five factors.[15] It was used more in teacher-organized than in peer-organized contexts, though the influence of this variable was stronger in the autumn term than in the summer term (see Table 6.10).

The most consistent differences in this complex interaction highlighted the contrast between girls and boys of low and high gender identity. In McCarthy School, high gender identity girls made greater use of the table than high gender identity boys in either term and in both organizational contexts. No differences were observed between girls and boys of low gender identity in their use of the table. By contrast, in Land School, girls made greater use of the table in peer-organized contexts, whatever their gender identity. In teacher-organized contexts, high gender identity girls used the table more than high gender identity boys in the autumn term. By the summer term, when high gender identity girls made less use of the table, the difference had disappeared. No differences were found between girls and boys with low gender identity in the autumn term, but by the summer term the girls were using the table more than the boys.

[15] Five-way interaction: $F = 4.82$; $df = 1,43$; $P < 0.05$.

Table 6.10 Mean proportions of observations at the table, by gender identity, sex, activity context, school and term

McCarthy School: peer-organized

| | Low gender identity | | High gender identity | |
	Autumn	Summer	Autumn	Summer
Girls	8.7	21.2	17.5	25.0
Boys	13.3	12.1	7.8	10.0

McCarthy School: teacher-organized

| | Low gender identity | | High gender identity | |
	Autumn	Summer	Autumn	Summer
Girls	33.5	25.0	43.4	40.0
Boys	33.6	28.6	31.5	15.7

Land School: peer-organized

| | Low gender identity | | High gender identity | |
	Autumn	Summer	Autumn	Summer
Girls	17.0	25.8	19.8	28.3
Boys	5.8	12.5	8.0	9.4

Land School: teacher-organized

| | Low gender identity | | High gender identity | |
	Autumn	Summer	Autumn	Summer
Girls	27.2	33.3	38.4	17.5
Boys	26.6	18.7	19.9	15.0

Use of the table is strongly influenced by the teacher, since it is frequently employed for instruction. Yet by the summer term, differences in the use of the table between organizational contexts had largely disappeared. What had emerged, though, were differences between the schools and between children, even within teacher-organized contexts. In McCarthy School in the summer term, there is a contrast between the girls and the boys. High gender identity girls were observed at the table more frequently than low gender identity girls, while low gender identity boys were observed more frequently at the table than high gender identity boys. Different results were found in Land School. In the autumn term, high gender identity girls were observed more frequently at the table than low gender identity girls, but the reverse was observed in the summer term.

The development of a local gender culture even within teacher-organized contexts is the most interesting feature of the complex results for the use of the table. As we have seen in other analyses in this chapter, the same resource becomes embedded in a different set of social practices in each classroom. Within each context, the table takes on distinctive gender meanings and becomes a focus for different groups of girls and boys. The expression of gender identities through the use of this resource reflects these differences. In McCarthy School, the differentiation is sharper, with the table being a focus for high gender identity girls and low gender identity boys. By the summer term in Land School, the table is a focus for low gender identity girls. As we have noted before in this chapter, the categories of high and low gender identity do not have any general meaning which can be applied to all children in all contexts. Rather, these categories reflect the way in which particular groups of girls and of boys establish a gender identity within the context of a specific classroom.

CONCLUSION

The significance of establishing a measure of gender identity independent of sex-group membership is revealed in these analyses of group size, material culture and space. They have also justified the utility of making a conceptual distinction between sex and gender. Both the sparseness and the complexity of the results, employing our index of gender identity, indicate that this is only a first approximation of an adequate measure. The overall result – that differences in gender identity are clearer for girls – poses a problem. It would appear that the proportion of observations in single-sex groups is not a measure which is sensitive to differences among boys. Boys, as we noted in Chapter 5, tend in any case to spend more of their time in single-sex groups than do girls, and this may be why an index based on this measure does not reveal interesting differences among boys. These analyses give an impression of greater variety in feminine styles than in masculine styles, which suggests a view of masculine socialization being more restrictive (cf. Archer, 1984).

An additional benefit of our analyses of gender identity is their demonstration of the emergence of local gender cultures within each school. The same resources did not carry equivalent gender markings in each classroom. No doubt the attitudes and actions of the teachers were an important influence on this process, but there were also important differences between the children in each class, particularly among the girls. Returning to the correspondence analyses in Chapter 5 (Figures 5.1–5.6), a further difference between the schools can be noted. In both schools, a number of well-defined groups of boys who regularly interacted with one another can be identified. Among the girls, however, there were more sharply defined groups in Land School than in McCarthy School. The implication is that high gender identity girls in Land School achieved their rating by forming close friendship groups, whereas in McCarthy School high gender identity girls were interacting less frequently with specific other girls.

It is important to look at differences between teachers and children in order to understand the characteristics associated with the emergence of local gender cultures in particular classrooms. In the next chapter, we look specifically at local gender cultures by examining our cross-sectional data drawn from four different schools.

7

The emergence of local gender cultures in reception classrooms

In Chapters 5 and 6, we compared the observational data collected from McCarthy and Land schools in both autumn and summer terms. A key theme which emerged from that longitudinal analysis was the significance of the local gender culture characteristic of each classroom. In this chapter, we explore this theme further by considering evidence for the emergence of local gender cultures in the first term of the reception year. To do this, we shall analyse an enlarged sample by drawing upon our observations of children carried out in the autumn term of the following year in George and Newby schools.

A point which needs to be borne in mind when considering the analyses in this chapter is that the index of gender identity used is based on the autumn term observations only. So far, our analyses have employed classifications of children from Land and McCarthy schools into high and low gender identity groups based upon summer-term observations. We noted in Chapter 5 that in both these schools there was considerable variation in the indices calculated for the autumn and summer terms.

The chapter begins with an overview of peer associations at the beginning of the year in George and Newby schools, in order to establish the index of gender identity. In the subsequent sections, we again consider the influence of gender identity, as well as sex-group membership and school, on the size of groups and the use of material culture and space in the classroom.

PEER ASSOCIATIONS IN THE AUTUMN TERM

The correspondence analyses for the autumn term in McCarthy and Land schools reported in Chapter 5 (cf. Figures 5.1–5.3) showed a general

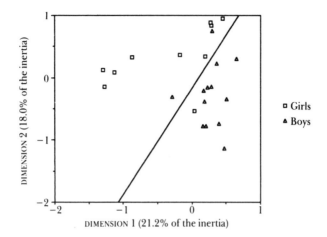

Figure 7.1 Plot of correspondence analysis for George
School: autumn term

tendency for children to associate with other members of the same sex
group, and also a tendency for children to form stable peer groups. Similar
analyses for observations in peer-organized contexts in George and Newby
schools are shown in Figures 7.1 and 7.2, and the same two features can also
be seen in these graphs.

In George School, two boys appear in the 'girls' side of the plot, while one
girl appears in the 'boys' side and another very close to it. A number of
groups can also be clearly identified, particularly among the girls. One
group can be seen on the left-hand edge and another in the top right-hand
corner. Interestingly, one of the atypical boys is also closely associated with
this latter group of girls. These four children are among the oldest in the
class; they are almost a year older than the youngest children in the class.
An explanation for this mixed-sex grouping cannot be found in age alone, as
there are other girls and boys who are almost the same age as this grouping,
but distant from them in the graph.

The graph for Newby School shows three boys in the 'girls' sector, but no
girls in the 'boys' sector. Again, a number of stable peer groups can be seen,
though these are more frequent among boys than girls. As in George
School, there is also a noticeable mixed-sex grouping involving one of the
atypical boys.

The structure of groups in George and Newby schools is similar to that in
McCarthy and Land schools. The generality of the earlier observations
presented in Chapter 5 is also seen in the quantitative analyses of different
types of group (see Table 7.1). Again, boys are observed more frequently in

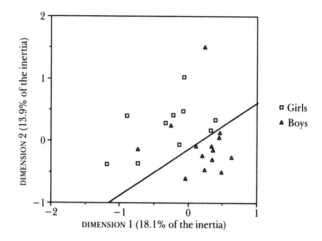

Figure 7.2 Plot of correspondence analysis for Newby
School: autumn term

single-sex and 'more boys' groups, and girls more frequently in mixed even
and 'more girls' groups.[1]

The only exception to this pattern occurred when children were observed
in activities organized by the teacher.[2] While boys (mean = 40.9 per cent)
were observed more frequently than girls (mean = 24.8 per cent) in single-
sex groups in peer-organized contexts, no difference between boys (mean =
10.5 per cent) and girls (mean = 10.0 per cent) was observed in teacher-
organized contexts.

The proportion of our observations of children in teacher-organized
contexts varied considerably across the schools, from nearly 50 per cent of
the time in Newby to about 16 per cent in George (see Table 7.2). These
differences reflect variations in pedagogical styles among the teachers. In
both Land and George schools, the teacher used methods of primarily
individual tuition. One consequence of this style is that the children tended

---

[1] The design for these analyses included sex group and school as between-subjects variables,
and organizational context as a within-subjects variable. Main effects for sex group (all df
= 1,92) in the analyses for 'single' (F = 21.8; P < 0.001), 'more boys' (F = 21.3; P < 0.001),
'mixed even' (F = 9.4; P < 0.01) and 'more girls' (F = 84.5; P < 0.001). In these analyses,
as for all of those reported in this chapter, the number of children in McCarthy School is
slightly greater than in the earlier chapters, as we have included data drawn from two girls
who had attended in the autumn term, but had left before the summer term.

[2] Sex by organizational context interaction (F = 14.9; df = 1,92; P < 0.001). As with the
other analyses reported in this chapter, *post hoc* comparisons for this interaction were made
using Tukey tests.

Table 7.1 Mean proportions of observations in each type of group, by sex and organizational context: autumn term (N=100)

	Peer-organized		Teacher-organized	
	Girls	Boys	Girls	Boys
Alone	9.5	5.4	4.0	4.5
Single	24.8	40.9	10.0	10.5
Mixed even	9.1	5.0	8.9	5.3
More girls	11.6	3.5	9.7	2.5
More boys	7.6	13.5	4.9	9.0
Total	62.6	68.3	37.5	31.8

Table 7.2 Proportions of observations in each organizational context in each school: autumn term (N=100)

	Peer-organized	Teacher-organized
McCarthy	59.0	40.9
Land	68.6	31.4
George	84.1	15.8
Newby	51.9	48.1

Table 7.3 Mean proportions of observations in single-sex groups, by school and organizational context: autumn term (N=100)

	Peer-organized	Teacher-organized
McCarthy	28.9	12.1
Newby	22.9	15.0
Land	41.1	9.8
George	42.6	4.1

to spend less time in teacher-organized activities than in the other two schools, Newby and McCarthy, where the teacher made greater use of group teaching methods. An indication of the influence of these different styles can be seen in the way that patterns of children's peer associations in the different activity contexts varied across the classrooms.[3] In particular, single-sex groups were more frequently observed in peer-organized than in teacher-organized contexts in all schools except Newby (see Table 7.3),

---

[3] School by organizational context interactions (all df = 3,92) in the analyses for 'single' ($F = 16.6$; $P < 0.001$), 'mixed even' ($F = 9.3$; $P < 0.001$), 'more girls' ($F = 5.2$; $P < 0.01$) and 'more boys' ($F = 4.5$; $P < 0.01$).

111

where the teacher's style was directed most strongly toward the organization of children's activity.

We have used the data in Table 7.3, based upon the influence of teachers on the formation of single-sex groups, to divide the four schools into two sets. On the one hand, Land and George schools are similar in having a high proportion of single-sex groups in peer-organized contexts and a low proportion in teacher-organized contexts. In McCarthy and Newby schools, on the other hand, there is a lower proportion of single-sex groups in peer-organized contexts and a higher proportion in teacher-organized contexts. This pattern challenges our original assumptions when choosing the two additional schools. Initially, we had believed it was important to select schools similar to Land and McCarthy in terms of their size, general organization and demographic characteristics. Our observational analysis suggests that within the classroom, however, it is the teacher's pedagogical style which is a more powerful influence on children's daily experience than those more objective factors.

These data also indicate that the pedagogical style adopted by the teacher was not influenced by the age range of children entering the reception class. George, as a one-form entry school, included in its reception class the full age range of children, while the class we observed in Land School contained only the youngest children. Conversely, there was a full age range in the one reception class in McCarthy, while the range in Newby School was restricted to younger children.

THE INDEX OF GENDER IDENTITY IN THE AUTUMN TERM

The proportion of observations in single-sex groups was used as the basis for an index of gender identity for the cross-sectional data, as it had been in the longitudinal data described in Chapter 5. Once again, girls and boys were divided into high and low gender identity groups by taking a median split. The resulting distributions are shown in Table 7.4.

GROUP SIZE

Again, the size of different types of group varied considerably, but separate analyses for each type of group indicated that sex-group membership only influenced this variation for single-sex groups.[1] Boys (mean = 3.2) were

[1] For each type of group the analysis was undertaken with gender identity, sex group and school as between-subjects variables, and organizational context as a within-subjects variable. For single-sex groups, the analysis produced main effects for sex group ($F = 51.0$; $df = 1,761$; $P < 0.001$), school ($F = 9.4$; $df = 3,761$; $P < 0.001$) and organizational context ($F = 3.9$; $df = 1,761$; $P < 0.05$). For 'more girls' groups, the analysis resulted in a main effect for school ($F = 3.1$; $df = 3,191$; $P < 0.05$).

Table 7.4 Numbers of children in low and high gender identity groups: in the autumn term, and the median of proportions of observations in single-sex groups

	Gender identity		
	Low	High	Median
McCarthy School			
Girls	5	5	0.236
Boys	7	7	0.323
Newby School			
Girls	7	3	0.100
Boys	6	8	0.300
Land School			
Girls	6	6	0.325
Boys	7	10	0.450
George School			
Girls	4	6	0.400
Boys	6	7	0.500
Total	48	52	

observed in larger single-sex groups than girls (mean = 2.6), and these groups were larger in peer-organized (mean = 3.1) than in teacher-organized (mean = 2.9) contexts. The size of single-sex groups also varied between the schools, being smaller in Land (mean = 3.0) and George (mean = 2.7) than in McCarthy (3.3) and Newby (3.2). These data offer further evidence of a similarity between Land and George schools and between McCarthy and Newby.

MATERIAL CULTURE

Table 7.5 shows the proportion of observations for each of the six categories of material culture in peer- and teacher-organized contexts. Although the data for the four schools observed in the autumn term is combined, the proportions are much the same as those recorded in the autumn term for McCarthy and Land schools alone (cf. Table 6.2). Once again, role play and activity play materials are very rarely used in teacher-organized contexts.

Here, sex-group membership was a significant influence on the use of these different categories of materials (see Table 7.6), with girls making greater use of creative play and directed play materials, and boys making

Table 7.5 Mean proportions of observations for each category of materials in each organizational context: autumn term

	Peer-organized	Teacher-organized
No materials	9.8	2.9
Creative play	9.6	4.4
Role play	8.0	0.8
Activity play	10.4	0.1
Constructive play	22.7	2.9
Directed play	5.8	22.6
Total	66.3	33.7

greater use of activity play and constructive play materials.[5] These differences echo those reported for the longitudinal data in Chapter 6.

A major difference between these cross-sectional analyses and the longitudinal analyses is in the influence of gender identity. The only categories of materials where gender identity played a systematic role were creative play[6] and activity play.[7] High gender identity girls made greater use of creative play materials in peer-organized contexts than did low

Table 7.6 Mean proportions of observations for each category of materials for each sex group: autumn term

	Girls	Boys
No materials	6.7	6.2
Creative play	8.6	5.8
Role play	10.4	6.3
Activity play	7.8	12.2
Constructive play	8.9	16.5
Directed play	16.5	12.6

Note: For role play and activity play, these figures are for observations in peer-organized contexts only.

[5] A separate analysis was undertaken for each category of material culture, with gender identity, sex group and school as between-subjects variables, and organizational context as a within-subjects variable. For activity play and role play, the within-subjects variable was dropped and the analysis undertaken on observations in peer-organized contexts alone. Main effects for sex group (all $df = 1,84$) in analyses for creative play ($F = 4.1$; $P < 0.05$), activity play ($F = 9.1$; $P < 0.01$), constructive play ($F = 29.5$; $P < 0.001$) and directed play ($F = 8.9$; $P < 0.01$).
[6] Gender identity by sex group by organizational context interaction $F = 4.84$; $df = 1,84$; $P < 0.05$.
[7] Gender identity by sex group by school interaction $F = 3.31$; $df = 3,84$; $P < 0.05$.

Table 7.7 Mean proportions of observations of creative play (cross-sectional data)

	Peer-organized		Teacher-organized	
	Girls	Boys	Girls	Boys
Low gender identity	8.2	7.7	6.5	4.7
High gender identity	16.4	7.8	3.5	3.3

gender identity girls, or either category of boys (see Table 7.7). In teacher-organized contexts, no differences were found in the use of these materials. By contrast, in the longitudinal analysis reported in Chapter 6 gender identity was not found to influence the use of creative play materials.

Analysis of the data for activity play (see Table 7.8) yielded no differences between low and high gender identity girls or boys within any of the schools, though differences were found between schools. Once again, the analysis indicated a distinction between the two sets of schools. The influence of gender identity on children's use of materials was similar in Land and George schools and different in McCarthy and Newby schools. High gender identity girls and low gender identity boys made greater use of activity play materials in Land and George schools than did the same categories of children in either McCarthy or Newby School.

These results for activity play contrast sharply with the results for the same materials reported in Chapter 6. In the longitudinal analysis, high gender identity girls made notably less use of activity play materials than other categories of children. As we noted earlier, we are employing different measures of gender identity in the two analyses, so direct comparisons are not possible. Nevertheless, our results from the autumn term data may throw some light on the longitudinal analysis. In the autumn term, activity

Table 7.8 Mean proportions of observations of activity play (cross-sectional data – peer-organized observations only)

	Girls		Boys	
Gender identity	Low	High	Low	High
McCarthy	6.2	3.5	5.2	10.8
Land	7.2	12.7	20.3	14.3
George	16.3	11.7	11.7	22.9
Newby	2.9	1.7	3.3	7.5

Table 7.9 Mean proportions of observations of each category of material culture in each school (cross-sectional data)

	McCarthy	Newby	Land	George
No materials	5.7	7.7	7.6	5.9
Creative play	6.1	3.3	7.8	9.2
Role play	5.6	1.9	11.0	13.0
Activity play	6.6	4.4	14.0	15.9
Constructive play	14.4	16.1	10.6	12.6
Directed play	15.7	21.5	11.2	9.0

Note: For role play and activity play, these figures are for observations in peer-organized contexts only.

play materials did provide a focus for those girls who spent more time in single-sex groups, at least in two of the schools. By the summer term, the attraction of playing with other girls may have led these girls away from the activity play materials.

Although gender identity had only a limited impact in the autumn term, there were significant differences between the schools in the use of each category of material culture.[8] Table 7.9 indicates that there is a consistent trend for the four schools to divide into two sets, with Land and George schools distinguished from McCarthy and Newby schools. In addition, the influence of organizational context in the analyses meant that this pattern was stronger in peer-organized contexts for constructive play and in teacher-organized contexts for directed play.[9]

Overall, the use of material culture in the autumn term is primarily influenced by sex-group membership and school. Gender identity has a less pervasive influence at the beginning of the first year of schooling. This suggests that the within-sex-groups differences reported in children's use of material culture in Chapter 6 do not emerge until later in the school year.

SPACE

The lack of any influence of gender identity early in the reception year is underlined by the absence of any intelligible effects for this factor in our analyses of children's use of space in the autumn term. As we noted in the

[8] Main effects for school (all df = 3,84) in analyses of no materials ($F = 3.3$; $P < 0.05$), creative play ($F = 4.1$; $P < 0.05$); role play ($F = 12.4$; $P < 0.001$), activity play ($F = 11.2$; $P < 0.001$), constructive play ($F = 5.3$; $P < 0.01$) and directed play ($F = 15.0$; $P < 0.001$).
[9] School by organizational context interaction (df = 3,84) for constructive play ($F = 2.8$; $P < 0.05$) and directed play ($F = 8.1$; $P < 0.001$).

Table 7.10 Mean proportions of observations in each zone in each organizational context: autumn term (cross-sectional data)

	Peer-organized	Teacher-organized
Home corner	4.9	0.3
Carpet	16.9	4.3
Book corner	1.1	1.5
Open spaces	22.1	2.0
Table	18.0	25.3
Other spaces	2.9	0.8
Total	65.9	34.2

longitudinal analysis, the use of space was strongly influenced by organizational context (see Table 7.10), with the carpet, open spaces, home corner and book corner being more frequently used in peer-organized contexts, and the table more frequently in teacher-organized contexts.[10] This pattern is broadly similar to that reported for the longitudinal data (cf. Table 6.7).

Sex-group membership was also a powerful influence on the use of space (see Table 7.11), with boys being observed more frequently on the carpet and in open spaces, and girls more frequently in the book corner and at the table.[11]

Table 7.11 Mean proportions of observations of each sex group in each zone: autumn term (cross-sectional data)

	Girls	Boys
Home corner	6.1	4.0
Carpet	11.0	12.1
Book corner	1.8	0.6
Open spaces	9.4	13.9
Table	24.6	19.5
Other spaces	2.6	1.3

Note: The figures for home corner and book corner are for peer-organized contexts only.

[10] A separate analysis was undertaken for each zone, with gender identity, sex group and school as between-subjects variables, and organizational context as a within-subjects variable. The home corner and book corner were so rarely used in teacher-organized contexts that the analyses for these zones were undertaken for peer-organized observations alone. Main effects for organizational context (all $df = 1{,}84$) were found in the analyses for carpet ($F = 129.1$; $P < 0.001$), open spaces ($F = 382.8$; $P < 0.001$) and table ($F = 19.3$; $P < 0.001$).

[11] Main effect for sex group (all $df = 1{,}84$) in the analyses for carpet ($F = 6.5$; $P < 0.05$), open spaces ($F = 14.6$; $P < 0.001$), book corner ($F = 4.4$; $P < 0.05$) and table ($F = 7.6$; $P < 0.01$).

Table 7.12 Mean proportions of observations on the carpet and in the open spaces (cross-sectional data)

	Peer-organized	Teacher-organized
Carpet		
Girls	11.8	5.2
Boys	20.5	3.6
Open spaces		
Girls	17.2	1.6
Boys	25.7	2.2

Again, this replicates the pattern reported for the longitudinal data (cf. Table 6.7).

For the carpet and the open spaces, the differences between the sex groups were a feature of peer-organized but not of teacher-organized contexts (see Table 7.12).[12] For the open spaces in particular, this result illustrates clearly the difference between the lack of influence associated with gender identity in the autumn term, and its significance in the summer term (where the use of open spaces by high gender identity girls varied considerably between the two schools; cf. Table 6.9).

The third major influence on the use of space was school.[13] As Table 7.13 shows, there was considerable variation between schools in the way different spaces were used. For the three most frequently observed spaces (carpet, open spaces and table), the pattern of differences between the

Table 7.13 Mean proportions of observations in each zone in each school: autumn term (cross-sectional data)

	McCarthy	Newby	Land	George
Home corner	4.4	0.2	8.4	5.9
Carpet	11.1	11.8	9.6	10.1
Book corner	2.5	0.6	1.3	0.0
Open spaces	9.4	5.7	13.4	19.7
Table	23.9	26.7	19.4	16.9
Other spaces	1.8	2.8	2.2	0.4

Note: The figures for home corner and book corner are for peer-organized contexts only.

---

[12] Sex group by organizational context interaction (all df = 1,84) in the analyses for carpet (F = 12.7; P < 0.01) and open spaces (F = 5.6; P < 0.05).

[13] Main effect for school (all df = 3,84) in the analyses for home corner (F = 12.2; P < 0.001), carpet (F = 7.0; P < 0.001), book corner (F = 4.1; P < 0.01), open spaces (F = 14.4; P < 0.001) and table (F = 7.9; P < 0.001).

Table 7.14 Mean proportions of observations on the carpet (cross-sectional data)

	Peer-organized	Teacher-organized
McCarthy	19.2	2.9
Newby	10.8	12.7
Land	18.2	0.9
George	18.9	1.3

schools once again associates Land and George, as distinct from McCarthy and Newby. In addition, for each of these three spaces differences between the schools also varied between organizational contexts.[14]

The carpet was used more in peer-organized than in teacher-organized contexts in all the schools except Newby (see Table 7.14). Indeed, the carpet was used less in peer-organized contexts and more in teacher-organized contexts in Newby than in any other school. Again, these data illustrate the particular style adopted by the teacher in Newby School.

The use of open spaces was always greater in peer-organized than in teacher-organized contexts (see Table 7.15), though there were differences between the schools in the extent to which they were used in peer-organized contexts. The greatest use was in George School, and the least, once again, in Newby. No differences were observed between the schools in the use of the open spaces in teacher-organized contexts.

In McCarthy and Land schools, the table was used more frequently in teacher-organized than in peer-organized contexts, though the reverse was the case in George, while in Newby no difference was observed in the use of the table between organizational contexts (see Table 7.16). The table was used more frequently in peer-organized contexts in Newby than in any other school, while in teacher-organized contexts the table was used less in George than in any other school.

Table 7.15 Mean proportions of observations in the open spaces (cross-sectional data)

	Peer-organized	Teacher-organized
McCarthy	16.9	1.9
Newby	8.3	3.1
Land	25.3	1.5
George	38.0	1.3

[14] School by organizational context interaction (all df = 3,84) in the analyses for carpet (F = 17.9; P < 0.001), open spaces (F = 24.9; P < 0.001) and table (F = 19.9; P < 0.001).

Table 7.16 Mean proportions of observations at the table (cross-sectional data)

	Peer-organized	Teacher-organized
McCarthy	12.8	35.1
Newby	28.3	25.0
Land	11.7	27.1
George	20.4	13.3

Lastly, the use of the table also varied between sex groups in the different schools.[15] Among the girls, the table was used less in George than in the other schools, while among the boys the analysis again showed the division of the four schools into two groups, with the table being used more in McCarthy and Newby than in Land and George. Only in Land School was the table used more by girls than boys (see Table 7.17).

Table 7.17 Mean proportions of observations at the table (cross-sectional data)

	Girls	Boys
McCarthy	27.3	21.5
Newby	25.5	27.5
Land	25.6	15.0
George	19.8	14.6

What stands out most clearly in these results for the use of space in the autumn term is the absence of any of the influences of gender identity observed in the longitudinal data. The influences of sex group and organizational context which were observed echoed, for the most part, those reported in Chapter 6. Boys made greater use of open spaces, and girls greater use of the table. Both the carpet and open spaces were more frequently observed in peer-organized contexts, and the table in teacher-organized contexts. Differences between the schools followed to some extent the division into two sets, though the use of space in Newby School often reflected the influence of the most consistent use of a teacher-directed style of pedagogical organization.

CONCLUSION

Where gender identity was observed to exercise a persistent and subtle influence on the longitudinal observations, in this review of our cross-sectional data there were few effects for gender identity. In the rare

[15] Sex group by school interaction in the analysis of table F = 3.9. df = 3,84; P < 0.05.

instances where gender identity did have a statistically significant effect, its influence was different from that found in the analyses undertaken on the observations collected across the first year of schooling. Our measure of gender identity does not reveal stable features of the social practices of girls or boys at the beginning of their reception year.

If gender identity is not yet a noticeable feature of classroom life, sex-group membership is a pervasive influence on the activities of children in the autumn term. The social identities which children bring into school appear to be largely tied to sex-group membership. Differentiation within sex groups according to gender identity may emerge through the course of the first year of schooling. The behaviour of girls in particular, as we saw in Chapter 6, could be differentiated in terms of our measure of gender identities.

The first year of schooling appears, then, to be a period in which some girls adopt a feminine identity which is differentiated from other girls. The culture of school seems not to impose any such obligation on boys, for whom a masculine identity remains solely based on their membership in a sex group. At first sight, this conclusion seems to run counter to the widely held view of the early years of schooling as a feminine environment, which would be expected to have a greater impact on boys than on girls. It may be that the female tone of the reception class allows for greater differentiation among girls than among boys. This suggestion is also compatible with the view that masculinity is a more restrictive social identity than femininity. It might also be the case that boys respond to the feminine atmosphere of school by emphasizing group solidarity. It is conceivable that both explanations might be true, in the sense that the same feminine environment of the reception class may evoke differentiation among girls and solidarity among boys.

This conclusion rests, of course, on the adequacy of our definition of gender identity in terms of the proportion of time children spend in single-sex groups. One difficulty with our measure is that it does not distinguish between different ways in which single-sex groups operate. For example, consider the analysis of peer associations in George School (cf. Figure 7.1), where two stable groups of girls were identified, all of whom were classified as high gender identity girls. Yet, as well as sharing the characteristic of associating frequently in all girls groups, these girls were also distinct in a significant way. The group on the extreme left-hand side of the graph in Figure 7.1 was located as far away from the boys as it was possible to be. These girls were constructing a femininity which was exclusively based on interacting with each other. The group in the top right-hand corner of Figure 7.1 not only interacted with each other, but was also located much closer to the boys, and particularly to one of the 'atypical' boys. These girls may be constructing a strong feminine identity, but it is not defined solely in opposition to boys. The differences between these two groups of girls suggest the need for some caution in interpreting Maccoby and Jacklin's (1987) claim that assertive and masculine girls are more likely to play with other girls. As this correspondence analysis indicates, groupings of girls can be organized around a variety of gender identities. Our measure of gender identity is not sensitive to this kind of distinction. A more sensitive measure might also reveal differences among boys.

The second general point to emerge from the analyses of the cross-sectional data concerns differences between the schools. Rather than reflecting the influence of criteria such as the age range of children, or the demographic characteristics of the locality, the distinction between types of school rests largely on the pedagogical style adopted by the teacher. In McCarthy and Newby schools, the teacher made greater use of collective work, setting tasks for small groups of children. In Land and George schools, the reception-year teacher organized children's activity by working with them individually, which ensures that each child benefits from the teacher's personal attention. A consequence of the teacher's attention to individual children is that children spend more time engaged in peer-organized activities. Both Land and George are schools in which stable groups of girls are a more prominent feature of peer-organized contexts than in McCarthy or Newby. It may be that the greater amount of time available for peer-organized activities encourages the differentiation among girls. The pedagogic style adopted by the teacher may have unintended consequences for the development of gender identities among the children. In this sense, pedagogic style may also contribute towards the emergence of a local gender culture within the classroom.

8

Children's knowledge of gender marking

In Chapters 5, 6 and 7, we examined the influence of sex group membership and social gender identity on children's activities through an analysis of classroom observations. We noted the growing significance of gender identities through the first year of schooling. In the first term, we recorded overall differences between sex groups in their patterns of association and their use of resources available in the classroom, principally in their use of objects (material culture) and of areas in the classroom (space). In the summer term, differences within sex groups were identified as feminine and masculine gender identities took shape, especially among the girls. At the same time, we also reported the appearance of local gender cultures within particular classrooms; the same resources did not necessarily carry the same gender markings in each classroom.

In this chapter, the focus of our attention shifts from children's practical activities to the knowledge of gender markings as expressed in three individual interviews. The Michael and Susan test investigates children's knowledge of the gender markings of toys and other materials in their classrooms; the Odd-one-out test is concerned with children's sensitivity to incongruity between sex group and gender marking; and the Figures test provided an opportunity to explore both issues in the context of children's guided re-creation of classroom life. At the end of the chapter, we consider data collected from some of the children in Land School about their knowledge of gender marking of linguistic forms. All these tests were described in Chapter 3.

Our reasons for undertaking these investigations of children's knowledge of the rules of gender were twofold. The first was a general expectation in developmental psychology of a disjunction between young children's practical activity and their knowledge or understanding of that activity. As Piaget (1977) has demonstrated, children are frequently able to achieve

123

practical solutions to problems before they are capable of providing an adequate explanation of what they have done. In our own earlier studies with pre-school children, we found a similar disjunction in relation to the gender marking of toys. Girls and boys clearly used gender-marked toys differently from an early age in their practical activity, but they experienced considerable difficulty in sorting photographs of toys by gender. Even by 4 years of age, children performed at chance levels, despite being able to sort pictures of male and female adults and children with almost perfect accuracy (Lloyd and Duveen, 1990). The picture which emerged from this research is that children's knowledge of gender is structured first around identifying the sex-group membership of people; only later is their understanding extended to the classification of objects in terms of gender markings.

Our second reason for exploring children's knowledge of gender stemmed from our general theoretical orientation. As we noted in Chapter 2, the perspective of social representations is concerned with social psychological structures which extend across the 'values, ideas and practices' (Moscovici, 1973, p. xiii) of social groups. The theory does not entail an assumption that there will be consistency across these three elements of representations. Indeed, Moscovici has himself coined the term 'cognitive polyphasia' to describe the ways in which social representations are capable of sustaining mutually contradictory elements (cf. Duveen and Lloyd, in press). For the researcher, the problem is first of all to recognize the inconsistent elements, and then, if possible, to offer an explanation as to why a particular social group constructs an identity drawn from a representation in which these inconsistencies appear. Sometimes inconsistencies can be observed within the values and ideas of particular social groups, as for example in Mugny and Carugati's (1989) study of the social representations of intelligence (see also Carugati, 1990). But there can also be contradiction between the values and ideas expressed by members of a social group and their actual practice – see, for example, Jodelet's (1991) exploration of the social representations of madness. In Chapter 4 we observed some examples of such cognitive polyphasia, both in the different voices which teachers use to talk about gender in the classroom, and, at times, in the inconsistencies between what teachers say and what they do.

As far as children are concerned, we expect to find a disjunction between their knowledge of gender and the practical activities observed in the classroom. From the point of view of the development of social representations, it is difficult to predict what the form or character of this disjunction might be. Children may have a well-structured understanding of gender marking by the time they enter school, even if this structure does not correspond to the ways in which they respond to the gender markings of resources in practice. Alternatively, children may still have a very weak understanding of gender marking, which would contrast with the clarity of the distinctions they make between differentially marked objects in their practical activity.

In the following sections, results from interviews are examined with these points in mind. Again, the longitudinal data is presented first and then the cross-sectional data. In each case, the framework for analysing the data has included both sex-group membership and gender identity. As our measure of gender identity is derived from observations of children in single-sex groups, the inclusion of this measure enables us to investigate the relationship between observations of children's practical activity and their responses to these individual interviews.

MICHAEL AND SUSAN TEST

Longitudinal data

In the Michael and Susan test, children first assigned eighteen photographs of materials from their classrooms to photographs representing either a prototypical boy or a prototypical girl. We analysed children's responses to determine whether there was any consensus regarding the gender markings assigned to these common classroom objects. Binomial tests were used to determine whether items were assigned more frequently to Susan or to Michael. Initially, we looked for consensus among children as a whole; that is, consensus which extends across both girls and boys. Table 8.1 shows the items for which significant results were obtained in each term.

As the table indicates, in both schools more items were gender marked by the end of the year than at the beginning of the year. Indeed, in the autumn term in Land School none of the items revealed any consensual marking. In McCarthy School, only two items were marked in the autumn term, the doll as feminine and the farm as masculine. In the summer term, three items were marked in the same way in both schools, the bricks and jigsaw as masculine (the jigsaw may seem an unlikely item to be marked as masculine; however, the picture on the jigsaw depicted a large red fire engine, and children may have responded to it as a vehicle rather than as a jigsaw), and the doll as feminine. In addition, in McCarthy School the trike was marked as masculine and the cooker as feminine, while in Land School the computer was marked as masculine and the clothes as feminine.

The items which were marked for gender can also be considered in terms of the categories used in the analysis of materials described in Chapter 6. By the summer term, a number of role play items (clothes, cooker and doll) were recognized as carrying a feminine marking, while those which carried a masculine marking were examples of constructive play (bricks and

125

Table 8.1 Michael and Susan test: items marked for gender in each term in each school (longitudinal data)

	Autumn term		Summer term	
	McCarthy	Land	McCarthy	Land
Bricks			M**	M**
Clothes				F**
Cooker			F*	
Doll	F***		F***	F*
Farm	M*			
Jigsaw			M**	M*
Trike			M*	
Computer	XX		XX	M*

Notes
F Feminine marked item.
M Masculine marked item.
XX Item not included.
*** P < 0.001
** P < 0.01
* P < 0.05

jigsaw) or activity play (trike). The pattern we identified across the year in both schools indicated a growing conventionality in the associations which children made between materials and gender, though in neither school did these consensual markings extend across a very wide range of items.

As well as consensus which extends across all children, there were also differences between girls and boys in the judgments made about items, and Table 8.2 shows the items which were clearly marked by each sex group.

Although the range of items which was marked for gender changed across the year, one important point to note is that the direction in which any item was marked was never reversed. Examining the way in which each sex group responded to the task also emphasizes the very sharp difference between the two schools in the autumn term. The most consistently marked item was the doll, which was seen as feminine in McCarthy School by both girls and boys in each term. Yet the same item was not seen as carrying any clear gender marking in Land School.

A greater range of items was recognized as being marked in the summer term than in the autumn term, but children displayed the greatest consensus about their own sex group. Girls tended to acknowledge feminine-marked items, while boys recognized masculine-marked items. The only exceptions were in McCarthy School, where girls saw the trike as being masculine-marked and boys viewed the doll as feminine. Noticeably, there were no instances of girls and boys marking the same item in different ways. The difference between girls and boys also led to a distinction in the kinds of material which they associated with each gender. Girls claimed as

Table 8.2 Michael and Susan test: items marked for gender by each sex group in each school (longitudinal data)

McCarthy School

	Autumn term		Summer term	
	Girls	Boys	Girls	Boys
Blackboard	M**			
Bricks				M**
Clothes		F*	F^a	
Cooker	F*			
Doll	F**	F*	F^a	F**
Farm		M*		
Jigsaw				M**
Lego				M*
Trike			M^a	
Number bricks			F^a	

Land School

	Autumn term		Summer term	
	Girls	Boys	Girls	Boys
Bricks				M*
Clothes	F*		F**	
Computer				M*
Jigsaw				M*
Paints	F*			
Trike				M*

Notes
F   Feminine marked item.
M Masculine marked item.
** $P < 0.01$
* $P < 0.05$
^{a} Items where the results just fail to reach a conventional level of significance ($P < 0.05$), but where only a single child has assigned the item to the opposite gender.

feminine role play items (clothes, cooker and doll), while boys claimed constructive (bricks, jigsaw and lego) or activity (trike) play items.

An explanation for this pattern is that children were assigning items to Michael and Susan differentially according to their own sex, so that boys assigned more items to Michael and girls more items to Susan. To investigate this possibility, difference scores were calculated between the numbers of items each child assigned to Susan and to Michael. For girls, this difference score was calculated by subtracting the number of items assigned to Michael from the number of items assigned to Susan. For the boys, the number of items assigned to Susan was subtracted from the number of items assigned to Michael. This procedure allowed for the possibility that both girls and boys were assigning more items to the character representing their own sex.

Analysis of this score showed that there were differences between girls and boys across the school year in the way they used a strategy of assigning items to their own sex group.[1] Girls gave more items to Susan than to Michael in both terms (mean difference in the autumn term = 3.4, in the summer term = 2.5). Boys, on the other hand, were more even-handed in their assignments in the autumn term (mean difference = 0.6), though by the summer term they too gave more items to their own sex (mean difference = 3.2). Although we identified each child in terms of our measure of gender identity, it did not influence the results.

In assigning items to Susan or to Michael, children were presented with a forced choice. In the second part of the test, they were asked to select four items for themselves. This preference data allowed us to ask whether any items were selected more frequently by girls or by boys. Chi-squares were computed to compare the numbers of girls and boys selecting each item among their four favourites (for these analyses, no account was taken of the order in which children selected items). In the autumn term, only the doll was selected more frequently by the girls,[2] and the lego by the boys.[3] In the summer term, the doll was again the only item to be selected more frequently by the girls,[4] while three items were more frequently selected by the boys, the blackboard,[5] the trike[6] and the lego.[7]

Children may have selected their four favourite toys on idiosyncratic grounds, believing them to be marked for their own gender, even if this belief was not consensually shared. In other words, a boy might have assigned an item to Michael, believing that it carried a consensual definition of a masculine marking, and then made a choice of personal preference on this basis. To investigate this possibility, children's preferences among the items were analysed in terms of their earlier assignment of each item. Differential preference scores for girls were calculated by subtracting the number of Michael-assigned items from the number of Susan-assigned items. For boys, the differential preference score was obtained by subtracting the number of Susan-assigned items from the

---

[1] Scores were analysed in a four-way design, with sex, gender identity and school as between-subjects variables, and term as a within-subjects variable. The only significant effect was the sex by term interaction ($F = 3.81$; df = 1,43; $P = 0.57$).

[2] Chi-square = 15.89; df = 1, $P < 0.001$.

[3] Chi-square = 3.63; df = 1; $P = 0.06$.

[4] Chi-square = 12.17; df = 1; $P < 0.001$.

[5] Chi-square = 7.54; df = 1; $P < 0.01$.

[6] Chi-square = 7.95; df = 1; $P < 0.01$.

[7] Chi-square = 2.99; df = 1; $P = 0.08$.

number of Michael-assigned items. Again, this procedure was adopted to allow both girls and boys to express a positive preference for items which they had assigned to their own gender.

Analysis of these differential preference scores revealed interesting tendencies.[8] In the autumn term, girls showed a preference for items which they had assigned to Susan (mean = 1.2) and boys preferred items which they had allocated to Michael (mean = 1.1). By the summer term, a clear difference had emerged, with boys showing a stronger tendency to select items they had assigned to Michael (mean = 1.8), while among girls the corresponding effect was very much reduced (mean = 0.5). Once again, gender identity did not influence this result.

By the end of the year, consistency between children's perceptions of the gender markings of items and their own preferences had become a more important issue for boys than for girls. This has an important consequence for the way in which social gender identities are shaped. The data on assignments suggested that, by the summer term, social identities were being elaborated by children 'claiming' some items as appropriate to their own sex group, with little consensus about the way items were marked for the opposite gender (and the differences between the schools in the markings of items emphasizes the importance of the local gender culture which emerged within each classroom). For boys, assignment to Michael was also associated with their own preferences. As we have noted in our earlier research (Lloyd and Duveen, 1990), the social identities which develop among boys encompass an impulse to mark the distinctiveness of their identity. The social identities which develop among girls do not stress an association between knowledge of gender markings and establishing a difference. As we have noted in Chapter 6, this may reflect the sense that the developmental pathway for boys is narrower than it is for girls.

Cross-sectional data

The results for George and Newby schools are broadly similar to those reported for McCarthy and Land schools in the autumn term. In George School, no items were marked for gender, either when all the children were considered together or when each sex group was considered separately. In Newby School, the computer and doll were marked as feminine and the bricks and the farm as masculine by all the children. The items marked by each sex group are shown in Table 8.3.

---

[8] Scores were analysed in a four-way design, with sex, gender identity and school as between-subjects variables, and term as a within-subjects variable. The only effect approaching conventional levels of significance was the sex by term interaction ($F = 3.07$; $df = 1,43$; $P = 0.08$).

Table 8.3 Michael and Susan test: items marked for gender by each sex group in Newby School (cross-sectional data)

	Girls	Boys
Blackboard	F*	
Bricks		M*
Computer	F**	F*
Doll	F*	
Farm		M*
Paints		M*
Scissors		M*

Notes
F   Feminine marked item.
M   Masculine marked item.
** $P < 0.01$
* $P < 0.05$

These results for Newby School illustrate once again children's tendency to 'claim' particular items for their own gender. Only one item, the computer, is recognized as carrying a feminine marking by both girls and boys in this school (and in this sense the local gender culture of this school is unusual – computers have more frequently been seen as masculine). In other respects, these results are a little different from those observed in the other schools. There is no clear parallel to the contrasting association of role play items as feminine and construction or activity play items as masculine that was reported in the longitudinal data. Most of the items which are clearly marked in Newby School are from the category of directed play (blackboard, computer, paints and scissors). This may reflect the greater amount of time which children in this school spent in teacher-organized activities.

Analysis of the difference scores for the number of items assigned to Susan and to Michael showed that across all four schools in the autumn term, girls (mean = 2.9) were more likely to favour Susan than boys (mean = 0.4) were to favour Michael.[9] This contrast is similar to that observed in the autumn term in Land and McCarthy schools.

Analysis of children's preferences in the second part of the interview showed that three items were more frequently selected by girls: clothes,[10] doll[11] and hat people; (dolls derived from the reading scheme employed in

[9] The scores were analysed in a three-way design, with sex, gender identity and school all as between-subjects variables. The only significant effect was for sex ($F = 7.00$; df = 1,84; $P < 0.01$).
[10] Chi-square = 13.11; df = 1; $P < 0.001$.
[11] Chi-square = 22.93; df = 1; $P < 0.001$.

McCarthy School;[12] and two items more frequently selected by boys: jigsaw[13] and lego.[14] In addition, three items showed a tendency to be selected more frequently by boys, though the results just fail to reach conventional levels of significance: blackboard,[15] crayons[16] and farm.[17]

As in the longitudinal analysis, differential preference scores were calculated to investigate whether girls and boys selected their favourite items from those which they had assigned to Susan or to Michael. The only significant effect in this analysis was for school.[18] Children in McCarthy (mean = 1.1), Land (mean = 1.0) and Newby (mean = 1.6) all showed some tendency to select their favourite toys from among the things which they had 'claimed' for their own gender. In George School (mean = −0.7), however, children showed a tendency to prefer items which they had assigned to the opposite gender.

Overall, the results from the cross-sectional analysis reinforced the picture of the autumn term observed in the longitudinal data. There was little clear gender marking of toys, though the results did provide an echo of the parallels drawn between the schools in the analysis of the observational data (see Chapter 7). Land and George schools were similar in the absence of any clearly recognized gender markings in the autumn term, while in both McCarthy and Newby schools there were some items which were clearly marked by all the children and some for which there was consensus within each sex group. Other aspects of the results revealed differences between schools, which point once again to the emergence of local gender cultures within each school.

ODD-ONE-OUT TEST

In this test, children were asked to select the odd item from triads of pictures showing children playing with toys. The six triads had been constructed so that it was possible for children to make their selection in one of three ways; on the basis of either the sex group of the actors, the gender marking of the objects or the mismatch between actor and object. Each type of choice was further identified in terms of specific gender markings. Choices on the basis

[12] Chi-square = 11.92; df = 1; P < 0.001.
[13] Chi-square = 4.72; df = 1; P < 0.05.
[14] Chi-square = 5.11; df = 1; P < 0.05.
[15] Chi-square = 3.20; df = 1; P = 0.08.
[16] Chi-square = 3.20; df = 1; P = 0.08.
[17] Chi-square = 2.86; df = 1; P = 0.09.
[18] The scores were analysed in a three-way design, with sex, gender identity and school all as between-subjects variables. The only significant effect was for school (F = 4.87; df = 3,84; P < 0.01).

Table 8.4 Odd-one-out test: mean scores for each type of choice (longitudinal data)

	Autumn term		Summer term	
	Masculine	Feminine	Masculine	Feminine
Actor	1.06	0.77	1.04	0.73
Object	0.98	0.69	0.98	0.48
Mismatch	1.25	1.25	1.29	1.48
Combined	3.29	2.71	3.31	2.69

of actors' sex group were separated into those identifying a boy as the odd one out and those identifying a girl as the odd one out. Similarly, object choices were divided into those identifying as odd masculine-marked objects and feminine-marked objects. Mismatch choices were divided between those identifying as odd a girl playing with a masculine toy, and a boy playing with a feminine toy. Across the three trials the total number of each type of choice made by children could vary from nought to three. Table 8.4 shows the mean scores for each type of choice in each term.

Table 8.4 indicates relatively little change across the year in choice pattern, when children's responses are examined all together. The influence of children's sex-group membership, gender identity and school were considered in a series of separate analyses for choices based on actors, objects and mismatches. There was a tendency for children to identify as odd a male actor (mean = 1.05) rather than a female actor (mean = 0.75).[19] A similar effect was found in the analysis for object choices,[20] with masculine-marked items (mean = 0.98) being selected as odd more often than feminine-marked items (mean = 0.59). In neither case were these differences influenced by either sex group or gender identity; the greater salience of male and masculine-marked items was common to both girls and boys. There was, however, a difference between schools in the number of object choices made. In McCarthy School, the number decreased from the autumn term (mean = 1.00) to the summer term (mean = 0.67), while in Land School it remained constant through the year (mean for the autumn term = 0.71; mean for the summer term = 0.79).[21]

[19] Each analysis was based on a five-way design, with sex group, gender identity and school as between-subjects variables, and term and marking as within-subjects variables. For choices of actor the main effect for marking was close to a conventional level of significance ($F = 3.41$; df = 1,40; $P = 0.07$).

[20] For object choices there was a significant effect for marking ($F = 5.37$; df = 1,40; $P < 0.05$).

[21] School by term interaction in the analysis for object choices ($F = 4.55$; df = 1,40; $P < 0.05$).

Table 8.5 Odd-one-out test: mean scores for mismatch choices (longitudinal data)

	McCarthy School		Land School	
	Autumn	Summer	Autumn	Summer
Girls				
Low gender identity	1.00	0.75	1.25	0.75
High gender identity	0.88	2.50	1.50	1.67
Boys				
Low gender identity	0.92	1.50	1.75	1.75
High gender identity	1.67	1.19	1.06	1.28

Given the salience which male and masculine markings had for actor and observer choices, it is surprising that no difference was found between mismatch choices according to the combination of markings. Boys playing with feminine objects were no easier or harder to identify as odd than girls playing with masculine objects.

Analysis of the mismatch scores showed that, across the year, there was a sharp increase in the extent of mismatch choices by high gender identity girls in McCarthy School (see Table 8.5).[22] No differences were found among the boys in McCarthy School, or among any of the children in Land School.

Mismatch choices are more cognitively complex than actor or object choices, because they demand a coordination between the two dimensions of actor and object.[23] For this reason, the sharp increase among the high gender identity girls in McCarthy School is all the more intriguing. Across the year, these girls have become more sensitive to mismatches between actor and object, which is not the case for the other girls in McCarthy School or for the boys. Our conjecture is that there is something in the local gender culture of McCarthy School which is supporting (or scaffolding) this development among high gender identity girls. The absence of similar effects in Land School also suggests that there are distinctive features in the local context of McCarthy School.

---

[22] Sex group by gender identity by school by term interaction ($F = 4.12$; $df = 1,40$; $P < 0.05$). Tukey tests showed that high gender identity girls in McCarthy School made more mismatch choices in the summer term than in the autumn term ($P < 0.05$), and that in the summer term in McCarthy School, the high gender identity girls made more mismatch choices than the low gender identity girls ($P < 0.05$).

[23] A sample of 7 year old children in Land School ($N = 20$) was also tested, and compared with the summer-term performance of the reception year children. They produced a greater number of mismatch choices (mean for 7 year olds = 2.03; mean for reception class = 1.23; $F = 7.30$; $df = 1,45$; $P < 0.01$). Identifying mismatches between actors and objects thus appears to be a developmental phenomenon.

Analyses of the cross-sectional data revealed no new patterns. For actor choices, male characters (mean = 1.22) were identified more often than female characters (mean = 0.84),[24] although no corresponding difference was found for object choices. The analysis for object choices showed that many fewer were made in George School (mean = 0.33) than in any of the other schools (mean for McCarthy = 1.00; mean for Land = 0.71; mean for Newby = 0.77).[25] No differences were found in the analysis of mismatch choices.

With the exception of the high gender identity girls in McCarthy School, differences in girls' and boys' gender identity did not influence their sensitivity to different aspects of gender marking. The Odd-one-out test is more specifically focused on children's knowledge of gender marking than the Michael and Susan test; it asks children about their knowledge of the rules of gender marking and leaves them no opportunity for expressing a preference of any kind. The influence of gender identity on children's responses to the Michael and Susan test was observed precisely when they were able to express a preference. As we noted in the conclusion to our studies with pre-school children, when children are asked only about their knowledge of gender marking, 'girls and boys display a similar competence' (Lloyd and Duveen, 1990, p. 45). This largely holds true for the first year of schooling as well.

FIGURES TEST

Through a guided reconstruction of a morning at school, the Figures test enabled us to explore children's understanding of the gender marking of various aspects of classroom life. The narrative took children through a series of events which were re-enacted with small wooden figures on a sketchmap of a classroom. At various points, children were asked to move the figures as they thought appropriate, or to respond verbally to questions (details of this test are presented in Chapter 3).

The classroom plan included a number of locations, each set out with specific materials. The eight materials were sand, bricks, paint, puzzles, home corner, train layout, Play-dough and work tables. Children were first asked to move the figures around these materials as they thought the teacher would have directed. Later, the narrative was manipulated so that children had the opportunity to move the figures around the same materials in ways they thought the children would have chosen. Through this comparison, the test attempted to examine children's grasp of the

[24] Main effect for marking in the analysis of actor choices (F = 6.51; df = 1,78; P < 0.05).
[25] Main effect for school in the analysis of object choices (F = 4.35; df = 3,78; P < 0.01).

distinction between teacher-organized and peer-organized activity contexts. In each case, children were asked to place pairs of figures in each location, so that they had a choice of placing two girls, two boys or a girl and a boy. These choices provided information about the extent to which children associated materials and gender.

Children in the longitudinal sample made few consistent associations between materials and gender. Each of the three possible choices was distributed more or less evenly across each of the materials. In teacher-directed contexts in both autumn and summer terms, fewer children placed two girls at the train layout than either two boys or a mixed pair.[26] In peer-organized contexts in the summer term, more children selected a boy and a girl for the puzzles and the work table than single-gender pairs.[27] When the data was examined separately for girls and boys, and for each class, very few materials were, again, associated with gender (the only consistent association being between the train layout and pairs of boys).

In the cross-sectional data, there were few consistent associations between materials and gender. In teacher-directed contexts, pairs of boys were more frequently assigned to the train layout.[28] In peer-organized contexts, a number of items attracted more mixed pairs than single-gender pairs (these included the sand, bricks, puzzles and paint;[29] analyses for each school showed that these effects were largely due to patterns in George and Newby schools).[30]

If children did not regularly associate individual materials with particular genders, was this because they adopted a particular style of responding to the test? Did they, for example, regularly choose to place two boys, two girls or a mixed pair with each of the materials? Table 8.6 shows the mean number of each type of choice in teacher-directed and peer-organized contexts in both autumn and summer terms. As the data in the table indicates, children tend to make more mixed-pair choices. Maccoby and Jacklin (1987) suggested that same-sex preferences were stronger in interviews with children than in observational data. This is not borne out in our own results in the Figures test, though in this interview children were not asked who they would choose to play with, but, which of the figures they

---

[26] In the autumn term, chi-square = 8.92; df = 2; P < 0.05. In the summer term, chi-square = 8.68; df = 2; P < 0.05.

[27] Chi-square for puzzles = 6.16; df = 2; P < 0.05. Chi-square for work tables = 6.13; df = 2; P < 0.05.

[28] Chi-square for train layout = 8.99; df = 2; P < 0.01.

[29] Chi-square for sand = 6.34; df = 2; P < 0.05. Chi-square for bricks = 9.12; df = 2; P < 0.01. Chi-square for puzzles = 8.67; df = 2; P < 0.05. Chi-square for paint = 6.34; df = 2; P < 0.05.

[30] In George School, chi-square for bricks = 6.10; df = 2; P < 0.05; chi-square for paint = 6.10; df = 2; P < 0.05; and chi-square for puzzles = 6.70; df = 2; P < 0.05. In Newby School, chi-square for bricks = 7.00; df = 2; P < 0.05.

Table 8.6 Figures test: mean number for each type of choice (longitudinal data)

	Autumn term		Summer term	
	Teacher-directed	Peer-organized	Teacher-directed	Peer-organized
Two girls	2.59	2.54	2.59	2.22
Two boys	2.54	2.52	2.61	2.26
Mixed pair	2.87	2.94	2.80	3.52

thought would play with the materials at each location. The differences between the studies may reflect differences in the task to which children were asked to respond.

Further analysis of these mixed-pair choices showed significant differences both within and between sex groups, as well as between the schools in different activity contexts.[31] The relevant mean scores are shown in Table 8.7.

The most striking contrast in Table 8.7 is that between organizational contexts for high gender identity girls in McCarthy School. In teacher-directed contexts, they made many more mixed-pair choices than they did in peer-organized contexts. As the data in the table indicates, the direction of this effect was unique to this group of girls. Every other group of children

Table 8.7 Figures test: mean number of mixed-pair choices, by sex, gender identity, class and organizational context (longitudinal data)

	McCarthy School		Land School	
	Teacher-directed	Peer-organized	Teacher-directed	Peer-organized
Girls				
Low gender identity	3.50	4.88	3.17	3.83
High gender identity	7.00	1.00	1.20	2.00
Boys				
Low gender identity	3.43	3.57	4.13	4.25
High gender identity	1.70	2.60	1.33	2.44

[31] The number of mixed-pair choices made by children were analysed in a five-way design with sex, gender identity and class as between-subjects variables, and organizational context and trial as within-subjects variables. The ANOVA produced a significant four-way interaction of sex by gender identity by class by organizational context ($F = 6.94$; df = 1,38; $P < 0.05$). Comparisons between mean scores were made by Tukey tests, and those quoted were significant at $P < 0.05$.

tended to make more mixed-pair choices in peer-organized contexts than in teacher-directed contexts (although none of these comparisons was statistically significant). We identified this group of girls as high gender identity on the basis of their tendency to associate exclusively with other girls. Their response to the Figures test is closer to their practice than the responses for any other group. These are the only children for whom there is a degree of congruity between practice and knowledge. In their responses to the Odd-one-out test, this same group of high gender identity girls in McCarthy School showed a strong increase across the school year in the number of mismatch choices which they made. They were the group which proved to be most sensitive to mismatches between persons and materials. Yet here in the Figures test, where they had an opportunity to select a gender-neutral choice, these girls took full advantage of it. It would appear that, while recognizing conflicts generated by the gender marking of materials, these girls took the opportunity offered by the Figures test to express a degree of resistance or dissatisfaction with this state of affairs.

In both schools, the number of mixed-pair choices made by low gender identity boys in teacher-directed contexts was higher than those made by high gender identity boys. In peer-organized contexts, no differences were found between these groups of boys in either school.

The influence of sex-group membership, gender identity and school on the number of mixed-pair choices which children made appeared when the longitudinal data was aggregated across the school year. In the cross-sectional data, drawn from the autumn term alone, the only significant effect was that children made more mixed-pair choices in peer-organized contexts (mean = 3.52) than in teacher-directed contexts (mean = 2.78).[32] This difference was consistent with the pattern noted in the longitudinal data. On the whole, children made more gender specific choices in teacher-directed contexts and more mixed-pair choices in peer-organized contexts.

A second set of analyses in the Figures test examined children's judgments about the gender markings of behavioural styles asserted by the teacher. In the narrative, a series of questions occurred in which the teacher was reported as saying 'Somebody's being very noisy, who is it?', and the child was asked to point out the figure whom they thought the teacher meant (in addition to noisy, the other behavioural styles were: silly, quiet, naughty, bossy and helpful). Binomial tests were undertaken to investigate whether male or female figures were significantly associated with each style. No consensus was found among all the children in the longitudinal

---

[32] The cross-sectional data was analysed in a four-way design with sex, gender identity and school as between-subjects variables, and organizational context as a within-subjects variable. The only significant effect in the ANOVA was for organizational context ($F = 5.24$; $df = 1,79$; $P < 0.05$).

Table 8.8 Figures test: associations between behavioural styles and gender (longitudinal data)

	Autumn term		Summer term	
	Girls	Boys	Girls	Boys
Noisy				
Silly			M*	
Quiet	F*		F*	
Naughty				
Bossy	M*			
Helpful	F**		F**	

Notes
M   Masculine.
F   Feminine.
** $P < 0.01$
* $P < 0.05$

sample, nor for each school. When the data for each sex group was examined, it appeared that girls made a number of associations between behavioural styles and gender, but boys made no such associations. These results are shown in Table 8.8, and it can be seen that in both terms girls claim the socially desirable styles (quiet and helpful) as feminine. The styles they identify as masculine are among the undesirable items (bossy in the autumn term and silly in the summer term).

A similar effect was also observed in the cross-sectional data, though in this larger sample some consensus emerged, too, across the children as a whole, associating helpful as feminine and bossy as masculine (see Table 8.9). Again, girls claimed socially desirable items as feminine (quiet and helpful), while ascribing undesirable (naughty and bossy) styles as

Table 8.9 Figures test: associations between behavioural styles and gender (cross-sectional data)

	All children	Girls	Boys
Noisy			
Silly			
Quiet		F**	M**
Naughty		M*	
Bossy	M*	M*	
Helpful	F**	F**	

Notes
M   Masculine.
F   Feminine.
** $P < 0.01$
* $P < 0.05$

Table 8.10 Figures test: judgments of responsibility (longitudinal data)

	All children	Girls	Boys
Autumn term			
Female figure			
hit	M**	M**	M*
Male figure			
hit	F**		F**
Female figure			
losing pencil	M**		M*
Male figure			
losing pencil	F**		F**
Summer term			
Female figure			
hit	M**	M**	M*
Male figure			
hit	F**		F**
Female figure			
losing pencil	M**	M**	M*
Male figure			
losing pencil	F**		F**

Notes
M   Masculine.
F   Feminine.
** $P < 0.01$
* $P < 0.05$

masculine. In this large sample, we also found the only example of boys associating a behavioural style with gender – they ascribed quiet as masculine. In this instance, then, the boys too claimed a socially desirable style for their own gender.

Overall, girls showed a much stronger sense of the ways in which behavioural styles enunciated by teachers may be gender marked. Girls considered socially desirable styles as feminine, and undesirable styles as masculine. This result suggests that girls construed gender identity in terms of intergroup comparisons. The failure of boys to make such clear associations between gender and behavioural styles might suggest that they were less likely to see behavioural styles in intergroup terms, but it might also reflect the context in which they were asked to ascribe these behavioural styles.

Some evidence in favour of the influence of context on the association between gender and behavioural styles comes from children's responses to a third set of questions in the Figures test. For these questions, the figures had been regrouped so that equal numbers of male and female figures were shown either working with the teacher at a table, or playing on the carpet. Both a boy and a girl left the carpet and complained to the teacher that someone had hit them, and children were asked to identify the culprit. A second behavioural style was investigated when a figure from the table complained to the teacher that someone had taken his or her pencil. Again, the question was asked for both a female and a male figure, and the children were asked to identify the guilty party. In response to each of the four questions, children could identify either a girl or a boy, and binomial tests were again used to analyse the choices they made.

In the longitudinal sample, a clear pattern was observed. The guilty party was always from the opposite gender to the injured figure (see Table 8.10), though the pattern was stronger among boys than among girls. While boys were prepared to identify masculine figures as responsible for these infringements, girls noticeably failed to identify feminine figures as guilty parties.

This pattern of responses was also observed in the cross-sectional sample (see Table 8.11). It appears that in a different context, where the behavioural styles were articulated by children, boys were more likely to construe the problem in terms of intergroup comparisons. The behavioural styles examined in this part of the Figures test (hitting and stealing) are both socially undesirable, and the key to girls' responses may be their reluctance to identify such styles as feminine. In this they were consistent with their responses to the questions relating to teacher-articulated styles. Boys both were more sensitive to the context in which behavioural styles were articulated, and would more readily associate their own gender with socially undesirable styles.

Table 8.11 Figures test: judgments of responsibility (cross-sectional data)

	All children	Girls	Boys
Female figure hit	M**	M**	M**
Male figure hit	F**		F**
Female figure losing pencil	M**		M**
Male figure losing pencil	F**		F**

Notes
M   Masculine.
F   Feminine.
**   P < 0.01
*   P < 0.05

Table 8.12 Figures test: judgments of responsibility within each school (cross-sectional data)

	McCarthy	Land	George	Newby
Female figure hit	M*	M**	M**	M**
Male figure hit	F**		F**	
Female figure losing pencil	M**		M*	M**
Male figure losing pencil	F**			

Notes
M   Masculine.
F   Feminine.
** $P < 0.01$
* $P < 0.05$

In this analysis of children's responses to questions about behavioural styles, no mention has been made so far of differences between the schools. For the teacher-articulated styles, no significant associations with gender were observed in any of the schools in either the longitudinal or cross-sectional samples. When the styles were articulated by children, however, the pattern of responses was stronger in some schools than in others (see Table 8.12). Intergroup comparison appeared to be more easily evoked in McCarthy and George schools than in Land or Newby schools, a result which may reflect differences in the salience of gender within the local culture emerging in each classroom (the summer term data shows a similar difference between McCarthy and Land schools).

Overall, the results from the Figures test show an interesting contrast. While children did not make any clear associations between materials and gender, they did consistently mark different behavioural styles for gender. There was an asymmetry between girls and boys in the associations which they made. Girls made associations in which socially desirable items were ascribed as feminine, and undesirable styles as masculine. They did this in contexts when styles were articulated by teachers or by children. Boys made less use of this strategy, and were more willing to ascribe undesirable styles to their own gender. In addition, boys responded differentially to the two contexts, making much stronger associations to peer-articulated behavioural styles than to styles articulated by teachers.

141

KNOWLEDGE OF LINGUISTIC GENDER STEREOTYPES

In addition to the three interviews already considered, we also examined children's awareness of linguistic gender stereotypes. Lakoff (1973, 1975) originally advanced arguments that certain linguistic forms were marked for gender in the speech practices of men and women. The question of whether linguistic forms are marked for gender in English-speaking adult communities is itself controversial. A number of authors have suggested that, while linguistic practices may not be as clearly marked as Lakoff claimed, there are powerful stereotypic beliefs associating each gender with particular linguistic forms. We studied the extent to which children's social representations of gender extend into the domain of language.

Lakoff (1973, 1975) claimed that men and women speak in distinctively different styles, or 'genderlects', as she described them. These styles are marked not only at the phonetic level by the higher pitch of women's voices, but also lexically and grammatically. On the basis of her linguistic intuitions, Lakoff asserted that women are more likely to use terms such as 'adorable', 'lovely' and 'divine'. They are also more likely to use tag constructions and other expressions of uncertainty, as in 'Flower arranging really is quite a charming way to spend one's time, isn't it?' In contrast, men were described as less polite in their requests than women and more likely to use swear words, expletives and other stigmatized forms. Lakoff's intention – to describe women's speech and position in society – produced a one-sided account of men and women's speech, consisting largely of the claim that women use expressions of uncertainty and triviality which mark their oppression.

Considerable effort has been devoted to testing Lakoff's intuitions on masculine and feminine speech styles in adults, utilizing observations of naturally occurring speech. This research, reviewed by Smith (1979, 1985), has provided little consistent support for the hypotheses. None the less, Lakoff's conjectures appear to represent stereotypes strongly held by linguistically naive native speakers. Edelsky (1976, 1977) was able to confirm that white, middle-class American adults, recruited at a parent–teachers meeting, shared many of Lakoff's intuitions. When presented with sentences containing such expressions as 'adorable' or 'my goodness', or tag questions, they judged them as more likely to have been spoken by a woman than by a man. Conversely, they ascribed sentences containing 'damn it' or 'I'll be damned' to male speakers. Edelsky also showed that sixth graders (12 year olds) had the same intuitions as adults and were, if anything, even more confident in their judgments. Even third graders (9 year olds) shared many of the same stereotypes. Among first graders (6 year olds), however, the evidence was much weaker. They only ascribed 'adorable' to women and 'damn it', rather uncertainly, to men. These results suggest that linguistic gender stereotypes for adult speech develop at least two to three years before the age at which Labov (1970) predicts children start to develop their stereotypes of the speech of different social classes.

Edelsky had taken care to present each linguistic form embedded in two sentences chosen for their neutral content, in an effort to ensure that her subjects relied on their linguistic, rather than cultural, intuitions. She also interviewed a randomly selected subset of her subjects and asked their reasons for their choices. Edelsky (1977) reported that very few of the first graders identified many of the linguistic forms with either male or female speakers. Instead, they responded on the basis of the sentence topics. This tendency was very strong, since 'When a sentence was presented with a conflicting form and topic, even when a form for which first graders had a stereotype (*Damn it, get me that perfume!*), topic outweighed form in saliency' (Edelsky, 1977, p. 234). Unfortunately, Edelsky's experimental procedure may not have been optimal for eliciting the youngest children's judgments. The children she interviewed were presented with stimuli in the form of sentences read aloud in a flat voice by either a male or a female speaker. This procedure, which presents children with an unnatural stimulus and an unfamiliar task, seems likely to underestimate their linguistic knowledge. Edelsky also noted that asking children for their judgments of adult speech was not a comparable task to asking adults for such judgments. This point takes on a new importance in the light of Labov's (1970) arguments that children, during their early years at school, are primarily influenced by the speech patterns of other children.

The study reported in this book was designed to use more realistic stimuli, based on a story about the activities of other children of comparable age. By embedding test items within this story format, it was hoped that the procedure would be more sensitive in eliciting the children's metalinguistic judgments than the isolated sentences used by Edelsky. The story presented the everyday activities of a boy (Simon) and a girl (Jenny) at school. Children were asked to help in the construction of the story by identifying which of the characters had uttered each of the test items (details of the story and the list of test items are given in Chapter 3).

Ten girls and ten boys in Land School were interviewed individually by the same female investigator (Dr Smith) in the autumn term and again in the summer term. In addition, a further twenty children (ten girls and ten boys) from the top year of the school were also interviewed in the autumn term. These children were 6 years old, and provided data comparable to that of Edelsky. All the children were asked on several occasions during their interview to explain their choices, but the number of probes varied according to children's attentiveness or restlessness. Each presentation of the story was tape-recorded, and the recordings were subsequently transcribed.

143

Among the reception-year children in the autumn term, both boys and girls allocated a majority of the masculine ('blast') items to Simon. Girls allocated a mean of 6.4 of the twelve feminine items to Jenny, but boys allocated a mean of 7.3 such items to Simon. These patterns of choice differ to a statistically significant extent.[33] Girls showed no clear sign of stereotyping on these items, while boys' choices contradicted the adult stereotype to a significant extent.[34]

Table 8.13 shows the sentences which were predominantly assigned to Simon or Jenny. Both boys and girls associated one 'Blast it' item with Simon, albeit different ones, and each claimed 'My goodness, it's time to go home' for the story-child of their own sex group. These results are similar to those of the 6 year olds. 'Oh dear, I dropped the crayons' was associated with Simon by both girls and boys, although 6 year olds had shown no strong agreement on this item. 'I am very tired' was given to Jenny by 6 year olds, but it is among the items allocated to Simon by 4 year old boys.

What is most noticeable about the reception children's performance at the beginning of the year is that boys did not systematically allocate any items to Jenny, but gave nine items to Simon, including no fewer than seven

Table 8.13 Reception-class children's allocation of test items to male (Simon) or female (Jenny) protagonists: autumn term

To Jenny	To Simon
By girls	
. . . sweet bear (7)	Blast it . . . spilt my tea (8)
My goodness . . . time to go home (7)	Oh dear . . . crayons (7)
By boys	
	+ Look . . . down (9)
	Blast it . . . broken (8)
	My goodness . . . time to go home (8)
	. . . sweet picture (7)
	Oh dear . . . crayons (7)
	Oh dear . . . scarf (7)
	Won't you please . . . teapot (7)
	. . . very tired (7)
	My goodness . . . mess we've made (7)

Notes
Figures in brackets specify the number of subjects out of 10 making a particular assignment.
Items are presented in the order of decreasing consensus.
+ $p < 0.03$ on a two-tailed sign test.

[33] Chi-square = 7.3; df = 1; $P < 0.01$.
[34] $P < 0.025$ on a two-tailed binomial test.

feminine items. This preference for their own sex was restricted to boys. The girls reached at least 7–10 agreement on four items, two each for Jenny and Simon.

In the summer term, the majority of boys and girls again allocated the masculine items to Simon. The girls assigned a mean of 7.9 of the twelve feminine items to Jenny,[35] while the boys assigned a mean of 7.2 such items to Simon.[36] Again, the boys' and girls' patterns of choice differed to a statistically significant extent,[37] with the girls' choices conforming to the adult stereotype and those of the boys contradicting it.

Table 8.14 shows that by the end of the year children differentiated sixteen items according to gender, of which girls marked seven and boys nine. The items which appeared for the first time in the summer term were '. . . aren't we?', '. . . can't I?', 'Look . . . down', and 'The water . . . very hot'. At the end of the first year of schooling, the assignments of the girls were congruent with adult stereotypes. They allocated both 'sweet' items,

Table 8.14 Reception-class children's allocation of test items to male (Simon) or female (Jenny) protagonists: summer term

To Jenny	To Simon
By girls	
+ . . . sweet picture (10)	+ Blast . . . broken (9)
+ . . . sweet bear (9)	
Won't you please . . . teapot (8)	
. . . very tired (7)	
. . . aren't we? (7)	
. . . can't I? (7)	
By boys	
. . . sweet picture (7)	+ My goodness . . . time to go home (9)
	My goodness . . . mess we've made (8)
	Blast . . . broken (8)
	Blast . . . spilt my tea (8)
	Look . . . down (8)
	Oh dear . . . scarf (7)
	The water . . . very hot (7)
	. . . very . . . tired (7)

Notes
Figures in brackets specify the number of subjects out of 10 making a particular assignment.
Items are presented in the order of decreasing consensus.
+ $p < 0.03$ on a two-tailed sign test.

[35] $P < 0.05$ on a two-tailed binomial test.
[36] $P < 0.05$ on a two-tailed binomial test.
[37] Chi-square = 16.6; df = 1; $P < 0.01$.

the two tag questions and one 'please' and one 'very' to Jenny. This pattern was closer to that of adults than the choices of 6 year olds, who listed only one tag question and added one 'my goodness' but dropped a 'please'.

After a year at school, boys still showed a marked preference for allocating speech to Simon. The one item they assigned to Jenny, 'I'm going to draw a sweet picture', can be considered the most strongly 'feminine' from a child's point of view, as it was assigned to Jenny by all 6 year olds and by the reception-year girls. It combines 'sweet', which was increasingly associated with girls' affairs, and the circumstance of table-based artwork, which was primarily a female domain in the classroom (cf. Chapters 6 and 7). 'Sweet bear' is a more ambiguous item, as many boys of this age possess teddy bears. Two items which were assigned to Simon by boys in the autumn disappear: 'Oh dear . . . crayons' and 'Won't you please . . . teapot'. On the second testing, boys assigned both 'Blast it' items to Simon. However, another 'very' item was also given to Simon. Three of the items which adults marked as masculine were now assigned to Simon by boys.

In the autumn term, 153 explanations were elicited from the reception-year children, eighty from boys and seventy-three from girls. A similar number, 160, were produced in the summer term, seventy-two from boys and eighty-eight from girls. The 6 year olds produced 159 explanations, which included eighty-two from boys and seventy-seven from girls. Most of these explanations focused on the content of the sentence rather than the gender of the speaker; for example, the assignment of 'sweet bear' to Jenny was explained by a 6 year old year saying 'because she wanted to pretend it was a baby'. Two categories of explanation did, however, invoke gender stereotypes of speech or of other behaviour. They were *linguistic form* – for example, 'Girls don't say "blast it"' – and *generalized behaviour* – for example, 'Because she's a girl and normally boys don't draw sweet pictures, they sort of draw fighting pictures' (a more detailed account of this analysis of children's explanations is given in Smith and Lloyd, 1989).

Among the reception-year children, these categories were hardly used at all. In the autumn term, linguistic form was used four times, though no such explanations were given in the summer term. In neither term did any reception-year child offer generalized behaviour as an explanation. Some increase in the use of both these categories of explanations was noted among the 6 year olds, with ten examples of linguistic form and eleven of generalized behaviour.

The rarity with which the children explained their choices in terms of linguistic form or generalized behaviour indicates that stereotypes were not salient in their decision making. Children were willing to provide explanations for their choices, but the great majority of these derived from the content of the stories, and none was used more frequently by children to justify their choice of either Simon or Jenny. Overall, children's explanations provide no evidence of gender stereotyping.

Gender identity, as indicated by our observational measure, did not influence either children's assignments of items to protagonists, or their explanations. As with many of the other interview-based measures, we found no evidence of any systematic relationship between gender identity and children's performance.

Both the pattern of children's assignments of speech items and the explanations they offer for them indicate that reception-year children had relatively weak stereotypes of the feminine speech style. Even by 6 years of age, this situation had hardly changed. Although these older children assigned speech to the girl in line with adult stereotypes, their assignments were not supported by explanations invoking linguistic form or generalized behaviour. This pattern of assignment was much weaker in the reception-year girls and absent in the reception-year boys, who allocated the majority of items of all types to the boy speaker, in both the autumn and summer terms. The diffuseness of children's grasp of feminine-marked speech styles contrasted with their grasp of the masculine association of at least one linguistic form – both boys and girls throughout the reception year assigned the expletive 'blast' items to Simon.

The most striking aspect of our findings is their similarity to Edelsky's work. Up to 6 years at least, children have weak stereotypes of masculine and feminine speech styles for child as well as for adult speakers. As they enter school, children's social representations of gender do not extend to the marking of language, and by the end of the reception year this situation has not changed.

CONCLUSIONS

At the beginning of this chapter, we suggested that children in the reception year would be likely to display a less sophisticated understanding of gender marking in individual interviews than we had observed in their practical activity in the classroom. By and large, the results we have presented support our expectations. Children made very few consistent associations between gender and the various materials in the classroom at the beginning of the school year. Their associations were limited to claiming particular items for their own gender group. While a stronger sense of the structure of gender marking was evident by the end of the reception year, it continued to be limited by personal concerns.

None the less, the analysis of preferences in the Michael and Susan test suggested that children saw gender as a significant dimension for organizing this aspect of their world. However, children appeared to mistake their own idiosyncratic vision of the gender marking of material culture for a consensual gender order (though, as we noted, this tendency changed across the school year, becoming weaker among the girls and stronger among the boys).

Results from the material culture parts of the Figures test are consistent with those from the Michael and Susan test; few items were consistently associated with one gender or another. A major difference between the two tests is the forced choice format of the Michael and Susan test, which offers only two categories – feminine and masculine. In the Figures test, children could also opt for a third, gender-neutral, response. It is not surprising that even fewer items appeared to be clearly marked for gender in the Figures test than in the Michael and Susan test (Zammuner, 1987, also noted that children make fewer marked choices when offered the possibility of a gender-neutral option).

The Figures test also explored children's knowledge of the gender marking of verbally identified behavioural styles. Where these styles were presented as being voiced by the teacher, a clear distinction emerged between the responses of girls and boys. Girls identified socially desirable styles as feminine and undesirable styles as masculine, while boys made no consistent associations between styles and gender. In contrast, where styles were voiced by children, boys responded systematically in terms of a framework of intergroup conflict. Both of the peer-voiced behavioural styles described socially undesirable styles, and boys responded by identifying the opposite gender as the culprit. Girls, by contrast, responded systematically only to the undesirable behaviours which could be attributed to boys. Where a framework of intergroup conflict suggests that a girl might have been responsible for an undesirable behaviour, the girls in our samples made no systematic choices. Girls were consistent in the way they responded to both teacher- and peer-voiced behavioural styles, while boys were more sensitive to those voiced by peers.

At first glance, these results suggest that girls are more influenced by issues of social desirability than are boys. Yet the situation may be more complex than this. The socially desirable behavioural styles voiced by teachers in the Figures test are also styles which are frequently associated as feminine (quiet, helpful), particularly in the classroom. The undesirable styles voiced by peers (hitting another child, taking another child's pencil) are also among those styles frequently associated as masculine. To ascribe them to boys, therefore, may be to see them as masculine in spite of their negative connotation. These styles may have an ambiguous status; negative or undesirable on the surface, but with an underlying or secondary characteristic which makes them more attractive to boys in so far as they confer a masculine identity.

There is an interesting contrast between children's responses to the

148

behavioural style items in the Figures test and to the linguistic stereotypes. Although children were able to mark behavioural styles for gender (particularly those voiced by peers), they demonstrated only a limited awareness of the gender marking of linguistic forms. Children were more responsive to the content of what was expressed in language than to its form.

A striking feature of the results of these individual measures is the general absence of effects associated with our measure of social gender identity, which was based upon observations of peer interactions. Rarely have we isolated any influence of this index on patterns of children's judgments. In addition, differences between the schools were less apparent in interviews than they were in observations. Individual children responding to an adult interviewer are isolated and deprived of the supportive network available in their ordinary interactions with other children. Expressing a gender identity is apparently closely tied to the pattern of relationships which children develop with their peers. If, as Durkheim and Mauss (1963) suggested, it is social practices which generate cognitive classifications, then children in the reception year can be described as more sophisticated practitioners who have not yet internalized the classifications implicit in their practice. Certainly there is evidence that older children are more consistent in their judgments about the gender marking of material culture (for example, Zammuner, 1987). Among these young children, the ability to recognize and respond to gender marking may be related to scaffolding provided by the collective patterns of interaction which children establish in their social lives.

9

Using language to mark gender and to explore sexuality

In Chapters 5, 6, 7 and 8, we presented findings based upon our systematic observations and interviews with children. Here we contemplate children's own expressions of their gender identities as these were conveyed through naturally occurring dialogue. We use this material to examine some linguistic constructions which are gender differentiated in adult speech and to analyse the specific content of the pretend play which is created with the aid of language. In Chapter 4, we analysed our ethnographic observations of children's and teacher's talk. Here children's own speech provides us with a window on their understanding of these issues.

We described these recordings in Chapter 3, noting that a corpus of natural dialogue was collected only in Land School. The autumn set was recorded during November, December and January, and the summer set at the end of the school year, in May, June and early July. To minimize the intrusiveness of the recording procedure, the apparatus was set up in a particular area of the classroom and allowed to run with as little attention as possible. The home corner and the carpet area were the main locations. Occasionally the directional microphone became the object of children's play, but adult interventions were rarely necessary.

When the autumn set of thirteen recordings was made, children attended school either for the morning or the afternoon, and the largest roll for a session was fifteen children. Usually there were fewer children in the classroom. During the summer term, children attended school all day and newly enrolled children also joined the school. There could be thirty-two children in the classroom at any one time. Since recording under these conditions was not feasible, children were invited to come into the classroom during the lunch playground break in groups of eight to ten. Once children volunteered to take part in a recording session, they remained in the classroom for the rest of the lunch break. As a consequence, the summer corpus differs from that collected in the autumn, when group composition in terms of sex-group membership was fluid. In the summer recordings it was more constant. The summer set of recordings was made in the classroom and the camera was focused, as it had been in the autumn term, on play either in the home corner or in the carpet area.

In Chapter 3 we described our partitioning of transcriptions into topic episodes which comprised talk and action focused on a single game or conversational theme. This was followed by the identification of actors or individual children who spoke or performed in an episode. Each of these active contributions was classified as a 'turn'. These turns were analysed further to determine whether they changed the topic of an episode, gave new direction to an episode or were responses or continuations of preceding turns in the same episode. 2,200 turns were identified in the autumn corpus and 2,800 in the summer corpus. In addition, all tag questions, politeness terms, swear words and expletives which appeared in the transcriptions were colour coded.

These recordings of natural dialogue provide information both about the linguistic characteristics of children's speech and about their topics of conversation. Although there was a great deal of domestic pretend and superhero adventure, we have focused on children's understanding of sexuality. We first report the linguistic characteristics of children's speech, in order to determine whether their usage is differentiated in terms of adult genderlects. The questions we consider are whether girls employ tag questions or politeness terms more frequently than boys and whether boys are more likely to use rude expressions or expletives. A more detailed account of our study of tag constructions is available in a book about the development of child language (Lloyd and Goodwin, 1992).

We also employ our record of children's natural dialogue to explore their understanding of sex, gender and sexuality by examining specific pretend themes. In Chapter 4, we reported our ethnographic observations of teachers' efforts to deal with the construction of social representations of gender. We argued, in Chapter 1, that the reproductive metaphor shaped social representations of gender. Following that theme, we consider children's re-creations of sexual behaviour and analyse their understanding of it. While teachers are guided by the explicit ideologies which we reviewed in Chapter 2, children are left to draw upon their imaginations when they construct their understanding of adult sexual behaviour and practice since adults are reluctant to intervene. The number of incidents related specifically to sexuality which we recorded is small. This may reflect children's early awareness of the unease which adults face in the wake of children's sexuality (cf. Best, 1983).

LINGUISTIC CHARACTERISTICS OF NATURAL DIALOGUE

The study of differences between the language of the sex groups, with a particular focus on women's speech, was given initial impetus by Lakoff's

(1975) vivid and widely quoted account. In it, she suggested that women's oppression is marked linguistically by heightened correctness, politeness and uncertainty in their language. She also proposed an account of the development of separate genderlects.

Lakoff suggested that children initially learn 'woman's speech' from their predominantly female caretakers. Girls retain this style but boys, under pressure from their peers, shift to a distinctly masculine style. Little peer pressure is expected before children enter school, and thus similar styles of speech are hypothesized for girls and boys entering school. Somewhat earlier, Labov (1970) proposed a developmental account for the acquisition of the full range of English speech. It is his second stage which is most relevant here. After an initial stage in which basic grammar and lexicon are mastered under the guidance of parents, peers become crucial in a second stage extending from 5 to 12 years of age. Labov proposes that

> the child learns the use of the local dialect in a form consistent with that of his [sic] immediate group of friends and associates. At this stage, neighbourhood dialect characteristics become automatically established responses in the pattern of everyday speech, and the influence of the parents is submerged under the influence of the peer group. (1970, pp. 288–9)

Labov had followed Hockett (1950) in creating his stage model. Hockett had observed that children do not necessarily grow up to speak their parents' dialect and that the most important environmental influence on the dialect of a child is the speech of other children. This raises at least two questions for us. The first concerns the similarity or difference in girls' and boys' speech when they enter school. The second, related question is whether school attendance in the first year is reflected in any further differences at the end of the school year.

Surveys of gender differences in the speech of pre-school children are relevant to both of these questions. Romaine (1984) and Warren-Leubecker and Bohannon III (1989) concluded that gender differences may appear as early as 4 years of age and are clearly present at 6 years of age. Although the situation before entry to school is uncertain, Local (1982), working in Tyneside in England, reported significant differences in girls' and boys' use of rising and falling tones in their speech before age 6. Sachs' (1987) report that American boys are more assertive in their use of directives than girls is based upon a pretend doctor play setting. Our recordings allowed us to observe speech in scenes determined to a considerable extent by children themselves.

The tag question construction with which we begin our presentation has been a particular object of interest ever since Lakoff identified it as a mark of women's insecurity when making assertions. Tag questions are syntactically more interesting than the politeness terms which she also suggested marked women's speech. She identified expletives and rudeness terms as characteristics of the speech of men. In Chapter 8, we noted that expletives are one of the linguistic gender stereotypes which children mark first.

TAG CONSTRUCTIONS

Tag constructions were classified according to their syntactic form, pragmatic function and intonation pattern. *Syntactic form* was coded in three categories as follows:

1. *Full tags.* These have four features:
   (a) The pronoun matches the subject of the declarative clause;
   (b) The verb phrase is shortened to the auxiliary or dummy form;
   (c) Polarity is reversed;
   (d) Subject and auxiliary are inverted; for example, 'We're baddies, aren't we?'
2. *Simple tags.* These are single words, such as 'OK' or 'right'.
   For example, 'I'm the mummy, OK?'
3. *Other tags.* This class includes tags attached to imperative clauses, tags matching the polarity of the declarative clause and ill-formed constructions.
   For example, 'Let's take baby to bed, shall we?'
   'I'm going to build a big snake, I am.'

The *pragmatic function* of tag constructions was classified according to the following six categories:

1. *Coercive.* A tag is coded as coercive when it follows a statement in which the speaker is trying to get someone else to do as they are told.
   For example, 'We're being sensible, aren't we?'
2. *Indirect coercive.* A tag is coded as an indirect coercive when it follows a statement in which the speaker is trying to get agreement for role allocation to another person or object or to the self.
   For example, 'We're robbers, aren't we, guys?'
3. *Permission.* A tag is coded as a permission when it follows a statement in which the speaker is seeking the other's agreement to an action by the speaker.
   For example, 'In the morning we can take you out, OK?'
4. *Question.* A tag is coded as a question when it follows a statement in which the speaker is seeking to determine a fact or condition which is not coded in the categories above.
   For example, 'We can have a feast, can't we?'
5. *Attention.* A tag is coded as attention when it is being used to elicit a response, to gain the attention of another.

153

For example, 'There's a fan in there. Makes you warm, you see.'
6. *Emphasis.* A tag is coded as emphasis when it is emphasizing what a child has said in the preceding statement.

For example, 'Then, he went on the yellow, you see.'

The *intonation contours* of the tag constructions were described as either rising, falling or flat. Each tag construction was coded by three coders, who observed the video record and agreed on the classification.

Syntactic form

Although there was a substantial rise in the proportion of full tags in the summer term, which indicated the increased maturity of the speakers, the autumn and summer distributions of tag types did not differ statistically.

Pragmatic functions

The pragmatic functions of full tags are shown in Table 9.1.

The most common function of full tags was that of questioning, although they were also used to try to coerce action on the part of others. This contrasts with the pattern of use of simple tags shown in Table 9.2.

The predominant function of simple tags was coercion. If we compare the relative proportions of questions versus other functions for the two syntactic types of tag, we find a statistically significant difference ($P < 0.001$, chi-square approximately 37.7, df = 9).

The individual sub-types of other tags occurred rarely. The simplest type was a form of 'long' short tag including a pronoun: 'you see' or 'you know' rather than 'see' or 'right'; for example,

Table 9.1 Pragmatic functions of full tags

	Coercive and indirect coercive	Question	Permission	Total
Autumn	14	28	–	42
Summer	25	58	3	86
Total	39	86	3	128

Table 9.2 Pragmatic functions of simple tags

	Coercive and indirect coercive	Question	Permission	Attention	Total
Autumn	15	–	4	–	19
Summer	14	5	2	3	24
Total	29	5	6	3	43

Then he went on the yellow, you see.
Mine is the biggest one, you know.

Six of these tags occurred in the autumn corpus, one with coercive function and the others with attention or emphasis functions. Children also produced seven tagged imperatives; for example,

Let's take baby to bed with us, shall we?

All of these served a clear coercive function.

Intonation

The overall distribution of intonation contours is given in Table 9.3. The information for full tags alone is given in Table 9.4. Full tags were normally pronounced with falling intonation while simple tags were very seldom pronounced with falling contours (see Table 9.5). The contrast between these two distributions is apparent, but the intonation contours of other tags offered no clear pattern.

The proportion of tags pronounced with a relatively flat intonation

Table 9.3 Intonation contours of all tags

	Rising	Falling	Flat	Total
Autumn	18	36	22	76
Summer	24	86	9	119
Total	42	122	31	195

Table 9.4 Intonation contours of full tags

	Rising	Falling	Flat	Total
Autumn	–	33	9	42
Summer	–	80	6	86
Total	–	113	15	128

Table 9.5 Intonation contours of simple tags

	Rising	Falling	Flat	Total
Autumn	13	–	6	19
Summer	21	2	1	24
Total	34	2	7	43

contour declined with age (see Table 9.3). This is expected, on the assumption that such cases arose largely by error and that children's control of intonation improves with age. However, careful listening to the video-recordings suggested that at least some cases of full tags with flat intonation were due not to poor control but to the deliberate use of a reduced form – for example, 'in't' rather than 'isn't it' – which was too brief to show a change in underlying pitch. Therefore, they do not challenge the conclusion that for these children full tags have a single intonation contour.

Influences of sex-group membership

The distributions of syntactic types of tag and of non-tag polar questions, and the proportions of total conversational turns produced by boys and girls, are given in Table 9.6.

In the autumn set, the proportion of girls' and boys' tags matched their respective production of non-tag polar questions, although girls produced only 40 per cent of total turns. However, in the summer this pattern was changed; there was no significant difference in girls' and boys' productions of non-tag polar questions, although girls produced 55 per cent of total turns. None the less, boys used tag questions substantially more often than girls did.

The distributions of pragmatic functions for full and simple tags produced by boys and girls are given in Table 9.7. The most notable feature in this data is the increase in the use of tags for questioning shown by boys in the summer recording. This accounts for the increase in boys' full tags shown in Table 9.6.

The lack of a clear expression of speaker uncertainty through heightened use of tag questions among girls, taken together with the increase in tag

Table 9.6 Syntactic types of tag, by gender

	Boys	Girls
Autumn		
Full	18	24
Simple	9	10
Other	12	3
Total tags	39	37
Total non-tag polar questions	55	57
Total turns	1308	883
Summer		
Full	62	24
Simple	6	18
Other	5	4
Total tags	73	46
Total non-tag polar questions	86	83
Total turns	1313	1504

Table 9.7 Pragmatic functions of full and simple tags, by gender

Function	Boys	Girls	Total
Autumn			
Question	12	16	28
Coercive and indirect coercive	11	18	29
Permission	2	2	4
Total	25	36	61
Summer			
Question	48	15	63
Coercive and indirect coercive	17	22	39
Permission	3	2	5
Attention	–	3	3
Totals	68	42	110

constructions to pose questions shown by boys in the summer corpus, challenge Lakoff's assertions (1975). Girls did not display consistently greater uncertainty of their opinions than boys, and the questions posed by boys were not indicative of doubt. To support our latter assertion, we consider the use of questions to maintain conversation in the next section.

Sustaining conversational cohesion

The nature of the discourse functions of both full and simple tags which appear in this analysis as questions or permissions requires further examination. In particular, it is necessary to determine why these tags are so often used to seek agreement. Our hypothesis is that questions are used to maintain conversational cohesion, a strategy shown to be particularly common to play in groups of boys in the summer term.

Although we have been able to infer the function of individual tag constructions from their context, this can only give us a partial view of what is going on. To get anywhere near the full richness of conversation, it is necessary to examine longer texts. Consider the following example: an episode from the autumn corpus in which five girls were playing with a train. In this example, pretend play was structured around a model railway. The difficulties which we encountered in transcribing from our video-recordings were described in Chapter 3 (discontinuities arising as the result of these problems in interpretation are marked in the text as follows. . . .).

1. Sally: Here's another rock fall. Fix the line!
2. Betty: Get out there. We're going to the village.
3. Sally: (Drives her train round track making 'vroom' noises.)

4. Lulu: Look at mine, then.
5. Lulu: Weeh!... Oh, never mind.
6. Sally: Look at mine, look at mine, then.
7. Lulu: Horrible.
8. Sally: (Points to train.) Mind!
9. Sally: Is mine nice?
10. Lulu: Yeah.
11. Sally: Yours is nice [. . . ?]
12. Lulu: They are all nice, aren't they?
13. Sally: Yeah. Lilly's not, though, is she – is it? Lilly's not.
14. Lulu: No.
15. Lilly: Well, I say yours is not nice.
16. Sally: We don't like Lilly, do we?'
17. Lulu: No-o.
18. Rachel: I do.
19. Lulu: But we like her, don't we?
20. Sally: Yeah, but we're afraid of her.
21. Lilly: Rachel, Rachel, are you afraid of me, are you?
22. Rachel: Yeah, I am.

Notice how tag constructions were consistently used to seek agreement to background propositions underlying the pattern of play.

After some friction in turns 4–7, Sally tried to put matters on a smoother course in turn 9 and received a favourable response in turn 10. She rewarded this in turn 11. Lulu then tried to confirm this general benevolence in turn 12. Sally provided this confirmation, but then sought to establish an exception (turn 13), which was accepted by Lulu (turn 14). In keeping, the victim replied in kind (turn 15). Sally then made clear her hostility and sought to establish a consensus about it (turn 16). This was accepted, slightly hesitantly, by Lulu but rejected by Rachel. Lulu promptly sought a reversal of Sally's proposition (turn 19). This was accepted by Sally but with a negative proviso (turn 20). The victim of these derogations, clearly rattled by them, sought to establish their truth (turn 21), only to have the last confirmed.

In the next example, also from the autumn corpus, four boys used tags to gain agreement on the assignment of roles.

1. (Alan on rocking horse, Teddy W. in front.)
2. Theo: And I'm a robber and I'm going to steal all the things.
               (Enters.) We're robbers, aren't we, guys?
3. Harry W.: (Enters.)
4. Teddy W.: Yeah, to steal the house.

5. Alan: (Pointing to the scarf tied over his mouth, cowboy fashion.) I'm wearing your thing, do you mind?
6. Theo: We're baddies, you're a goody, aren't you? Soon you gonna be dead.
7. Theo: [. . . ?] (To Teddy W.) Let's go.
8. Harry W.: I know, we gonna get the money.
9. Alan: (Dismounts.) Yeah, the money!
10. Teddy W.: We're baddies, aren't we?

In these exchanges, there was no disagreement on the assignment of the roles which served to structure the pretend play. Clearly, the boys knew what being a robber involved, even down to the appropriate dress required (turn 5), and what happens to people who oppose robbers (turn 6). So common agreement that they should be robbers had a powerful structuring effect on the boys' play.

Episodes such as these provide clear and firm evidence of the function of full tags in seeking agreement to an underlying proposition and thereby maintaining the structure of the play episode. The available evidence does not allow us to determine whether boys' greater use of tag constructions to maintain conversational cohesion in the summer term reflected frequent disputes about or lack of clarity in the underlying propositions on which boys' pretend play is constructed.

POLITENESS

Lakoff (1975) originally suggested that individuals use politeness in speech to reduce friction and maintain their position in social interaction. Since then, there have been suggestions that politeness is necessary to the creation of ordered social life (Gumperz, 1987) and that women's use of politeness is linked to their use of more formal speech, both of which reflect their subordinate status (Brown, 1980). Although there is considerable debate concerning the use of politeness forms to infer functional intentions (Trudgill, 1983), we need not resolve the issue, as our analysis is restricted to an examination of the frequencies with which such terms are employed by girls and boys. Even then, the rarity of instances and individual differences in their use make conclusions relevant to their employment in the expression of social gender identities problematic.

Politeness terms such as 'please' were colour coded on the transcriptions of natural dialogue by Dr Smith and the first author. Greetings such as 'Hi' were not included. Any disagreements between the coders were resolved through discussion. Table 9.8 shows the frequencies of politeness terms for

Table 9.8 Use of politeness terms

	Autumn	Summer
Boys		
Number	23	16
% politeness	1.8	1.2
Total turns	1308	1313
Girls		
Number	17	25
% politeness	1.9	1.7
Total turns	883	1504

girls and boys in the autumn and summer recordings. They are also presented as a percentage of girls' and boys' turns in each corpus.

The pattern of results across the first year of school suggests that children's use of politeness terms was changing in line with adult stereotypes. In the autumn, there was little difference in their use by girls and boys, but boys used fewer politeness terms in the summer. However, examination of the particular children who contributed to these totals permits a clearer picture to emerge. In both sets, the child who used politeness terms most frequently was Saul – twelve (52 per cent) of all boys' uses in the autumn, and eleven (69 per cent) in the summer. But for Saul's contribution, the pattern of a declining use of politeness expressions among boys would have been even sharper. Saul's adoption of a style more typical of a feminine gender identity obscured a trend among other members of his sex group to adopt a masculine style.

There was no girl who contributed in the manner of Saul, though there was one consistently high contributor. Betty produced six politeness terms in the autumn and five in the summer (35 per cent and 20 per cent respectively). These differing proportions were not indicative of a change in the proportion of girls' politeness terms, but were in line with the increased number of turns recorded for girls in the summer corpus.

RUDE TERMS AND EXPLETIVES

Once again, it was Lakoff (1975) who suggested that men employ rude words and use expletives more than women. In the last chapter, we noted that one of the linguistic stereotypes children first acquire is the masculine use of expletives; in our interview, 'blast'. Swear words and expletives, including name calling, were coded on the transcriptions by the same method used for identifying politeness terms. Frequencies for both rude terms e.g. 'bum' and 'stupid', and expletives such as 'frigging' are presented in Table 9.9.

Table 9.9 Use of rude terms and expletives

| | Autumn | | Summer | |
	Rude terms	Expletives	Rude terms	Expletives
Boys				
Number	32	6	2	6
%	2.4	0.5	0.2	0.5
Total turns	1308		1313	
Girls				
Number	3	3	15	29
%	0.3	0.3	1.0	1.9
Total turns	883		1504	

Although our results for the autumn set of recordings were congruent with adult stereotypes, there was a marked decline in boys' absolute use of rude terms in the summer corpus, although their use of expletives remained constant. Girls, however, used vastly more rude terms and expletives in the summer recordings. Examination of most frequent contributors is not as revealing as it is for politeness terms. Saul, who produced the largest proportion of politeness terms, also produced eleven rude terms (34 per cent of the total) in the autumn, but none in the summer. Neither Theo nor Charley, who had contributed a similar total number in the autumn (five and six respectively) contributed to the summer totals. There is no obvious explanation for this decline, as Saul was still the most frequent contributor of politeness terms in the summer. Lulu, with eight entries, was the most frequent producer of rude terms among the girls in the summer, followed by Joan, who produced four. Together they account for 75 per cent of entries. The nineteen expletives used by Joan account for 66 per cent of them.

Here we have a pattern again at variance with sex-group membership. At the risk of special pleading, we suggest that while Saul's exceptional use of politeness and rude terms in the autumn recordings, and his failure to produce any rude terms in the summer, might be explained in terms of the assertion of a feminine social gender identity, Joan's use of expletives, displaying a masculine gender identity, may be her only way to express the frustration occasioned by a series of health problems and hearing impairment. As we noted at the beginning of this section, the limited numbers of entries per child and the very wide individual differences restrict the conclusions which we are able to draw about the use of these linguistic constructions as resources for the expression of a social gender identity.

SEXUAL PRACTICES

In Chapter 1, we suggested that the reproductive metaphor sustained a binary classification in which members of the same sex group were held to be similar to each other and fundamentally different from those in the other group. Further, it supported a view that heterosexuality was normal and any deviation from this practice was pathological. In addition, it was suggested that this image strengthened a belief in the biological origins of difference between men and women. In that discussion, we considered the research of psychologists and biological scientists and the theorizing of psychoanalysts.

Here we consider children's own understanding of sex and gender. Adults experience difficulty in considering behavioural variability within sex groups and confound sex-group membership and gender identity, and children are even more rigid in their views. In order to demonstrate children's understanding of sex, gender and sexuality, we examine five episodes of pretend play; three are drawn from the autumn corpus of natural dialogue, and the remaining two from the summer set. In these episodes, children attempted to re-create the roles of mummy–wife and daddy–man, but there was never mention of the term 'husband'. In this pretend world, members of the two sex groups were viewed almost exclusively as potential sexual partners, and intimate contact between sex-group members was construed in terms of marriage. Best (1983) has described the attitude of older primary school children who, in a similar vein, viewed mixed-gender friendship as invariably sexual. She also recounts her efforts to change this attitude to intergroup relations. Our examination of these pretend episodes demonstrates that, in children's sharply polarized world of gender representations, sex-group membership and sexuality are confounded. Intergroup relations result in marriage, which in turn regularly leads to procreation.

Best (1983) offers a useful insight into American 4 year olds' particular understanding of adult sexuality, and there is little doubt that they intend their mummy/daddy pretend play to have a sexual meaning. But their meaning is constructed within a system not yet congruent with adult understanding. Thus Best writes 'When asked what they were doing, they would answer either that they were playing "Mommy and Daddy" or that they were "fucking," apparently synonymous terms in their minds . . . "fucking" did not mean penetration but, rather, the rubbing together of genitals' (p. 121).

The themes in the first script (G), given below, are fragmentary, and fuller meaning depends on preceding turns. Our attention is drawn to Theo's attempts to position Henrietta as his wife (turns 1 and 4). Henrietta categorically rejected both of his summons (turn 6). She sought to enter a

162

scene which Charley had created as Santa, complete with sleigh. Her counter-intention – to establish herself as Santa's helper – ultimately succeeded (turn 8). Henrietta's success may have been a function of a relatively incoherent discourse, or the disjointed quality of the interaction may have reflected competing aims. The wish to position a girl as a grown woman/wife is none the less clear, and Henrietta's shrill laughter (turn 7) may reflect her relief at a narrow escape.

Script G
1. Theo: There's, there's Supergirl, she's my . . .
2. (Charley advances towards Steve and Theo swinging steering wheel, which is now a weapon.)
3. Henrietta: (To Steve, who is aiming at her.) No! Oi!
4. Theo: You [. . .?] my wife.
5. (Boys scuffle.)
6. Henrietta: (Gets off sleigh. Says very emphatically, with gesture.) No, I'm not a wife. I'm his helper, Theo. (Points to Charley.)
7. (Theo collapses on floor, copied by Steve. Henrietta laughs piercingly.)
8. Henrietta: (Henrietta climbs back into sleigh.) Now I can do it.

Script J is much longer, but it still contains competing themes. Although Enid and Bob Z. established their relationship as husband and wife in turns 1, 2 and 7, there was a sequence, starting with Rob Z. in turn 8 and continuing until his turn 23, during which the husband/wife theme was ignored. Despite these intrusive bids from Rob Z. and Mark to establish a pretend world of superhero activity, and Bob Z.'s ambiguous contribution in turn 15, he and Edna sustained their mummy/daddy pretend and close physical contact. The discord between Mark and Rob Z. about the aims of their pretend, whether to have a party or not in turns 9, 10 and 11, may inadvertently have contributed to the success of the mummy/daddy pretend. The success of the Bob Z./Enid pretend was surprising, because Bob Z. and Rob Z. were twins, who usually played together in a manner which was somewhat idiosyncratic to them and less mature than the play of the other children. The sexual implications of the theme were evidenced in turns 27 and 29, with the introduction of a baby who was taken to bed with its parents. The meaning of this sequence for the participants was confirmed in turns A and B. Rob Z., who had been competing to establish a superhero theme, verified the mummy/daddy pretend in response to the teacher's inquiry about the nature of their game.

Script J
1. Bob Z.: And its Superwoman. (Pulling Enid to him with his arm round her neck.) And here's Superwoman. And here's Superwoman.

2. Enid: (Giggles.) And you're [Superman?] (Muffled as she gets pulled into his chest . . .)
3. Mark: I'm Superted.
4. Rob Z.:   I'm, I'm Superman's body! I'm Superman's body! I'm, I'm, I'm [. . . ?] tee holder I'm tee holder.
5. (Laughter and indistinct repetition from Mark and Bob Z.)
6. Rob Z.:   I'm Vinegarman and Superman.
7. Bob Z.:   Oh! Get out of our bedroom!
8. Rob Z.:   Vinegarman and Superman. I'm Superman, Superman, oh no, Superman (half singing) vinegar, vinegar.
9. Mark: We're having a party. We're having a party. We're having a party.
10. Rob Z.: No, we're not, no, we're not, no, we're not. (Quick, indistinct voice.)
11. Mark: Yes we are. Hey. Ow. Hello-hello-hello? Are you coming? What's your name?
12. Peter: Peter.
13. Mark: We're . . . we're all well we're – er – this is all my friends.
14. Mark: Come on then Superman, hurry up.
15. Bob Z.: And a apple.
16. Mark: Vinegarman
17. Rob Z.: Yeah, I'm Vinegarman and Vinegarman and Superman.
18. Mark: What?
19. Rob Z.: I'm Superman. I'm Superman. I'm Superman. (Sings.) Superman.
20. Mark: Vinegarman?
21. Rob Z.: No, I'm Superman. I'm Superman. I'm Superman. (Sings.) Superman.
22. Mark: I am as well.
23. Rob Z.: [. . . We're going on break. Going on break . . . ?]
24. Bob Z.: (To Enid.) That's our cover.
25. Bob Z.: Get out of our bed.
26. (Some indistinct turns.)
27. Bob Z.: This is our house. Let's take baby to bed with us, shall we?
28. (Indistinct turns.)
29. Enid: Aah – you are a baby. Let's get to bed.
30. Bob Z.: Yeah, let's get to bed.
31. Mark: Come on, bedtime, bedtime . . .

A   Teacher: (Asks what their game is – mummies and daddies?)
B   Rob Z.: Mummy and daddy game.

In Script K, Enid was again engaged in a mummy/daddy pretend, this time with the other twin, Rob Z. (turns 3–4 and 14). Enid assumed an organizing role in turns 5 and 9, but the pretend appeared less satisfying to her. She started another theme by complaining about a headache in turn 16, and rejected the ongoing bed scene in turn 19. We are left to puzzle whether this is the simulation of an adult woman's efforts to avoid sexual activity. The introduction of a physical complaint was confirmed as a doctor routine when Rob Z. said in turn 20 that he would phone the doctor.

Our corpus includes a number of doctor pretend episodes, but this is the only one which developed from a couple sharing their 'marital' bed. Our doctor routine appears less clandestine than that of American children. Best (1983) maintains that American children are aware of adult concerns about the behaviour underlying the doctor game, and would not engage in doctor pretend openly. The shift from a sexuality constructed in terms of marriage and procreation to fantasies about the body suggests a shift from an explicit sexual theme.

Script K
  1. Rob Z.:   (With a cushion in each hand.) That's not yours, that's that's, that's his, that's his, he sleeps on the floor.
  2. Mark: (Snatching cushion.) Gai!
  3. Rob Z.:   We sleep on the furniture, don't we?
  4. Enid: Yeah.
  5. Enid: (Goes to sleep on the sofa with Rob Z.) And you (indicating Mark) have to sleep . . . (in squeaky voice) Ah, where's our cushions?
  6. Rob Z.:   Yeah.
  7. (Scuffle between the boys.)
  8. Mark: Ow! Ow!
  9. Enid: (Picks up cushion from floor.) That's ours!
 10. Mark: (Goes to sit in corner behind sofa.) [. . .?]
 11. (Laughter.)
 12. Rob Z.:   Get to bed. (Yawns.)
 13. Enid: (Throws herself back on cushions.) Daaah!
 14. (Sleeping noises from Enid and Rob Z.)
 15. (Break and several uninterpretable turns.)
 16. Enid: [. . . gotta headache . . .?]
 17. Rob Z.:   All ready to get to bed, Enid. (Pushing her down on sofa.)
 18. Mark: You get to bed.
 19. Enid: I don't want to.
 20. Rob Z.:   I ring up, I'll ring up the doctor.

This excerpt is one of two drawn from the summer corpus. Script T contained a long domestic pretend episode which features mummy, daddy, their bed, their babies and marriage. Oscar asserted his role and responsibilities as daddy in turns 1, 4 and 5. Once again members of the sex groups were construed as mummy and daddy. Sally initiated a scene shift from domesticity to courtship with princesses in turn 17. Adults were portrayed as actively searching for partners who presumably, upon marriage, became mummies and daddies. Physical contact between a boy and girl inevitably resulted in marriage, as Sally proclaimed in turn 27. Betty's somewhat ambiguous comments in turn 28 left little doubt that the princess's marriage involves procreation. These episodes provide us with a glimpse of children's understanding of family life. It is based upon a view of adult sex-group membership which offers little role choice or within-group variability. Sexuality is heterosexual and procreative.

Script T
Oscar is daddy, Rachel the mummy, and Betty the baby. There have been prior turns about eating and mending things.

1. Oscar: (On mattress.) I'm the daddy.
2. Sally: (To Rachel.) Dinner's not ready, so just wait.
3. Betty: (To Oscar.) And you hear my crying a-ha-aah-aah.
4. Oscar: (Goes to Betty, who is still crying.) Be quiet, baby, be quiet.
5. Oscar: I put that by your bed in case you wanted some dinner. (He goes back to bed.)
6. Rachel: (Joins Oscar.) No – aah!
7. Oscar: That's my bed. It's my bed. (They both lie on it.)
8. (Break, followed by:)
9. Sally: This is mummy's and daddy's bed. (Lying down on bed. Oscar goes over to her.)
10. (Character shift and Sally becomes Mummy.)
11. Rachel: (Rolling on bed.) Hello, Mum.
12. Sally: No! Get off Mummy's and Daddy's bed. You're being a very naughty girl today.
13. Betty: (Crawling over to them.) Googa googa.
14. Sally: Will you get that cover, baby?
15. Betty: (Hands cover to Sally.)
16. (Going to bed, baby crying, tap dripping – relevant?) . . .
17. Sally: I'm the princess. (Sits down on her bed.)
18. Betty: Pretend, pretend, I want, pretend you was a bit beautiful and I was . . .
19. Oscar: I'm the prince.
20. Betty: . . . beautiful. We were both beautiful. Decide who you want to marry . . .
21. Oscar: I'm the prince.

22. Betty: You can searching for a beautiful woman . . .
23. (Oscar pretends to dip between Sally and Betty. Meanwhile Rachel is pulling at his trouser leg.)
24. Rachel: I caught him! I caught him! I caught him! I caught him! I caught him! I caught him!
25. (Sally wins the dip and Oscar goes and puts his arms around her, sits beside her on bed, puts his head on her shoulder.) . . .
26. Betty: [. . .]
27. Sally: He marries me.
28. Betty: [. . . ?] Yes, Yes, and I have to be the [. . .?] princess, but with you little girl. Pretend you got married and you, you had a [. . . ?] grown up. And I had to go to school.

The fragment of Script Y which is reproduced below illustrates once again children's belief that physical/'sexual' contact between sex-group members needs to be validated through marriage. Oscar was chased for some time by the girls, but once he was kissed by Christine, perhaps somewhat to his surprise, he proclaimed in turn 16 that he was going to marry her. Children create a simple world in which physical contact between sex-group members is construed as sexual and involves marriage. In this world, actions have direct and predictable consequences.

Script Y
1. Edith: . . . and Lulu kiss, uhm, Oscar. Go on.
2. Christine: I'm not playing now.
3. Edith: Go away, then.
4. Lulu: No, you kiss Oscar and I kiss Darren.
5. Edith: I know. Look. You [Joan] kiss him, Darren.
6. Lulu: And I'll kiss Oscar.
7. Edith: Joan kiss Oscar.
8. Edith: Joan kiss Darren, and Oscar kiss . . . you!
9. Joan: (Starts for Darren, who runs.) Hey!
10. Edith: Come here. (Grabs Lulu and moves her towards Oscar, not unwillingly.) No, kiss! Kiss her on the lips. Kiss her on the lips. Come on!
11. Lulu: No way!
12. Edith: Go on. Kiss her. Kiss her.
13. Christine: (Makes a dash for Oscar.) I kissed him.
14. Oscar: I kissed *her*!
15. Edith: Oooh!
16. Oscar: (Points at Christine.) I'm going to marry her.
17. Edith: (With Lulu, no longer struggling, very close.) Kiss her.
18. Oscar: I'm going to marry her.

19. Sally: (Also closing in on Oscar.)
20. Oscar: All right. (But which one should he kiss?)
21. Sally: Kiss me. (They kiss.)
22. (All laugh. Oscar throws himself back on sofa.)

We conclude by reproducing some evidence from our ethnographic observations to support the inferences we have drawn from children's pretend play. In the first exchange, a girl struggled with her belief that there is little variability in the adult roles of sex-group members; women become mummies and men become daddies. In the second exchange, another girl wrestled with her images of marriage and procreation; it is typical of those current in children's representations of sexuality. Gerard recorded this conversation with Lulu.

Lulu: Are you a daddy?
Gerard: No.
Lulu: Are you just a man?
Gerard: Yes, just a man.

In the second exchange, Katherine assures Gerard and herself, no doubt, that some people get married but don't have babies.

Katherine (playing with the sand) tells me that she went all the way to Newcastle to be a bridesmaid. 'Who got married?' I ask. 'Katy, she got married, but she's not having a baby, people sometimes don't.'

We have reproduced fragments of five pretend episodes and two conversation exchanges to support our assertion that, for children in reception classes, the reproductive metaphor sustains a simple binary classification, in which members of the same sex group were held to be similar to each other and fundamentally different from those in the other group. For children sexuality is not problematic; it is heterosexual and inevitably procreative.

Part III

The development of gendered identities

10

Conclusions

We begin this final chapter by reviewing the empirical findings which we reported in Part II. This summary is structured by the following four questions:

1. Is there evidence to suggest that differences are emerging among sex-group members in their expression of social gender identities across the school year?
2. Do different organizational settings influence the structure of children's interaction with one another and, in particular, do teachers have an identifiable influence?
3. Can different social gender identities be observed more clearly in practical activity or in intellectual understanding?
4. Is the expression of social gender identities moderated by particular classroom experiences?

After considering the evidence relevant to our four empirical questions, we return to a core problem and consider our success in measuring social gender identities. This examination includes both methodological and theoretical issues in our research. We have already commented upon the unidimensional nature of our measure of gender identity, which derived from children's patterns of association. We evaluate our conceptual gains against this manifest limitation.

Our discussion of the theoretical consequences of our procedures in assessing social gender identities leads on to a wider examination of the conceptual consequences of our study in reception classes. Our ideas have changed in the course of the research. We drew a theoretical distinction between sex and gender in our 1986 paper; realizing it in practice has led us to revise some of those ideas and given us an awareness of their

171

shortcomings. We have found that our original understanding of social identities (Duveen and Lloyd, 1986) requires modification. In reconsidering our earlier conceptualization, we examine identity in relation to intergroup relations, social representations and the nature of the distinction between sex and gender.

In the final section of this chapter, we return to empirical issues and examine the contributions of teachers and children to the construction of social gender identities. We view this as a starting point from which to reflect upon educational practices.

EMPIRICAL REVIEW

In order to answer our first question, pertaining to the emergence among sex-group members of differences in their expressions of social gender identities across the school year, we review findings both from our cross-sectional comparison of four reception classes, reported in Chapter 7, and from our longitudinal study, described in Chapter 6. In Chapter 7, we compared observations of children's practical activity in the autumn term in reception classes in four schools: Land, George, McCarthy and Newby. Membership in a sex group accounted for differences in peer association; boys were observed more frequently in single-sex and 'more boys' groups, and girls more frequently in mixed even and 'more girls' groups. The single-sex groups in which boys were observed were larger than those of girls, but in teacher-organized contexts girls and boys were observed equally often in single-sex groups. Sex-group membership also influenced the nature of children's play, with boys more often engaged in activity and constructive play, and girls more often seen in creative and directed play. In addition, girls were observed more frequently in the book corner and at the table, while boys appeared in open spaces and on the carpet more regularly. But in terms of the emergence of different patterns of activity within sex groups, the most important finding was our failure to uncover reliable within-group effects; that is to say, there were few significant influences of our measure of gender identity on the organization or nature of children's activity in the autumn term in any of the classes.

In the longitudinal analyses for Land and McCarthy schools, reported in Chapter 6, a number of significant effects of gender identity were recorded, but they varied for girls and boys, between autumn and summer terms, and for schools. Here we used a measure of gender identity derived from summer-term activity patterns, and it revealed that differences within the group of girls were more salient than gender identity differences among boys. The influence of gender identity on the association patterns of girls varied between the two classrooms. In the reception class in Land School alone, girls of low gender identity were observed more frequently in larger-sized groups than were the boys in the class, and in larger 'more boys' groups than high gender identity girls. Turning to the nature of play, we found that high gender girls were less frequently observed in activity play than boys, as a group, or than low gender identity girls. High gender identity girls were, however, observed more frequently than low gender identity girls or than boys in directed play. The frequent appearance of high gender identity girls in constructive play settings in Land School only emphasized once again the importance of the teacher's specific interventions for understanding children's patterns of activity. The teacher had set aside time in the week when girls were given access to the large blocks. In McCarthy School, high gender identity girls spent more time at the table, whether in peer-organized or teacher-organized activity, but in Land School this effect was only significant in the autumn term in teacher-organized contexts. Gender identity influenced boys' participation in constructive play, but in different directions and only for low gender identity boys. In Land School, these boys were observed more frequently in constructive play in the summer term than in the autumn term, but in McCarthy School less frequently in the summer term.

Taken together, these findings support the conclusion that the influences of gender identity and sex-group membership on patterns of activity cannot be separated when children enter school in the autumn, but by the end of the first year, particularly among girls, there is evidence to support an assumption of emerging gender identities within sex groups.

To answer our second question, concerning the influence of different organizational settings on the structure of children's interaction with one another, we turn to Chapters 5 and 6 and examine the effects of peer and teacher organization on the types and size of group in which we observed girls and boys. We observed children in Land and McCarthy schools in peer-organized contexts about two thirds of the time and in teacher-organized contexts the remaining third. In each of these contexts, both girls and boys spent about half their time in single-sex groups. By the end of the school year, girls had become more similar to boys in this; that is, they were observed more in single-sex (all-girl) groups in peer-organized contexts, but less frequently when their activity was arranged by the teacher. A further effect of context was the occurrence of larger 'more girls' groups when activity was organized by the teacher; this may reflect the willingness of boys to join groups when they are centred upon the teacher. We can conclude from these observations that the teacher influences both the gender composition of children's groups and their size, as well as, indirectly, their expression of gendered identities.

In order to compare the salience of gender identities for practical activity and knowledge of gender – our third question – it is necessary to consider the influence of gender on the interview tasks reported in Chapter 8 as well as on the observations reported in Chapters 5, 6 and 7. We begin by considering the results of the four interview measures. The Michael and Susan test, which required children to assign classroom objects to a boy or a girl, revealed little overall gender marking. Consistent choices increased over the year, but this pattern was shaped by children's eagerness to make assignments to their own sex group. Only in McCarthy School did girls allocate the trike to Michael and the boys the doll to Susan. There were no disagreements, in the sense that the same item was assigned by both girls and boys to their own group, and there was no recognizable influence of gender identity (that is to say, systematic within-sex-group variation in assignments). As a group, boys showed greater consistency in displaying preferences for items which they had previously assigned to Michael than did girls in choosing items which they had given to Susan. The only exception to this pattern was in George School, where children tended to prefer items they had assigned to the other gender.

On the Odd-one-out test, where children could chose the actor, the object or the mismatch between actor and object as odd in sets of three drawings, both male actors and masculine objects were more frequently selected than female actors or feminine items. This was as true for boys and girls as for high and low gender identity children. The salience of masculine marking did not hold for mismatch choices generally, but high gender identity girls in McCarthy School made significantly more mismatch choices at the end of the school year than other children.

Children were asked in the Figures test to assign models of girls and boys to locations in the classroom that were designed to assess connections between materials and gender, and to designate the gender of the actor performing certain stereotypic behaviours described by teachers and peers. Although there were few consistent associations between materials and gender, pairs of boys were more frequently assigned to the train in the teacher-directed context. In peer-organized contexts, children tended to assign a girl and a boy to different materials, though the effect was strongly influenced by the responses of children in George and Newby schools. Low gender identity boys in Land and McCarthy schools made more mixed-pair choices in teacher-organized contexts, but their responses did not differ from those of other boys in peer-organized settings. Again, it is high gender identity girls in McCarthy School who stand out. They made many more assignments of mixed pairs in teacher-directed contexts, while all other groups of children made more mixed-pair assignments in peer-directed contexts. When asked to assign socially desirable and undesirable behavioural styles, girls were consistent in claiming desirable behaviours such as 'quiet' and 'helpful' for girls, and actions such as 'hitting' and 'losing a pencil' for boys, in both peer- and teacher-articulated contexts, while boys

174

were prepared to make negative assignments to boys, particularly in peer contexts.

Our investigations of children's awareness of linguistic stereotypes revealed that both girls and boys showed some knowledge that expletives are stereotypically assigned to boys, but boys tended to claim stereotypically feminine items for their own sex group as well. There was no evidence that gender identity influenced children's choices.

This review of the very limited influence of gender identity on the Michael and Susan test, the Odd-one-out test and the Figures test, and in relation to awareness of linguistic stereotypes, allows us to conclude that social gender identities exert a greater influence on children's practical activity than on their theoretical understanding of gender.

Evidence relevant to our fourth and final question, concerning the effects of particular classroom experiences on the expression of social gender identities, is presented in Chapters 4, 6, 7 and 8. The results we reported in Chapter 8 offer only limited evidence of the influence of local cultures of gender on children's reflective knowledge. Although we noted that children in Land and McCarthy schools differed in their initial assignments of classroom objects to Michael and Susan, the absence of any consensual gender marking in Land School cannot be ascribed to classroom practice. Many of these children were interviewed before they started school. There was more consensual marking of items in McCarthy School in the summer term (the cooker as feminine and the trike as masculine), and this result accords with our view of the greater salience of gender issues in McCarthy School. Our interpretation is supported by results on the Figures and the Odd-one-out tests. High gender identity girls in McCarthy School stand out; they were particularly sensitive to gender mismatch between actor and object on the latter test, and they made more mixed-pair choices when asked to place figures in play settings organized by the teacher. In this they were unlike other children, who organized peer contexts to include more mixed pairs. The results for girls in McCarthy School suggest that our measure of gender identity has some construct validity, since differential participation in single-sex groups was echoed in differential assignment of figures by these girls.

It is our analyses of observations of children's practical activity in Chapters 6 and 7, and episodes reported in our ethnographic account in Chapter 5, which provide stronger evidence of the influence of local cultures of gender on gender identities. Our initial analyses suggested that size of group might be indicative of masculine and feminine identities, but when we examined data across the year in Land and McCarthy schools, we found that associating in large groups generally was not a masculine style. On the other hand, the participation of girls in 'more boys' groups differentiated high and low gender identity girls, but only in Land School, where low gender identity girls were more frequently observed in these groups. Further evidence of local cultures of gender emerged from our analyses of material culture. High gender identity girls in Land School were observed more frequently using constructive play materials in the summer term, and we were able to link this finding directly to the teacher's intervention in setting aside time for girls to use them. The group of children least often observed with constructive play materials was high gender identity girls in McCarthy School. Here, there is consistency between their practical activity and their reflective knowledge. Patterns of organization and use of materials have different meanings in different classrooms, and provide evidence of classroom differences in social representations of gender. We can speculate that the differences we recorded between girls in Land and McCarthy schools reflect differences between their teachers, whose influence may operate through girls' identification with them.

In Chapter 7 we suggested, on the basis of comparisons of our autumn-term observations in four schools, that pedagogic style is an important source of variation in local gender cultures. We found that variables such as the proportion of time children were observed in teacher-organized versus peer-organized activity or in single-sex groups, and the size of these groups, were influenced by styles of teaching, and in particular by teachers' use of group work as opposed to individual tuition. Land School had been matched to Newby, and McCarthy to George, in terms of the age range of children in the classroom and demographic factors such as the social class composition of the catchment area, but it was teaching style which accounted for the similarity in the structure of our observations of children's activity in Land and George schools, and McCarthy and Newby schools. These results, which suggest that teachers who impose a structure on classroom activity by their demands for group work reduce children's opportunities to organize their activity along sex-group lines, are unexpected. If we considered the beliefs of teachers reported in Chapter 4, we would expect less gender differentiated activity in Land School than in McCarthy. To our surprise, pedagogic style, as practice, has unintended consequences, in the sense that it influences collective behaviour in ways that are not explicitly intended by teachers. There is a mismatch between the two teachers' social representations of gender, as described in Chapter 4, and the consequences of their choice of pedagogic styles. Both our cross-sectional and longitudinal data lends support to the view that social representations of gender vary across classrooms and that schools offer local gender cultures which operate alongside official, local-authority-guided procedures.

MEASURING SOCIAL GENDER IDENTITIES

In presenting a summary of our research findings, we have focused upon our success in distinguishing between sex-group membership and social gender identities. Although this strategy was necessary in order to provide a coherent overview, we now need to consider the methodological adequacy of our measure of gender identity and the conceptual benefits of discriminating between sex-group membership and gender identity.

In Chapter 5, we recounted the process through which we decided to employ participation in single-sex groups as our measure of gender identity, and our use of a median split to distinguish high and low gender identity children. As a consequence of these decisions, we depended upon this unidimensional measure in our subsequent analyses, but we noted the methodological limits of this procedure in Chapters 5 and 7. The lack of consistency between autumn and summer terms in the identification of children who displayed a high or low gender was considered in Chapter 5. With the data we collected, we are unable to determine whether the inconsistency is a feature of our measure or a characteristic of young children's interpersonal behaviour.

A further difficulty we encountered was in interpreting the designations of high and low gender identity children. We warned that the terms had different meanings for girls and boys, since boys, as a sex group, tended to associate together, whereas there was variability among girls in their patterns of association. Some but not all girls chose to associate exclusively with other girls. Even within the group of girls identified as displaying a high gender identity through their frequent appearance in single-sex groups, we noted differences in their patterns of association. Inspection of Figure 7.1 showed that the two definable single-sex girl groups located themselves differently in relation to the boys in the class. The group seen in the plot in the left-hand corner was as far from boys as possible, while the group in the right-hand corner was nearer the boys and was often joined by one of the boys who did not associate frequently with members of his own sex group. Our success in differentiating behaviour due to gender identity differences, particularly within the group of girls, suggests that there are conceptual gains despite the limitations we have identified.

In Chapter 1, we traced the use of the terms 'sex' and 'gender' in psychological writings and noted Maccoby's (1980) position. Her objection to the systematic use of '*sex*' to identify variables such as chromosomes as biological, and occupations which are socially constructed as '*gender*' determined – because this practice prejudged questions of causality – carried weight, in view of her observation that in empirical research sex and gender had not been separated. One of the aims of this study was to demonstrate that such a separation is possible. In the course of our research, we found that a simple distinction between sex and gender was inadequate. However, we have demonstrated that it is useful and meaningful to distinguish between children's membership in a sex group and their display of a particular gender identity. We would argue, further, that despite the limits of our measure of gender identity, this distinction allows us to clarify a number of issues in this domain.

First of all, we suggest that membership in a sex group involves both dimensions, sex and gender. Although initial assignment to a sex group is based upon biological criteria, once that assignment is made, membership in a particular group is a signal for gender-differentiated socialization and the basis for the construction of stereotypes. The symbolic significance of membership in a sex group has meaning both for the individual and for others. We reported that children starting school do not differentiate between sex-group membership and gender identity, but for older children and for adults these categories are important.

In Chapter 4, we reported teachers' interest in a girl they described as a tomboy. At nursery school, she had played with boys and adopted their style of activity. In no sense was she perceived as a member of the sex group 'boys', but her particular behaviour placed her in a category, a gender identity, which distinguished her from other members of her sex group.

We draw upon an illustration from *Sex and Gender* (Archer and Lloyd, 1986) to argue that the separation of sex-group membership and gender identity helps us to explore possible gender identities within the two sex groups. In *Sex and Gender*, we described the Omani Xaniths, men who adopted a style of women's dress, who were allowed in a strict Muslim society to associate with women and, it was argued, formed a third gender. Again, in no sense were the Xaniths construed as members of the women's sex group, and if they were able to consummate marriage to a woman, they regained their full position in the men's group. This second example of the variety of gender identities within a sex group alerts us to the significance of reproduction in the construction of the sex-group category. While trans-sexuals attempt, through biological interventions, to alter their member-ship in a sex group, the issue at stake for individuals of bisexual or homosexual preferences is one of gender identity and not of sex-group membership. The distinction between sex-group membership and gender identity allows us to mark this variation and consequently to achieve greater clarity in a conceptually confused area.

THE DEVELOPMENT OF GENDERED IDENTITIES

In Chapters 1 and 2, we outlined our approach to the development of social gender identities based upon theories of social representations and intergroup relations. We argued that it is as social identities that social representations become psychologically active for individuals. We proposed that children in reception classes re-construct the social gender identities which they elaborated in the pre-school years as they encounter new social representations of gender embedded in new institutional structures. In this section, we reflect upon our model in the light of our empirical research.

A social identity, viewed as an enduring psychological process (structure) which facilitates the organization of meanings and the positioning of social actors, also locates the self in the social world. We described children's practice as the *expression* of their social identities because we assumed that it was social identities which organized their activity. We noted that for young children meanings are more clearly established through their practical activity than through intellectual understanding.

The concept of social identities functions theoretically to mediate between the interpersonal and the intrapersonal, and avoids an assumption of a direct relationship between social practices and individual functioning. Our finding that children mistook their idiosyncratic beliefs about the gender marking of toys on the Michael and Susan test for consensual beliefs suggests that convergence of the two is a developmental achievement.

Perhaps more importantly, the concept of social identity allows us to contemplate variation within social categories as well as between them. Tafjel's (1981, 1982) theory of intergroup conflict highlights differentiation between categories, and where it examines the theme of gender it has focused on differentiation between sex groups. We have argued (Duveen and Lloyd, 1990a) that even within the domain of gender, where social representations impose an imperative obligation on individuals to adopt a social gender identity, different gender identities are available within sex groups. Masculinity and femininity have a variety of definitions, and these different social gender identities provide children with a means for orienting themselves in the social world of the classroom in the present, and with a pathway towards the development of their gender identities in later years.

The development of social gender identities refers, then, to children's adoption of positions within sex groups which are marked by social representations of gender, and not to individual resolutions of the question of positioning in the world of gender. Positioning in this sense has rarely been examined in research on social representations, where the emergence of group differences in social representations has been the primary focus. Mugny and Carugati's (1989) study of the positioning of parents, teachers and other groups in relation to social representations of intelligence, and the related research of Molinari and Emiliani (1990) on differences between the social representations of children held by groups of mothers, are exceptions. These inquiries have studied the process through which the same representation can give rise to different social identities, but they have not considered the way in which the process develops over time.

In our comparisons of high and low gender identity children in the autumn and summer terms in Chapter 5, we reported on the effects of time on social gender identities. Although gender identities varied considerably across the first year of school, we were unable to draw simple conclusions, but the dimension is too important to ignore. The adoption of some positions may offer restricted opportunities for change in the future; the girls in George School who defined their femininity around the exclusion of boys will have little opportunity for interaction with boys, particularly in peer-organized contexts.

Our notion that positions occupied by different social gender identities may vary in the extent to which they constrain future development affects our understanding of the influence of peer interaction on social representations. From our point of view, children's social identities both lead them into particular social interactions and influence the negotiation of meanings which is achieved. Our interest in the time dimension thus leads us to take issue with social-psychological theories which draw upon post-structuralist thought to argue that children's 'subjectivity' is 'constituted and reconstituted through the various discursive practices in which they participate' (Davies, 1989, p. 229). These theories emphasize the positioning of the self in relation to specific discourses, but they do so in terms which rarely reach beyond the immediate horizons of a particular interaction. It is as though positions can be endlessly taken up and changed as children move in and out of different interactions. Our view is that different positions constrain the kinds of interaction children enter, as well as generate a more fixed identity than such theories allow. A belief that social representations themselves are structured in such a way as to render particular positions possible, is a corollary to our theory of social identity in relation to positioning. According to this view, boys and girls do not spontaneously divide into segregated sex groups. Rather the divisions that appear in their social world reflect the influence of social representations of the culture into which they were born and are developing. It is in this sense that we argued in the first chapter that it is necessary to take account of the influence of the existing social order on the development of social gender identities. If there are developmental pathways (Archer, 1992) to the construction of gender identities, these pathways are mapped out within the social representations of gender. As these social representations change new pathways may emerge, but at any given time the social representations of gender constrain the available pathways to identity.

Conclusions

SEXUALITY AND CHILDREN'S
REPRESENTATIONS OF GENDER

In Chapter 1, we described the significance of the reproductive metaphor for social representations of gender. This metaphor offers an image of gender as a bipolar opposition which is acquired by children at a very early age, and which persists into adulthood. Although we considered the organizing function of images in theoretical terms in Chapter 2, and referred to the way in which children represent gender as a bipolar opposition in Chapter 9, we did not discuss the importance of the image for the development of social gender identities through the influence of social representations. Here we examine its function as the figurative nucleus of bipolar opposites, which sustains a conceptualization of classroom life in terms of two complementary but exclusive sex groups.

In Chapter 9, we showed that sexuality, marriage and domestic life are connected in pretend play by a bipolar image. In these constructions, sex and gender are reduced to a single dimension and it is the difference between the sex groups which is emphasized, while differences within each of these social categories are obscured.

In Chapter 1, we reviewed evidence which suggests that children are the most conservative social actors in the gender culture of the classroom. We can account for their conservatism in terms of the image of bipolar opposition as the figurative nucleus of their social representations of gender. As an image, it offers a degree of clarity and simplicity which is consistent with children's capacity for cognitive elaboration. Their resistance to the influence of equalitarian voices in shaping social representations of gender is a bid to preserve a clear and sharp image of their social world.

In crystallizing children's social representations of gender, the image of bipolar opposition fuses the form of knowledge (its categorical structure) with the content of knowledge (the separation of things masculine and feminine). The relationship between masculinity and femininity is one of power. Masculine objects tend to cohere together, acquire prestige and separate from things feminine, so that the bipolar image of gender represents hierarchy as well as difference. We observed the shadow of this inequality in disputes which broke out over access to resources. Both girls and boys held some masculine objects to be more valuable than feminine objects, and teachers, in the pursuit of equity, invoked special rules to safeguard shared access for girls and boys.

Viewed in this light, it is hardly surprising that it is girls who are most willing to abandon a social organization and gender marking based upon a strict bipolar opposition. In our ethnographic observations, we recorded a number of episodes in which girls challenged this image by competing with boys for masculine-marked resources. Though girls' attempts to cross the binary divide were infrequent, they serve to show that even for children in reception classes gender is not an entirely uncontested terrain, and that girls are the social actors most often prepared to violate the relations of power evoked by consensual representations of gender.

GENDER IDENTITIES AND EDUCATION

Although gender was represented as a distinction between masculinity and femininity in the four classrooms we observed, there was considerable variation in the way this distinction was used to mark resources. For individuals concerned with education, the emergence of local gender cultures is one of the most important aspects of our research. It highlights the particular contribution of social interaction in the development of social representations.

Besides identifying the emergence of local gender cultures through children's use of gender-marked resources, we noted that local gender cultures are associated with pedagogic styles which have unintended consequences for the development of children's gender identities. The key contrast lay in the amount of time each style allowed for peer-organized activity. When teachers adopted a style based on individual tuition, children spent more time in peer-organized contexts in which stronger patterns of gender differentiation appeared. When a group-based pedagogic style was employed, children spent more time in teacher-organized contexts. These styles are not linked directly to the child-centred ideology discussed in Chapter 1, and they are not directly related to teachers' views on gender. In McCarthy and Newby schools, where the reception-class teachers we observed adopted group-centred styles, they differed in their approaches to both group work and gender. The teacher in McCarthy School divided her class into four colour groups of six to eight children and seated them according to membership in these groups. Her assignments reflected individual differences in age and achievement. In Chapter 4, we noted this teacher's views on the naturalness of gender inequalities. By contrast, in Newby School, children were organized in small groups of two, three and four children. The teacher in Newby School was notable for her efforts to organize children in groups composed of equal numbers of girls and boys.

The connection between pedagogic style and emerging gender identities in the classroom has been a focus of recent sociological research. Valerie Walkerdine (1981) has observed that, in following the dictates of a child-centred ideology which places emphasis on children's self-expression, teachers leave uncontrolled children's interactions with other children.

182

Conclusions

Thus the most conservative social actors inadvertently regulate the expression of gender identities. Looking beyond gender categories, Bernstein (1990) has sought to describe the consequences of pedagogical discourse for the identities which children develop. These investigations do not yield a prescription for a radical pedagogy from which gender identities might take on a different form.

Our results should not be read as a prescription for the development of less differentiated gender identities. We grant that group work reduces peer-organized activity and thus reduces the emergence of differentiated gender identities in relation to peers; but the consequences of greater contact with the teacher are not yet apparent in the first year of school. Our observations in teacher-organized contexts are not informative about the nature of the gender identities which are yet to emerge in children's role as pupils. A more valuable approach to the link between pedagogic styles and gender identities is to emphasize the contribution which children make to this process. It was in peer-organized contexts that we have been able to identify differentiated gender identities. We may speculate that our success was achieved as a consequence of children's limited development, which results in a representation of gender grounded in an image of bipolar opposition. Perhaps the question for adults to consider is the extent to which our understanding moves beyond that of the children we study or attempt to educate.

References

Agar, M.H., 1986, *Speaking of Ethnography*, Beverly Hills, CA: Sage.

Archer, J., 1984, 'Gender roles as developmental pathways', *British Journal of Social Psychology*, *23*, pp. 245–56.

Archer, J., 1992, 'Childhood gender roles: social context and organization', in H. McGurk (ed.) *Childhood Social Development*, Hove: Erlbaum, pp. 31–61.

Archer, J. and Lloyd, B., 1974, 'Sex roles: biological and social interactions', *New Scientist*, 21 November, pp. 582–4.

Archer, J. and Lloyd, B., 1986, *Sex and Gender*, Cambridge: Cambridge University Press.

Bem, S.L., 1974, 'The measurement of psychological androgyny', *The Journal of Consulting and Clinical Psychology*, *42*, pp. 155–62.

Bem, S.L., 1981, 'Gender schema theory: A cognitive account of sex-typing', *Psychological Review*, *42*, pp. 354–64.

Bem, S.L., 1991, 'Gender and social theory', seminar at the London School of Economics, 8 July.

Berger, P.L., 1963, *Invitation to Sociology*, New York: Anchor.

Berger, P.L. and Luckmann, T., 1966, *The Social Construction of Reality*, Garden City, NY: Doubleday.

Bernstein, B., 1990, *The Structuring of Pedagogical Discourse*, London and New York: Routledge.

Best, R., 1983, *We've All Got Scars: What Boys and Girls Learn In Elementary School*, Bloomington, IN: Indiana University Press.

Boyd, J., 1989, *Equality Issues in Primary Schools*, London: Paul Chapman.

Brown, P., 1980, 'Why and how women are more polite: some evidence from a Mayan community', in S. McConnell-Ginet, R. Borker and N. Furman (eds) *Women and Language in Literature and Society*, New York: Praeger, pp. 111–36.

Burgess, R.G. (ed.), 1984, *The Research Process in Educational Settings: Ten Case Studies*, London: The Falmer Press.

CACE, 1967, *Children and their Primary Schools* (The Plowden report), London: HMSO.

Carpenter, C.J., Huston, A.C. and Holt, W., 1986, 'Modification of pre-school sex typed behaviors by participation in adult-structured activities', *Sex Roles*, *14*, pp. 603–15.

Carugati, F., 1990, 'From social cognition to social representations in the study of intelligence', in G. Duveen and B. Lloyd (eds) *Social Representations and the Development of Knowledge*, Cambridge: University of Cambridge Press, pp. 126–43.

Chombart De Lauwe, M.J., 1984, 'Changes in the representation of the child in the course of social transmission', in R.M. Farr and S. Moscovici (eds) *Social Representations*, Cambridge: Cambridge University Press, pp. 185–209.

184

References

Connell, R.W., 1987, *Gender and Power: Society, the Personal and Sexual Politics*, Cambridge: Polity Press.

Croll, P., 1986, *Systematic Classroom Observation*, Lewes: Falmer Press.

Croll, P. and Moses, D., 1985, *One in Five: The Assessment and Incidence of Special Educational Needs*, London: Routledge & Kegan Paul.

Croll, P. and Moses, D., 1991, 'Sex roles in the primary classroom', in M. Woodhead, P. Light and R. Carr (eds), *Growing Up in a Changing Society*, London and New York: Routledge, pp. 271–91.

D'Alessio, M., 1990, 'Adolescents' representation of infancy and childhood,' in G. Duveen and B. Lloyd (eds) *Social Representations and the Development of Knowledge*, Cambridge: Cambridge University Press, pp. 70–90.

Davenport, W.H., 1976, 'Sex in cross-cultural perspective', in F.A. Beach (ed.) *Human Sexuality in Four Perspectives*, Baltimore and London: Johns Hopkins University Press, pp. 115–63.

Davies, B., 1989, 'The discursive production of the Male/Female dualism in school settings', *Oxford Review of Education*, 15, pp. 229–41.

Deaux, K., 1984, 'From individual differences to social categories: Analysis of a decade's research on gender', *The American Psychologist*, 39, pp. 105–16.

Delamont, S., 1980, *Sex Roles and the School*, London: Methuen.

Delamont, S. and Hamilton, D., 1984, 'Revisiting classroom research: a continuing cautionary tale', in S. Delamont (ed.) *Readings on Interaction in the Classroom*, London: Methuen, pp. 3–37.

Dobert, R.L., Habermas, J. and Nunner-Winkler, G., 1987, 'The development of the self', in J. Broughton (ed.) *Critical Theories of Psychological Development*, New York: Plenum, pp. 275–301.

Durkheim, E. and Mauss, M., 1963, *Primitive Classification*, Chicago, IL: University of Chicago Press.

Duveen, G., 1984, *From Social Cognition to the Cognition of Social Life*, D.Phil thesis, University of Sussex.

Duveen, G. and Lloyd, B., 1986, 'The significance of social identities', *British Journal of Social Psychology*, 25, pp. 219–30.

Duveen, G. and Lloyd, B., 1990a, 'Introduction', in Duveen, G. and Lloyd, B. (eds) *Social Representations and the Development of Knowledge*, Cambridge: Cambridge University Press, pp. 1–10.

Duveen, G. and Lloyd, B., 1990b, 'The developmental asymmetry of gender', paper presented to the IVth European Conference on Developmental Psychology, Stirling.

Duveen, G. and Lloyd, B. (In press). The influence of teachers on the expression of social gender identities in the first year of school.

Duveen, G. and Shields, M.M., 1984, 'The influence of gender on the development of young children's representations of work roles', paper presented to the 1st European Conference on Developmental Psychology, Groningen.

Eckert, P., 1989, 'The whole woman: Sex and gender differences in variation', *Language Variation and Change*, 1, pp. 245–67.

Edelsky, C., 1976, 'The acquisition of communicative competence: recognition of linguistic correlates of sex roles', *Merrill-Palmer Quarterly*, 22, pp. 47–59.

Edelsky, C., 1977, 'Acquisition of an aspect of communicative competence: Learning what it means to talk like a lady', in S. Ervin-Tripp and C. Mitchell-Kernan (eds) *Child Discourse*, New York: Academic Press, pp. 225–43.

Edwards, D. and Mercer, D., 1987, *Common Knowledge*, London: Methuen.

Erickson, E., 1946, 'Ego development and historical change', *Psychoanalytic Study of the Child*, 2, pp. 359–96.

Erickson, E., 1950, *Childhood and Society*, New York: Norton.

References

French, J., 1986, 'Gender and the classroom', *New Society*, 7 March, pp. 405–6.

Freud, S., 1905, 'Three Essays on the Theory of Sexuality', in *The Standard Edition, Vol. VII*, London: Hogarth Press, 1953.

Furth, H., 1981, *Piaget and Knowledge*, Englewood Cliffs, NJ: Prentice-Hall.

Furth, H., 1983, 'A developmental perspective on the societal theory of Habermas', *Human Development*, 26, pp. 181–97.

Glton, M., Simon, B. and Croll, P., 1980, *Inside the Primary Classroom*, London: Routledge & Kegan Paul.

Goffman, I., 1963, *Stigma: Notes on the Management of Spoiled Identity*, Engelwood Cliffs, NJ: Prentice-Hall.

Goldfoot, D.A., Wallen, K., Neff, D.A., McBrair, M.C. and Goy, R.W., 1984, 'Social influences upon the display of sexually dimorphic behaviour in rhesus monkeys: Isosexual rearing', *Archives of Sexual Behavior*, 13, pp. 395–412.

Goldmann, L., 1976, *Cultural Creation in Modern Society*, St Louis, MI: Telos Press.

Gould, S.J., 1991, 'The birth of the two-sex world', Review of T. Laqueur, *Making Sex: Body and Gender from the Greeks to Freud*, *The New York Review*, 13 June, pp. 11–13.

Gumperz, J. (ed.), 1982, *Language and Social Identity*, Cambridge: Cambridge University Press.

Gumperz, J., 1987, 'Preface', in P. Brown and S. C. Levinson, *Politeness: Some Universals of Language Use*, Cambridge: Cambridge University Press.

Gurin, P. and Markus, H., 1990, 'Cognitive consequences of gender identity', in S. Skeffington, and D. Baker (eds) *The Social Identity of Women*, London: Sage, pp. 152–72.

Habermas, J., 1984, *The Theory of Communicative Action, Vol. 1*, Oxford: Polity Press.

Hammersley, M. (ed.), 1986, *Case Studies in Classroom Research*, Milton Keynes: Open University Press.

Hartley, D., 1985, *Understanding the Primary School*, London: Croom Helm.

Henley, N.M., 1977, *Body Politics, Power, Sex and Non-Verbal Communication*, Englewood Cliffs, NJ: Prentice-Hall.

Herzlich, C., 1972, 'La représentation sociale,' in S. Moscovici, *Introduction à la Psychologie Sociale, vol. I*, Paris: Librarie Larousse, pp. 303–325.

Hockett, C.F., 1950, 'Age-grading and linguistic continuity', *Language*, 26, pp. 449–57.

Holmberg, A.L., 1969, *Nomads of the Long Bow*, Garden City, NY: Natural History Press.

Huddleston, R., 1984, *Introduction to the Grammar of English*, Cambridge: Cambridge University Press.

Huston, A.C., 1983, 'Sex-typing', in P.H. Mussen and E.M. Hetherington (eds) *Handbook of Child Psychology, Vol. 4, Socialization, Personality and Social Behavior*, New York: Wiley, pp. 387–467.

Huston, A.C., 1985, 'The development of sex typing: Themes from recent research', *Developmental Review*, 5, pp. 1–17.

Huston, A.C. and Carpenter, C.J., 1985, 'Gender differences in preschool classrooms: The effects of sex-typed activity choices, in L.C. Wilkinson and C.B. Marrett (eds) *Gender Influences in Classroom Interaction*, London: Academic Press, pp. 143–65.

Jodelet, D., 1991, *Madness and Social Representations*, Hemel Hempstead: Harvester Wheatsheaf.

Kelly, A., 1988, 'Gender differences in teacher-pupil interactions: a meta-analytic review', *Research in Education*, 39, pp. 1–23.

Kessler, S.J. and McKenna, W., 1978, *Gender: An Ethnomethodological Approach*, New York: Wiley.

King, R., 1978, *All Things Bright and Beautiful*, Chichester: Wiley.

Kirk, R.E., 1968, *Experimental Design Procedures for the Behavioral Sciences*, Belmont, CA: Brooks Cole.

Kohlberg, L., 1966, 'A cognitive-developmental analysis of children's sex-role concepts and attitudes', in E.E. Maccoby (ed.) *The Development of Sex Differences*, Stanford, CA: Stanford University Press, pp. 82–173.

References

Kuhn, D., Nash, S.C. and Brucken, L., 1978, 'Sex role concepts of two- and three-year olds', *Child Development*, *49*, pp. 495–7.

Labov, W., 1970, 'Stages in the acquisition of standard English' in H. Hungerford, J. Robinson and J. Sledd (eds) *English Linguistics: An Introductory Reader*, Glenview, IL: Scott, Foreman, pp. 274–302.

Lakoff, R., 1973, 'Language and woman's place', *Language in Society*, 2, pp. 45–80.

Lakoff, R., 1975, *Language and Woman's Place*, New York: Harper & Row.

Laqueur, T., 1991, *Making Sex: Body and Gender from the Greeks to Freud*, Cambridge, MA: Harvard University Press.

Livesley, W.J. and Bromley, D.B., 1973, *Person Perception in Childhood and Adolescence*, London: Wiley.

Lloyd, B., 1987, 'Social representations of gender', in J. Bruner and H. Haste (eds) *Making Sense: The Child's Construction of the World*, London and New York: Methuen, pp. 147–62.

Lloyd, B. and Duveen, G., 1989, 'The reconstruction of social knowledge in the transition from sensorimotor to conceptual activity: the gender system', in A. Gallatly, D. Rogers and J. Sloboda (eds) *Cognition and Social Worlds*, Oxford: Oxford University press, pp. 83–98.

Lloyd, B. and Duveen, G., 1990, 'A semiotic analysis of the development of social representations of gender', in G. Duveen and B. Lloyd (eds) *Social Representations and the Development of Knowledge*, Cambridge: University of Cambridge Press, pp. 27–46.

Lloyd, B. and Goodwin, R., 1992, 'Intonation and function of four year old's tag constructions', in D. Messer and G. Turner (eds) *Critical Influences on Child Language Acquisition and Development*, London: Macmillan, pp. 179–94.

Local, J., 1982, 'Modelling intonational variability in children's speech', in S. Romaine (ed.) *Sociolinguistic Variation in Speech Communities*, London: Arnold, pp. 85–103.

Maccoby, E.E. , 1967, *The Development of Sex Differences*, London: Tavistock.

Maccoby, E.E., 1980, *Social Development*, New York: Harcourt Brace Jovanovich.

Maccoby, E.E., 1988, 'Gender as a social category', *Developmental Psychology*, *24*, pp. 755–65.

Maccoby, E.E. and Jacklin, C.N., 1974, *The Psychology of Sex Differences*, Stanford, CA: Stanford University Press.

Maccoby, E.E. and Jacklin, C.N., 1987, 'Gender segregation in childhood', in H. Reese (ed.) *Advances in Child Development and Behaviour, Vol. 20*, London: Academic Press, pp. 239–87.

Masson, J., 1984, *The Assault on Truth*, London: Faber & Faber.

Mitchell, J., 1974, *Psychoanalysis and Feminism*, London: Allen Lane.

Molinari, L. and Emiliani, F., 1990, 'The structure of mothers' images of the child and their influence on conversational styles', in G. Duveen and B. Lloyd (eds) *Social Representations and the Development of Knowledge*, Cambridge: Cambridge University Press, pp. 91–106.

Money, J., 1988, *Gay, Straight and In-Between: The Sexology of Erotic Orientation*, New York: Oxford University Press.

Moscovici, S., 1973, 'Foreword' to C. Herzlich, *Health and Illness*, London: Academic Press.

Moscovici, S., 1976a, *La Psychanalyse, son image et son public*, Paris: Presses Universitaires de France.

Moscovici, S., 1976b, *Social Influence and Social Change*, London: Academic Press.

Moscovici, S., 1981, 'On social representations', in J. Forgas (ed.) *Social Cognition*, London: Academic Press, pp. 181–209.

Moscovici, S., 1984, 'The phenomenon of social representations', in R. Farr and S. Moscovici (eds) *Social Representations*, Cambridge: Cambridge University Press, pp. 3–69.

Moscovici, S., 1988, 'Notes towards a description of social representations', *European Journal of Social Psychology*, *18*, pp. 211–50.

Mugny, G. and Carugati, F.F., 1989, *Social Representations of Intelligence*, Cambridge: Cambridge University Press.

Neitz, M.J., 1982, 'Comment', *American Sociologist*, *17*, pp. 37–8.

References

Oakley, A., 1981, *Subject Women*, Oxford: Martin Robertson.

Paley, V.G., 1984, *Boys and Girls Superheroes in the Doll Corner*, Chicago, IL: University of Chicago Press.

Piaget, J., 1926, *Language and Thought in the Child*, London: Routledge & Kegan Paul.

Piaget, J., 1934, *The Moral Judgement of the Child*, London: Routledge & Kegan Paul.

Piaget, J., 1970, *Main Trends in Interdisciplinary Research*, London: George Allen & Unwin.

Piaget, J., 1971, *Biology and Knowledge*, Edinburgh: Edinburgh University Press.

Piaget, J., 1977, *The Grasp of Consciousness*, London: Routledge & Kegan Paul.

Pluckrose, H., 1987, *What is Happening in Our Primary Schools?*, Oxford: Basil Blackwell.

Rogoff, B., 1978, 'Spot observation: An introduction and examination', *The Quarterly Newsletter of the Institute for Comparative Human Behavior*, 2, pp. 21–6.

Romaine, S., 1984, *The Language of Children and Adolescents: The Acquisition of Communicative Competence*, Oxford: Blackwell.

Sachs, J., 1987, 'Preschool boys' and girls' language use in pretend play', in S.U. Philips, S. Steele and C. Tanz (eds) *Language, Gender and Sex in Comparative Perspective*, Cambridge: Cambridge University Press, pp. 178–88.

Schaffer, R., 1977, 'Problems in Freud's psychology of women', in H.P. Blum (ed.) *Female Psychology*, New York: International Universities Press Inc., pp. 331–60.

Serbin, L.A., Connor, J.M. and Citron, C.C., 1981, 'Sex-differentiated free play behavior: Effects of teacher modelling, location and gender', *Developmental Psychology*, *17*, pp. 640–6.

Smith, C. and Lloyd, B., 1978, 'Maternal behavior and perceived sex of infant: revisited', *Child Development*, *46*, pp. 1263–5.

Smith, M. and Lloyd, B., 1989, 'Linguistic measures of developing social gender identity', *York Papers in Linguistics*, *13*, pp. 317–28.

Smith, P.M., 1979, 'Sex markers in speech', in K.R. Scherer and H. Giles (eds) *Social Markers in Speech*, Cambridge: Cambridge University Press, pp. 109–46.

Smith, P.M., 1985, *Language, the Sexes and Society*, Oxford: Blackwell.

Spence, J.T. and Helmreich, R.L., 1978, *Masculinity and Femininity: The Psychological Dimension, Correlates and Antecedents*, Austin, TX: University of Texas Press.

Spender, D., 1982, *Invisible Women: The Schooling Scandal*, London: Writers and Readers Cooperative.

Stoller, R.J., 1968, *Sex and Gender*, New York: Science House.

Stone, G.P., 1962, 'Appearance and the self', in A.M. Rose (ed.) *Human Behavior and Social Processes*, Boston, MA: Houghton Mifflin, pp. 86–118.

Streeck, J., 1983, *Social Order in Child Communication*, Amsterdam: John Benjamins Publishing Co.

Tajfel, H., 1981, *Human Groups and Social Categories: Studies in Social Categories*, Cambridge: Cambridge University Press.

Tajfel, H. (ed.), 1982, *Social Identity and Intergroup Relations*, Cambridge: Cambridge University Press.

Teaching and Learning in English Urban Schools, 1991, London: Council of Greater London Schools. (reference from THES, 17 May 1991)

Thorne, B., 1986, 'Girls and boys together . . . but mostly apart: gender arrangements in elementary schools', in W.W. Hartup and Z. Rubin (eds) *Relationships and Development*, Hillsday, NJ: Erlbaum, pp. 167–84.

Trautner, H.M., 1991, 'Intraindividual changes and interindividual differences in the development of sex-typing during childhood', paper presented at the ESF Conference on Longitudinal Research: Challenges for the Future, March 1991, Budapest.

Trautner, H.M., Helbing, N., Sahm, W.B. and Lohaus, A., 1989, 'Beginning awareness–rigidity–flexibility: A longitudinal analysis of sex-role stereotyping in 4 to 10 year old children', paper presented at the SRCD Conference, April 1989, Kansas City.

188

References

Trudgill, P., 1983, *On Dialect: Social and Geographical Perspective*, Oxford: Basil Blackwell.

Walkerdine, V., 1981, 'Sex, power and pedagogy', *Screen Education*, *38*, pp. 14–21.

Walum, L.R., 1977, *The Dynamics of Sex and Gender: A Sociological Perspective*, Chicago, IL: Rand McNally.

Warren-Leubecker, A. and Bohannon III, J.N., 1989, 'Pragmatics: Language in social contexts', in J.B. Gleason (ed.) *The Development of Language*, 2nd Edition, Columbus, OH: Merrill, pp. 327–68.

Weigert, A.J., Teitge, J.S. and Teitge, D.W., 1986, *Society and Identity*, New York: Cambridge University Press.

Weinreich-Haste, H., 1979, 'What sex is science?', in O.Hartnett, G. Boden and M. Fuller (eds) *Women: Sex-role Stereotyping*, London: Tavistock, pp. 18–27.

Wenger, M., 1983, 'Gender role socialization in an East African community: Social interaction between 2- to 3-year-olds and older children in social ecological perspective', Ph.D. Dissertation, Harvard Graduate School of Education. Reported in Whiting and Edwards.

Whiting, B.B. and Edwards, C.P., 1988, *Children of Different Worlds The Formation of Social Behavior*, Cambridge, MA: Harvard University Press.

Wilcox, K., 1982, 'Ethnography as methodology and its applications to the study of school: A review', in G. Spindler (ed.) *Doing the Ethnography of Schooling: Educational Anthropology in Action*, New York: Holt, Reinhart & Winston, pp. 456–88.

Zammuner, V.L., 1987, 'Children's sex-role stereotypes: A cross-cultural analysis', in P. Shaver and C. Hendrick (eds) *Sex and Gender, Review of Personality and Social Psychology, Volume 7*, Beverly Hills, CA: Sage, pp. 272–93.

Author index

Author index

Kuhn, D., 50

Labov, W., 143, 152
Lakoff, R., 142, 152–3, 157, 159, 160
Laqueur, T., 19
Livesley, W J., 8
Lloyd, B., vii, 7, 9, 15, 20, 23–5, 27, 29–32, 34, 43, 77–8, 87, 124, 129, 134, 146, 151, 172, 178–9
Local, J., 152
Lohaus. A., 5, 8, 11
Luckmann, T., 30

Maccoby, E. E., 8, 11, 15, 16, 23, 36, 47, 76, 122, 135, 177
Markus, H., 28
Masson, J., 24
Mauss, M., 149
McBrair, M. C., 18
McKenna, W., 15
Mercer, D., 59
Mitchell, J., 24
Molinari, L., 60, 179
Money, J., 15, 17–18
Moscovici, S., 20–3, 25, 27–8, 30, 31, 59, 78, 124
Moses, D., 33–5, 100
Mugny, G. 124, 179

Nash, S. C., 50
Neff, D. A., 18
Neitz, M. J., 16
Nunner-Winkler, G., 29, 30

Oakley, A., 15

Paley, V. G., 5, 7, 9–10, 14, 28, 68

Piaget, J., 23, 30, 60, 123
Pluckrose, H., 11

Rogoff, B., 45
Romaine, S., 152

Sachs, J., 152
Sahm, W. B., 5, 8, 11
Schaffer, R., 18
Serbin, L. A., 84
Shields, M. M., 7
Simon, B., 34
Smith, C., vii
Smith, M., 146
Smith, P. M., 142
Spence, J. T., 6, 8
Spender, D., 33
Stoller, R. J., 5
Stone, G. P., 29
Streeck, J., 59

Tajfel, H., 27–8, 30–1, 179
Teitge, D. W., 28, 31
Teitge, J. S., 28, 31
Thorn, B., 28, 84
Trautner, H. M., 5, 8, 11
Trudgill, P., 159

Walkerdine, V., 182
Wallen, K., 18
Walum, L. R., 23
Warren-Leubecker, A., 152
Weigert, A. J., 28, 31
Weinreich-Haste, H., 23
Wenger, M., 45
Whiting, B. B., 45
Wilcox, K., 59

Zammuner, V. L., 148–9

Subject index

193